CONSENT CULTURE
AND TEEN FILMS

CONSENT CULTURE AND TEEN FILMS

Adolescent Sexuality in
US Movies

MICHELE MEEK

INDIANA UNIVERSITY PRESS

This book is a publication of

Indiana University Press
Office of Scholarly Publishing
Herman B Wells Library 350
1320 East 10th Street
Bloomington, Indiana 47405 USA

iupress.org

© 2023 by Michele Meek

All rights reserved
No part of this book may be reproduced or utilized in any form or by any means, electronic or mechanical, including photocopying and recording, or by any information storage and retrieval system, without permission in writing from the publisher. The paper used in this publication meets the minimum requirements of the American National Standard for Information Sciences—Permanence of Paper for Printed Library Materials, ANSI Z39.48-1992.

Manufactured in the United States of America

First printing 2023

Cataloging information is available from the Library of Congress.

ISBN 978-0-253-06573-5 (cloth)
ISBN 978-0-253-06574-2 (paperback)
ISBN 978-0-253-06575-9 (e-book)

To Chase and M

CONTENTS

Acknowledgments ix

Introduction *1*

1. Regulating Adolescent Sexuality in US Cinema: From Censorship to Child Pornography Laws *21*
2. Flipping the Heterosexual Script and Race-Based Sexual Stereotypes in Teen Comedies of the 2010s and 2020s *61*
3. Queering Consent: Navigating Performative and Subjective Consent in Queer Teen Films *89*
4. "I Was Not Lolita": Child Sexual Abuse and Children's Agency in *The Diary of a Teenage Girl* and *The Tale* *118*
5. The (In)Visibility of Trans Teens: *3 Generations*, *Adam*, and *Boy Meets Girl* *149*

Conclusion: Adolescent Sexuality and the Adult Imagination *180*

Filmography 193

Bibliography 197

Index 221

ACKNOWLEDGMENTS

NUMEROUS SCHOLARS OFFERED THEIR FEEDBACK on portions and stages of this manuscript, and I am grateful to all of them. Thank you especially to Aiden James Kosciesza and Laura Stamm for providing comments on a particular chapter that warranted their expertise. Thank you also to Roxanne Harde and Ann Smith for their thoughts on my 2021 essay in *Girlhood Studies* that iterated arguments about affirmative consent in teen films and to Lisa Funnell and Ralph Beliveau for their responses to my chapter on consent in teen films in *Screening #MeToo: Rape Culture in Hollywood Film*. Both of those writings proved formative in developing the ideas for this book. Thank you also to Kristen Hatch who generously provided comments on several chapters. I am also greatly appreciative to my anonymous peer reviewers who offered essential questions, thoughts, and suggestions—thank you for taking the time to read and review my manuscript so carefully and thoughtfully. Thank you to Rebecca Geiger, whose attention to detail I could not have done without, and to Daniel McGinn for introducing us. Thank you to Belle Tuten and Spencer Owens for assistance with the index. And, of course, thank you to my editor Allison Blair Chaplin and everyone at Indiana University Press who helped make this book a reality.

I am also beholden to the many teen film scholars who have written invaluable texts that I reference here. Thank you especially to my colleagues in the Society for Cinema and Media Studies Children's and Youth Media and Culture—especially Frances Smith, Andrew Scahill, Barbara Brickman, and Julia Alekseyeva who joined me on a panel, Youth Beyond the Binaries, in April 2022. And thank you to Tim Shary for being such a generous colleague to youth media studies scholars. I could not have been more thrilled to receive an honorable mention for the inaugural Timothy Shary Prize for Best Essay in Children's and Youth Media Studies in 2022 for my essay "Exposing Flaws of Affirmative Consent through Contemporary American Teen Films."

The first glimmer of my focus on sexual consent emerged through my doctoral studies and my subsequent dissertation on "consent puzzles" in 1990s literature and film. While very few films that I discussed then overlap with this book, the research on sexual consent that I conducted at that time enabled me to lay the groundwork for this project. I am absolutely indebted to my major professor Jean Walton and so grateful for the advice and thoughts I received from my other committee members Carolyn Betensky, Patricia Morokoff, Naomi Mandel, and Tiffani Kisler. Their feedback not only greatly impacted my thinking and writing but also solidified my determination to pursue my line of research and ultimately publish this book.

There are many teen films to consider in a work like this, and I am so appreciative to Nicholas Romano who helped me parse the list of hundreds of teen films considered for this book. Thank you also to Kyra Clarke who shared with me a list of teen films from her own research. I am in awe of the many filmmakers who have spent their time and money creating the many teen films I discuss. I had the opportunity to interview Jennifer Fox and Martha Coolidge for my book *Independent Female Filmmakers*, and I am grateful to them both for sharing their thoughts about their work and the industry—both of which come up again in this book.

I was pleasantly surprised to receive a fan letter from James and Nita Kincaid for my *Ms. Magazine* review of *Promising Young Woman*. Since then, I have been grateful for Jim's thoughts on how the media shapes stories of adolescent and childhood sexuality. Thank you also to Roxanne Szal from *Ms.* for providing me such an esteemed outlet for public writing and to Aviva Dove-Viebahn for first interviewing me in *Ms.* in 2019.

I am fortunate to have received grants from both the Center for the Advancement of Research and Scholarship and the Martin Richard Institute for Social Justice at Bridgewater State University to fund this project. I am grateful to all my colleagues at BSU who have been so supportive of my research.

Writing a book requires relentless persistence—and I am so thankful to the friends and colleagues in my Mastermind Failure Club—Moriah Harris, Margaret Owens, Stephanie Alvarez-Ewens, Betsy Stubblefield Loucks, Amy Walsh, and Holly Wach. This group has kept me honest in so many ways—especially to myself and my aspirations. And thank you to the many friends like Geoff Gunter, Susan Gunter, Michael Klein, and Laura Stroud who were always willing to indulge my conversations about consent and teen films.

Finally, thank you most of all to my family who have tolerated my near total obsession with teen films and have heard me say what feels like countless times "I'll be working on my book." Thanks to my mom, Laura Travaglino, who taught me at a young age to think critically about movies and is always eager to be a sounding board. Thank you also to Geoff, whom I have known since the time I was an adolescent myself—you picked up the slack, talked through my arguments, and cheered me on to the finish line. And last and most of all, thank you to M and Chase for being you. Perhaps without knowing it, you have helped me consider what my research means for actual youth, and your wisdom and compassion are constant reminders that maturity is not simply about being a specific age.

CONSENT CULTURE AND TEEN FILMS

INTRODUCTION

BY 2019, THE CONCEPT OF affirmative consent ("yes means yes") had become so prevalent in US culture that it was edited into the film *Good Boys*. While the word *consent* does not appear in an April 4, 2017 version of the script, the released film includes numerous instances of verbal consent—even one when the tween boys decide to practice kissing on what they think is a "really pretty CPR doll" but is actually a sex toy. In the scene, Max leans in for a kiss on the doll, and his friend Lucas yells, "Stop! What are you doing? . . . You can't kiss someone without their permission. Remember from assembly?" So Max asks the doll (a stand-in for his crush Brixlee), "Can I kiss you?" to which Lucas (playing Brixlee) ultimately responds, "I consent." The humor of the scene, drawn from the absurdity of obtaining affirmative consent from a sex toy, emphasizes the impacts of consent culture, or what we might call the cultural prioritization of obtaining clear consent in all interactions—particularly sexual ones. In an interview with *The Hollywood Reporter* about the film, director and cowriter Gene Stupnitsky says, "[Consent] is very real and something that should be addressed. . . . There's a long history of movies being on the other side of that, and I think going forward it's imperative for filmmakers, as the world evolves, to evolve with it."[1] Clearly, Stupnitsky intended *Good Boys* to be on the "right" side of consent culture and that meant explicitly taking sexual consent into account.

Such attention to consent in contemporary teen films represents a significant change from decades earlier. In 1980s teen films, boys routinely treat consent as irrelevant by spying on young women in locker rooms and bedrooms and tricking or coercing girls into sex. However, as affirmative consent has been increasingly culturally prioritized, studios and filmmakers have adapted the plots and scenes accordingly. Date rape is no longer a joke, and young women's

Fig. 0.1. In the 2019 film *Good Boys*, the boys practice consent on what they think is a CPR doll, but is actually a sex toy.

desires are no longer transgressive. In addition, as actors, directors, and audiences have demanded greater diversity in representation, queer teens are no longer relegated to the sidelines, and leading roles in teen films now span a range of racial and ethnic identities.

However, despite these transformations, consent has remained complex for teens in films, even in the first few decades of the twenty-first century. Girls are still shown navigating subtle and not-so-subtle coercion, while boys often are portrayed as always already consenting. Queer teens are depicted forcing themselves into unpleasant heterosexual encounters, and trans youth are shown subjugated by parents who control decisions about their gender-affirming care. Numerous contemporary teen films reveal how consent in practice can be much more perplexing than implied by "no means no" and "yes means yes." In *Consent Culture and Teen Films: Adolescent Sexuality in US Movies*, I trace the history of adolescent sexuality in US movies and look at dozens of early twenty-first-century teen films in which youth are shown as having ambiguous control over their bodies and their sexualities—despite the advances of consent culture. These moments, I argue, reveal the biases and flaws in our affirmative consent framework as well as in our assumptions about youth sexuality, ultimately exposing the need for a more nuanced way forward.

FROM RAPE CULTURE TO CONSENT CULTURE: THE EMERGENCE OF AFFIRMATIVE CONSENT

Sexual consent is a slippery concept to define, leading one scholar to declare flatly, "There is no consensus on an encompassing definition of sexual consent."[2] While consent's "moral magic" or its power to distinguish a permissible act from an impermissible act is largely agreed on, the specific interpretation of consent can vary widely depending on individual contexts.[3] Peter Westen in *The Logic of Consent* argues that although we have a "general sense" of what the term means, distinct cases expose how, in fact, we "have only vague and conflicting notions of what we mean by consent."[4] These "diverse meanings" can result in "theorists who seem to be directly debating each other" instead "talking past one another."[5] As Westen suggests, this disconnect carries the "risk" of "failing to think and communicate clearly about normative values to which we are committed."[6] In other words, while most people support a consent framework, it is not always clear what is meant by the term or how it manifests in practice.

Even as a legal construct, consent can be hard to pin down with definitions that vary state by state in the United States. Some states avoid defining consent at all, instead articulating the meaning of nonconsensual acts like sexual assault and rape.[7] Nevertheless, researchers, scholars, sex educators, schools, institutions, and governments routinely do attempt to define sexual consent. In its simplest form, sexual consent is permission for a sexual act. When broken down further, consent can be understood as "an internal experience" and/or "external communication."[8] In other words, consent can be intangibly thought/felt and/or embodied via what one says/does. Westen similarly breaks down consent into "attitudinal" consent (i.e., willingness) and "expressive" consent (i.e., verbal or other articulation of consent) and notes that in the eyes of a legal jurisdiction, consent might be defined as either or both. The contemporary discourse of affirmative consent emphasizes a clear articulation of verbal consent with the presumption that an eager yes would correspond to an internal willingness. Many related policies and guidelines thus highlight several components as necessary to validate consent, such as Planned Parenthood's definition, which outlines how consent must be "informed," "specific," "freely given," "enthusiastic," and "reversible."[9]

Consent culture represents a concerted effort to shift our cultural norms from trivializing nonconsent to focusing on clearly expressed consent. In short, consent culture is a response to rape culture. For decades, many have argued that widespread sexism has created a society that accepts and even encourages sexual assault through cultural ideas, educational practices, laws, institutional policies, and media representations. As Sarah Projansky in *Watching Rape: Film and Television in Postfeminist Culture* suggests, "depictions of rape are a pervasive part of this culture, embedded in all of its complex media forms, entrenched in the landscape of visual imagery." Such ubiquity "naturalizes rape's place in our everyday world, not only as real physical events but also as part of our fantasies, fears, desires, and consumptive practices."[10] In an attempt to address rape culture in the 1980s and 1990s, many educators, activists, and others began to stress "no means no."

Since then, the sex-positive movement, which advocates women's and girls' sexual agency, revised the mantra to "yes means yes." While no should be respected, ensuring consent requires not only the lack of a no but also an enthusiastic yes. At its core, consent culture is based on this principle of affirmative consent—hearing and articulating yes is the key to making an interaction valid. Consent culture is guided by a widespread conviction that consent matters deeply and the belief that free, informed, and mutual consent is a key to building a better world without domination, without force, and without violence. Consent culture stresses that sexual interactions are but one (albeit important) instance of consent and that consent is a learned cultural behavior—for example, children develop consent skills from being asked, not forced, to hug a relative and from learning that they too need to ask before hugging a friend.

In 2008, Jaclyn Friedman and Jessica Valenti published the volume *Yes Means Yes!: Visions of Female Sexual Power and a World without Rape*, in which they highlight their move toward affirmative consent. In the introduction, they write, "So often it seems as if the discourse is focused solely on the 'no means no' model—which, while of course useful, stops short of truly envisioning how suppressing female sexual agency is a key element of rape culture, and therefore how fostering genuine female sexual autonomy is necessary in fighting back against it."[11] Friedman and Valenti distinctly stress the necessity of cultural change, stating that the contributors seek "to heal a sexual culture that is profoundly broken" and to "explore how creating a culture that values genuine female sexual pleasure can help stop rape, and how the cultures and systems that support rape in the United States rob us of our right to sexual power."[12] Ultimately, they suggest how a turn towards consent culture or affirmative consent might best address the roots of rape culture.

While the phrase *consent culture* had been used occasionally during the twentieth century in the contexts of labor, government, and healthcare, it appears that in the 2010s, the term suddenly became widely adopted by US media.[13] Although it would be difficult to pinpoint an exact source for this surge, Kitty Stryker's blog, *Consent Culture*, is often cited as bringing prominence to the term.[14] By 2014, *consent culture* had become mainstream enough for inclusion in Urban Dictionary which states, "A consent culture is one in which the prevailing narrative of sex is centered around mutual consent. It is a culture with an abhorrence of forcing anyone into anything, a respect for the absolute necessity of bodily autonomy, a culture that believes that a person is always the best judge of their own wants and needs." The definition clarifies that "consent culture is also one in which mutual consent is part of social life as well," meaning that consent is required for *all* interactions—from hugging and tickling to talking to someone, even stating, "Don't want to try the fish? That's fine."[15] In 2017, Stryker published the compilation *Ask: Building Consent Culture* with the goal of encouraging conversations "not just about the issues around consent in daily life, but also what we can do about them—a friendly yet firm call to action."

There is no one precise moment when consent culture came into being. However, numerous journalists and scholars often highlight the first college affirmative consent policy developed by the feminist student organization Antioch Womyn in 1990 at Antioch College as a historical moment. Their Sexual Offense Prevention Policy (SOPP), revised over the years, outlined tenets such as "consent is required each and every time there is sexual activity" and "each new level of sexual activity requires consent." It also included specifics such as intoxication and sleep invalidate consent; consent can be withdrawn at any point; and "silence is not consent." In their emphasis on "yes means yes," the policy clarified that "body movements and non-verbal responses such as moans are not consent" and stated that it was the responsibility of the sexual initiator to obtain consent and the recipient to respond verbally.[16]

In 1993, this policy became the object of national ridicule when it was parodied on *Saturday Night Live*'s "Is It Date Rape?" sketch with Mike Myers with lines like "May I elevate the level of sexual intimacy by feeling your buttocks?" Affirmative consent, at this time, seemed excessive and preposterous—it was "held up as the apotheosis of political correctness," according to Kristine Herman, one of the Antioch Womyn authors. Meanwhile, the policy had already been in effect for two years without controversy; students took it to be "normal and status quo."[17] Decades later, such a policy is now commonplace at colleges across the United States.

The evolving discourse of consent culture has been negotiated by and through legislation and landmark cases regarding sexual consent on college campuses. A 1985 study with over six thousand undergraduates conducted by *Ms.* and Mary P. Koss concluded that one in four undergraduate women "had an experience that met the legal definition of rape or attempted rape."[18] The study later became adapted into the book *I Never Called It Rape* published in 1988. Several US Supreme Court cases in the 1990s then established that Title IX must protect student victims of sexual violence and harassment: a 1992 decision confirmed student victims of sexual harassment could be awarded monetary damages in certain cases, and a 1999 decision concluded that Title IX covered both student-student sexual harassment and teacher-student harassment.[19] These judicial battles played out alongside growing mainstream awareness of campus sexual assault. In the aughts, campus sexual assault continued to be recognized as a serious and pervasive issue, with cases from the Air Force Academy, Rutgers University, Duke University, and numerous others making national headlines.

A tipping point came in 2011, when the Obama administration's Department of Education Office of Civil Rights (OCR) presented schools a nineteen-page "Dear colleague" letter that outlined the specific steps to prevent and respond to accusations of sexual harassment and violence under Title IX. The letter defines "sexual violence" as "physical sexual acts perpetrated against a person's will" and states that drugs, alcohol, and certain disabilities can invalidate consent. There is no explicit mention of affirmative consent in the letter. Still, the effects of the OCR's actions would prove significant. Colleges had long tried to sweep campus rapes and sexual assaults under the rug by suppressing reports and statistics. Suddenly, this tacit strategy was outed as a national issue, and federal funding was on the line for compliance in handling such cases according to the OCR guidelines. In May 2014, the OCR took it even further with the "unprecedented step" of publishing the names of fifty-five colleges and universities under investigation for Title IX compliance, which included elite institutions like Harvard Law School and Princeton University; public universities like Michigan State University and Ohio State University; and private institutions such as Boston University and Sarah Lawrence College.[20] As R. Shep Melnick states in his Brookings report "Analyzing the Department of Education's Final Title IX Rules on Sexual Misconduct," the OCR in 2014 articulated a "'new paradigm' for sexual harassment regulation" one intended to "change the culture on the college campuses . . . to cure the epidemic of sexual violence." This paradigm shift, Melnick states, "replaced the courts' focus on identifying and punishing the perpetrators of on-campus sexual misconduct with a much broader effort to change social attitudes and to mitigate the effects of sexual assault wherever it occurs."[21] Such a statement points to how the OCR saw the transition from a rape culture to a consent culture as necessary to solving the complex problem of campus sexual assault. In 2014, California became the first state to require colleges to specify affirmative consent policies for students. Others have since followed.

In 2015, *Saturday Night Live* once again performed a consent sketch, "Teacher Trial," which depicted a teen boy (played by adult Pete Davidson) in a court detailing his sexual assault by two women teachers. A straight-faced attorney questions the student who expresses how pleasurable their three-way was and how it earned him respect from his peers, all of which attracts approving nods from his dad and fist bumps from the judge. The joke implies the impossibility of a young man's being sexually assaulted by an adult woman teacher, perpetuating an unfortunate belief that men and boys are always already consenting to sex. However, this time, *SNL* got more than laughs—the skit immediately received abundant backlash on Twitter with viewers calling the sketch "gross and unnecessary," "Not cool. Not funny," and "a new low."[22] Consent culture clearly had changed how viewers reacted to such sketches, and the rise of social media facilitated their ability to communicate their dissatisfaction to each other and *SNL* itself. As I elaborate further in chapter 5, consent culture can be viewed as linked to what has been termed *cancel culture* as audiences demand accountability from public figures, celebrities, and media.

The shift to consent culture has been the result of countless voices advocating change. In between these two *SNL* skits, there have been essays, blog posts, hashtags, conversations, court cases, and, of course, films, television, and other media that together have transformed the mainstream way of thinking about consent. As an example of how long and how many voices it can take to shape a cultural transition, consider the #MeToo movement. Tarana Burke first posted the hashtag on MySpace in 2006, but it wasn't until 2017 that Alyssa Milano tweeted, "If you've been sexually harassed or assaulted write 'me too' as a reply to this tweet." The response was overwhelming and went much further than simply direct replies to Milano. At that moment, many felt comfortable posting their stories publicly for the first time, partly because they were no longer isolated survivors but members of a growing movement highlighting the harms of rape culture and demanding a better way forward.

A SEX-CRITICAL APPROACH TO CONSENT

Consent culture is not without flaws. Harvard Law School professor and attorney Janet Halley, in "The Move to Affirmative Consent" in *Signs*, argues that the move to affirmative consent is actually a "conservative" one that "poses the possibility of a vast new criminalization"; "install[s] traditional social norms of male responsibility and female helplessness"; and "foster[s] a new, randomly applied moral order that will often be intensely repressive and sex-negative."[23] Halley pinpoints the central question often asked when using consent as the key to ethical or legal interactions: Should consent be defined as "subjective" or "performative"[24], that is, as a "state of mind" or a "performative act"?[25] Halley argues that discrepancies could result in an individual verbally consenting to a sexual act that they *do not want* and refusing to verbally consent to a sexual act they *do want*. In other words, an emphasis on performative consent "come[s] at the cost of enabling people to punish their sex partners for engaging in sex that the complainants passionately desired at the time."[26]

This confusion over consent impacts real-world interactions. In focus groups, college students often express that they are either unfamiliar with their school's consent policies or are unable to determine how to put the policies into practice. In one study, students described how nonsexual/sexual and nonconsensual/consensual interactions "blur into one another" leading the researchers to call for consent to be thought of as a "cumulative phenomenon" as opposed to a single consensual or nonconsensual event.[27] In addition, many theorists note how consent for sexual acts is often interpreted by participants through nonverbal cues like body language, making affirmative consent even more confusing.[28] Other ambiguities can derive from the fact that consent frequently is given "prospectively" (beforehand) or "retrospectively" (after the fact) and not "contemporaneously" (in the moment), as Westen notes.[29] For example, one might consent to a sexual act but feel differently as that sexual act begins and proceeds. Or one can engage in an act and then feel differently about it afterward.

The fact that consent proves to be an incredibly ambiguous and tenuous framework for sexual interactions is often glossed over, except by certain sex researchers and legal scholars.[30] Yet I would argue that Michel Foucault's 1978 prediction appears to have become true: "sexuality will no longer be a kind of behavior hedged in by any precise prohibitions, but a kind of roaming danger, a sort of omnipresent phantom." This scenario, Foucault suggests, ushers in a "new regime for the supervision of sexuality," one in which legal and medical institutions "try to get a grip through an apparently generous, and at least general, legislation."[31] In other words, it is no longer particular sexual behaviors and relationships (sodomy, miscegenation, etc.) that are controlled; rather, sex itself has become understood as a "roaming danger" that needs constant attention, regulation, and enforcement.[32] Yes, consent culture emerged out of a legitimate and urgent need to protect individuals from sexual harassment, assault, and exploitation. But consent culture has also elicited a new era of discussing and policing sexual relations. And ironically, affirmative consent does *not* automatically resolve a key concern amid rape culture—eradicating the abundance of unwanted and pressured sexual interactions. When verbal assent is emphasized as the essential factor in ethical and legal sexual interactions, unwanted sexual encounters can still be consensual. In other words, a yes might not always mean yes. Such an issue also has been raised by radical feminists like Catharine A. MacKinnon who argue that "the sharp line drawn by liberals between consensual and nonconsensual sex falsifies the degree of coercion imposed upon women by men in our ordinary sexual lives."[33] Some radical feminists take this argument quite far, suggesting the impossibility of women's heterosexual consent—not a stance I would support. Still, it is quite possible that affirmative consent has provided a deceptive sense of security about how rape culture can be addressed and resolved.

In recognition of all the complexities of consent, I position myself within a sex-critical approach to consent, seeking to bridge the common schism in feminism between sex-positive and radical feminist ideologies. This approach recognizes the urgency of critiquing and disrupting rape culture and prioritizing consent while avoiding value judgments about the range of sexualities, gender identities, desires, and practices. A sex-critical approach emphasizes the importance of examining, calling out, and rewriting dominant "sexual scripts" that imply primarily one way of being sexual—typically "penile-vaginal intercourse that happens between one cisgender man and one cisgender woman," as Milena Popova observes in the book *Sexual Consent*. Such scripts, Popova contends, create a "clear line of progression" between "the starting point of sex somewhere around kissing and touching, and the endpoint at a cisgender man's ejaculation."[34] Lisa Downing, who coined the phrase *sex critical*, underscores that in this approach, "all forms of sexuality and all sexual representations should be equally susceptible to critical thinking and interrogation about the normative or otherwise ideologies they uphold."[35] I would add that this way of thinking also offers an opportunity to look more critically at sexual consent itself, by seeking to understand and unravel complexities instead of avoiding them through oversimplifications.

In looking at how consent culture impacts teen films, I aim not to provide pat answers but rather to demonstrate some of the more troubling aspects of consent depicted through this body of films. I recognize too that adolescent sexuality is not a single monolithic idea but rather a range of desires, experiences, and subjectivities, some of which are more visible than others in the genre. For example, trans, nonbinary, gender-questioning, and bisexual teens remain less commonly depicted—even now. Topics, themes, characters, and plots for teen films are not only crafted by adults but also filtered by an industry that relies on producing popular content marketed to a wide audience for economic gain. Thus, I would argue that omission does not necessarily suggest the lack of importance of an issue among actual youth but rather signals a lack of mainstream focus and acceptance in adult society. Adolescent sexuality ultimately exists within an adult world of laws, rules, and cultural meanings and yet is also full of its own rebellions, contradictions, and resistances.

A DEFINITION OF TEEN FILM

While there are numerous interpretations of what we mean by "teen films," for the purposes of this study, I define them as coming-of-age movies marketed to youth and/or adults. Ultimately, I am interested in how portrayals of youth by adults have shaped and continue to shape our ideas of adolescence, sexuality, and consent. For this reason, I have chosen not to limit my definition to films marketed to teens. Certainly, teen audiences have comprised a formidable demographic for the genre, even the industry as a whole. In *Signifying Female Adolescence*, Georganne Scheiner argues that "a clear teen culture came into being" as early as the 1920s, and that it was that culture which shaped both the content and marketing of films for decades to come.[36] Others highlight the 1940s as the era when the concept of a "teenager" emerged and the industry became more conscious of youth as drivers of ticket sales, ultimately taking the form of "teenpics" in the 1950s, as Thomas Doherty suggests. Other shifts in the genre over the last half century have also been driven by youth. In the book *Generation Multiplex*, Timothy Shary argues that the 1980s represented a particular flourishing of the teen film due to adolescents who flocked to movies in malls and theaters. In the early twenty-first century, youth audiences again have been instrumental in bringing about the transition from in-person theatrical screenings to video on demand (VOD) platforms like Netflix and Hulu.

Still, I do not view teen films as being solely *for* youth. Many contemporary teen films are rated R by the Motion Pictures Association (MPA), so teenagers under age seventeen would be unable to watch them in a theater without an accompanying adult. Similarly, numerous VOD teen films like Hulu's *Plan B* (2021) are rated TV-MA or "mature" and designated only for logged-in users over the age of eighteen.[37] So, it seems no leap to argue that teen films are not exclusively for youth. I would even contend that teen films have long been positioned for adults—the teen sex comedy, in particular, with its nudity and sexual humor is often marketed as voyeuristic entertainment for adults. Such R-rated films explicitly target adults nostalgic for the teen films of their own generation—*Blockers* (2018) brings parents into the foreground of the teen sex comedy plot, *The To Do List* (2013) takes place in the 1990s, and *Good Boys* mixes adult humor with naive preteen boys.

In fact, adults might be partial to the youth genre because, as Shary says, "teen films hold a special place in the hearts of almost all moviegoers, since we have fond and frustrating memories of the films that spoke to us in our adolescence."[38] Catherine Driscoll too notes that the "sensibility" of the teen film—marked by Robert Benayoun's description of "normal qualities of youth: naïveté, idealism, humor, hatred of tradition, erotomania, and a sense of injustice"— ensures an "appeal" beyond teens.[39] Universal themes alongside the simple fact that every adult experienced their own youth draws adults into the potential, if not always the intended audience. And ultimately, in this book, I seek to unravel what teen films suggest about cultural notions of adolescent sexuality—whether they are marketed to adults, youth, or both.

Perhaps quite obviously, teen movies are generally not *by* teens. As Shary notes in his book *Teen Movies: American Youth on Screen*, there is no "cinematic tradition of movies made by children, unlike many other marginalized groups in U.S. history." While youth certainly produce their own media, they typically are not involved in the writing, directing, and producing of feature-length films. The prevailing assumption has been that "adults could portray the youth experience based on their personal memories and current observations; the only creative input young people actually had was in performing the roles adults designed for them."[40] As a result, Shary notes, "screen images of youth have always been traditionally filtered through adult perspectives."[41] Even sporadic exceptions, such as books written by teen girls and adapted into movies such as *The Outsiders* (1983) and *The Kissing Booth* (2018) or scripts written in collaboration with teens such as *Thirteen* (2003), still involve adult screenwriters, directors, and producers who ultimately shape the resulting visual narrative.

The fact that teen films are made by adults, not adolescents themselves, presents a unique question for the study of the genre not always acknowledged by critics and scholars—might teen films lag in their resonance by years or decades as a result of their adult points of view? Of course, the adolescents in teen films are not necessarily representative of actual youth in any period—as Driscoll in the book *Teen Film: A Critical Introduction* suggests, "probably few people have ever felt their adolescence was accurately portrayed by teen film."[42] In fact, teen films so often draw on a stock set of characters and themes, one cannot help but wonder if they are less drawn from any past or present reality but are rather, as Driscoll suggests, more indicative of Fredric Jameson's concept of "pastiche," or imitation without an original or referent.[43] The teens conjured by "teen films" reside more in adults' imaginations than in reality, and the plots often contain recycled narrative patterns.

While teen films are fictional, they are also a manifestation of the discourses around youth. Jon Lewis argues that teen films are "the *principal* mass mediated discourse of youth"—one "that rather glibly and globally re-presents youth as a culture."[44] Teen films both reflect and influence ideas about adolescents, even though they are not always representative of actual youth. Jacqueline Rose makes an analogous argument in a study of children's literature stating, "There is no child behind the category 'children's fiction,' other than the one which the category itself sets in place, the one which it needs to believe is there for its own purposes."[45] Ironically, children's fiction, as Henry Jenkins describes, "tell[s] us far more about adults, their values, their aspirations, their emotional needs, than such stories tell us about children's actual experiences."[46] Similarly, teen films imaginatively conjure and invent the notion of the "teen." At times, teen films appear to be a double fiction—not necessarily accurately representing youth nor created for them. Rather the concerns that emerge through the teen films of each era represent the fears and beliefs of the adults who make them, watch them, and regulate them.

Aligning with numerous other scholars of adolescence in film, I allow my definition of teen movies to blur beyond the strict limits of characters aged thirteen to nineteen. In the teen movie genre, *teen* often serves as a stand-in for *youth* or *adolescent*, terms that imply a stage of life rather than a specific age. The definition of an adolescent is itself a moving target, currently characterized by individuals between the onset of puberty through their twenties. In general, I look here to films that depict the journey of a sexual coming of age in adolescence, whether the characters are tweens (such as in *The Tale* and *Good Boys*) or are in college and beyond (such as in *Boy Erased*). That said, most protagonists in the films included in my study are high school age—and there seems to be a particular prevalence within teen romance/sex films to set the story during senior year of high school or the summer before college, likely to position the characters as mature enough for sexual exploits.

Teen films, of course, encompass an array of subgenres. Shary breaks down the US contemporary youth genre into five categories: school films (usually comedies), delinquency dramas, horror films, science films, and love/sex films.[47] I focus largely on the dramas and comedies of this last subgenre—love/sex films. Like Shary, I view horror films as a distinct subgenre, so they are not included in my study. I also do not focus on G-rated children's films such as animated Disney features since I also consider them a distinct subgenre. Within the love/sex subgenre, as Shary notes, are stories about the desire for (and obstacles to) sexual knowledge/experience and stories about the desire for (and obstacles to) romance. I add in other subcategories including stories about sexual abuse that prioritize the adolescent's point of view, such as *Precious* (2009), *Diary of a Teenage Girl* (2015), and *The Tale* (2018); stories that focus on gender transitioning, such as *3 Generations* (2015); and stories that focus on a teen's experience in conversion therapy, such as *The Miseducation of Cameron Post* (2018) and *Boy Erased* (2018).

Furthermore, my focus on teen *films* precludes my delving into how adolescents have been depicted on television, VOD, or web series. My omission of episodic programming in this study does not suggest its irrelevance but is simply a result of my examining the through line of over one hundred years of the teen film as a specific and unique genre. Although it is certainly possible, perhaps even likely, that shorter form and episodic content will eventually supplant feature-length films, the teen film remains a robust genre with strong market potential. In fact, some of the most watched films on Netflix in recent years have been teen films, such as *The Kissing Booth* and *To All the Boys I've Loved Before* (2018), both of which inspired trilogies.

I limit my study in this book to films produced in the United States.[48] Teen films, of course, are an international art and product. There is no doubt that US cinema is influenced by work and trends across the globe, just as it wields influence around the world, and some of the most groundbreaking work indeed has emerged from filmmakers outside of the United States. For example, there are numerous instances of trends that began in Europe—such as European films' depicting explicitly queer youth protagonists years before US films. However, my exclusive focus on US cinema enables an examination of teen films in direct relation to cultural forces and laws regarding visual culture and youth sexuality that are unique to the country. For example, the United States has some of the strictest laws against child pornography in the world, a fact that continues to shape visual depictions of youth sexuality even now.

One of the limitations in reviewing any aspect of US film history is the fact of an industry that has been long guided by racism, sexism, classism, heteronormativity, ableism, and cis sexism. Youth of different races, ethnicities, classes, gender identities, abilities, and sexualities have been omitted from most of film history, just as directors, producers, and executives have tended to be white cis men for over a century. Groundbreaking films by women and people of color have long been excluded from awards like the Oscars and archives like the National Film Registry. These obstacles have made it frustratingly difficult to find depictions of diverse teens from a range of perspectives throughout US cinema history. As a result, the definition of "teen film" has leaned white, heterosexual, and cisgender. In this study, I have made a conscious effort to seek out a more diverse range of teen films from the independent film arena—both in recounting the history of sexuality in the genre and in selecting twenty-first-century films for my study. While many studies in teen films tend to omit or gloss over early cinema, I also attempt in chapter 1 to illuminate some early examples worth another look. However, one chapter cannot comprehensively represent a complete history of the genre, and there clearly remains a continued need for more studies emphasizing race and the range of sexualities and gender identities in teen films throughout US history.

Perhaps the single most important characteristic of the teen films included in my study is a clear point of view from the youth's perspective. For this reason, I tend to exclude films where childhood is shown as the stepping-stone to a story about adulthood, such as *Riding in Cars with Boys* (2001), as well as films in which the adolescent's point of view is not primary, such as in *The Kids Are All Right* (2010). However, I do include a film like *The Tale* since writer/director Jennifer Fox specifically prioritizes the child's (Jenny's) voice alongside that of her adult self (Jennifer). In fact, Jenny's voice is one of the key features of the film, so much so that in one scene Jenny looks into the camera and insists that she is the hero of the story. Although I recognize the tenuousness of adolescent subjectivity within *any* story told by adults, I look to stories that provide the illusion of such subjectivity. In other words, I do not argue that teen films depict an actual contemporaneous adolescent point of view but rather suggest how this imagined subjectivity articulates the current cultural concerns, fears, and fascinations of adults regarding adolescence.

SEXUALITY IN TEEN FILMS IN THE EARLY TWENTY-FIRST CENTURY

Consent culture has undoubtedly curbed certain depictions in film and television, while encouraging others to flourish. As the arbiter of depictions of adolescent sexuality, filmmakers of teen films undoubtedly respond to cultural pressures and norms. In many ways, consent culture provides filmmakers a new production "code"—one that suggests not what is morally decent, but rather what is ethical in contemporary society. In subsequent chapters, I address how consent culture influences specific thematic depictions of adolescent sexuality in teen films during the early twenty-first century—and how these films reveal some of the tacit dilemmas of consent.

In chapter 1, "Regulating Adolescent Sexuality in US Cinema: From Censorship to Child Pornography Laws," I provide an overview of the history of US regulation of adolescent sexuality—from the silent era to contemporary films. I examine the impact of key movements of censorship, rating systems, and child pornography legislation, and I highlight several films that circumvented barriers with groundbreaking or surprising representations of adolescent sexuality. Concern for protecting children has significantly shaped and continues to shape how adolescent sexual behavior is visualized through film. As I reference dozens of teen films throughout the decades, I demonstrate that although anxiety for adolescents' exposure to ideas about sex through film has waned, concern over the sexual exploitation of minors has grown. Ultimately, this chapter provides a context for those that follow, tracing a history of adolescent sexuality in US teen films from the inception of cinema in the 1890s through the twenty-first century.

In chapters 2 and 3, I show how teen films expose specific flaws in the affirmative consent discourse. In chapter 2, "Flipping the Heterosexual Script and Race-Based Sexual Stereotypes in Teen Comedies of the 2010s and 2020s," I look to a number of recent US sex comedies like *The To Do List*, *Banging Lanie* (2020), *Blockers* (2020), *American Pie: Girls' Rules* (2020), and *Sex Appeal* (2022) and romances targeted to younger audiences like *To All the Boys I've Loved Before*, *Sierra Burgess Is a Loser* (2018), and *The Half of It* (2020) that rewrite the stereotypical heterosexual script by placing girls in the role of the sexual aggressor. In many ways, these films represent the gains of consent culture, feminism, the call for more women directors, and demands for greater diversity in films. Many of the girls playing aggressors are also multiethnic—Aubrey Plaza (*The To Do List*) is Puerto Rican American; Leah Lewis (*The Half of It*) is Chinese American; Lana Condor (*To All the Boys I've Loved Before*) is Vietnamese American; Piper Curda (*American Pie: Girls' Rules*) is Korean American; Madison Pettis (*American Pie: Girls' Rules*) is Black American; and Geraldine Viswanathan (*Blockers*) is Indian Swiss. As a result, these films push against not only the heterosexual script but also race-based sexual stereotypes. However, such films persist in problematic narrative patterns, such as relying on nonconsent as part of the plot and perpetuating the stereotype that teen boys are always already consenting. In particular, many of these films use nonconsent as humor or plot device—and such a structure only seems possible amid consent culture by switching genders. Ultimately, I argue that these teen films expose affirmative consent as a highly gendered discourse where consent is taken into account for girls more than boys.

In chapter 3, "Queering Consent: Navigating Performative and Subjective Consent in Queer Teen Films," I describe how queer US teen films highlight another failing of the affirmative consent discourse—how it can be ineffective at protecting against undesired and unpleasant sexual encounters. Here, I outline how queer teens moved from the sidelines into leading roles of independent teen films in the late 1990s, culminating with *Love, Simon* (2018), the first Hollywood film to feature a homosexual protagonist in the genre. However, many recent cis queer and questioning characters in films such as *Alex Strangelove* (2018), *Blockers*, and *A Girl Like Grace* (2015) depict consent as troubling—the teens are shown as initially not consenting to their own sexual impulses and thus force themselves into heterosexual encounters that they neither want nor enjoy. Furthermore, recent films such as *Boy Erased* and *The Miseducation of Cameron Post* depict older teens "consenting" to conversion therapy, which again accentuates how constrained and coerced affirmative consent can be. I conclude the chapter by looking at the film *Princess Cyd* (2017), which rewrites the queer script in a nuanced and affirming way, recognizing nonconsent but also underscoring sexuality as a continuum and open-ended exploration.

In chapters 4 and 5, I highlight how teen films resist oversimplifying consent and agency regarding youth. In chapter 4 "'I Was Not Lolita': Child Sexual Abuse and Children's Agency in *The Diary of a Teenage Girl* and *The Tale*," I look at two recent US films that recount the statutory rape of cis girls by adult men—situations that imply the impossibility of consent. In earlier eras, young girls were frequently depicted as sexually precocious in films such as *Taxi Driver* (1976), *Pretty Baby* (1978), *Manhattan* (1979), and *Blame It on Rio* (1984) or even as dangerous sexual aggressors/predators toward older men in *Poison Ivy* (1992), *The Crush* (1993), and *Election* (1999). With the passing of the Victims of Trafficking and Violence Protection Act of 2000, the sexualization of girls discourse, and increased recognition of childhood sexual abuse (CSA), twenty-first-century films clearly avoided blaming girls for statutory rape and incest. However, what became lost in this turn is the acknowledgment of girl survivors' sexual desire, curiosity, pleasure, and choices. For example, the 2009 adaptation *Precious* omits the girl's orgasms so prominent and discomfiting in the original novel *Push*, begging the question of whether it would have been impossible to highlight her status as a victim with that aspect in the film. In this chapter, I suggest that two recent films, *The Diary of a Teenage Girl* and *The Tale*, present a new way of imagining CSA stories as more complex narratives of girls who voice desires and make choices even while depicting them as exploited by adult men. These films challenge us to rethink the Lolita narrative and recognize how youth might assert choices and maintain a distinct point of view, even in stories where consent is ethically impossible.

In chapter 5, "The (In)Visibility of Trans Teens: *3 Generations*, *Adam*, and *Boy Meets Girl*," I look at how US trans teen films render visible a unique problem regarding consent—how can we even know that youth consent to the stories told about them? After over a century of near invisibility, trans teens have finally started to emerge in a handful of recent independent breakout movies. President Biden repeatedly has called trans rights the "civil rights issue of our time." I would add that for youth, trans rights are also a consent issue of our time. Adolescents must rely on parents to consent to their gender-affirming care, and over a dozen US states are weighing bills to prevent minors from obtaining this care even *with* parental consent—such a law passed in Arkansas in April 2021 and other states since have followed suit.

In this chapter, I look at how audiences express dissent (or nonconsent) for specific depictions of trans youth pointing out the intrinsic link between consent culture and "cancel culture," the movement to hold people accountable publicly for undesired actions and representations. While trans activists clearly advocate more stories by and about trans individuals, they also protest the visibility of films with problematic plots and insensitive elements. Two recent films, 3 *Generations* and *Adam* (2019), received abundant social media backlash as audiences and activists sought to erase them. In recognition that these stories cannot be detached from the many extratextual elements that impact actual trans youth's lives, I consider what is rendered (in)visible through these two films and the more affirming under-the-radar independent feature *Boy Meets Girl* (2014). While *Boy Meets Girl* did not find a large audience despite its overwhelmingly positive reviews from critics and fans, 3 *Generations* and *Adam*, along with the issues they raise, also were largely overlooked due to their being "canceled." Such continued invisibility for trans youth in the genre has forced the issues that these films raise about gender and sexuality—such as the unspoken cisness of the affirmative consent discourse—to remain in the background.

In my conclusion, "Adolescent Sexuality and Adult Imagination," I draw together key issues raised in my earlier chapters—the flaws embedded within the affirmative consent discourse; the challenge of accessing stories from a youth's point of view; and the urgency to attribute sexual agency to youth. At the same time, I shift my discussion from the fictional to the nonfictional world via a discussion of youth "sexting," the practice of sending and receiving sexual images and videos. Teen films represent a fundamental problem of representation—the sexual stories about youth are not by youth, nor would youth necessarily find them accurate portrayals of their lives. So what happens when young people take cameras into their own hands to display their sexual selves to each other? Although teen films routinely imagine adolescents in sexual situations, there remains quite a bit of apprehension in the

United States around youth sexuality. In this chapter, I detail how the sexting discourse initially was shaped by adults' anxieties around a toxic connection between youth and sexuality. However, youth not only wrested back this story but also altered the legal ramifications of their actions by the sheer prevalence of the behavior. As adults were forced to recognize the ubiquity of teen sexting, it became unsustainable to prosecute and impossible to label the behavior deviant. Ultimately, I suggest how adolescent sexuality discourses might be framed by adults, but youth nevertheless wield formidable power both to create their private sexual selves and transform public discourses about their sexuality.

As I elaborate throughout the following chapters, consent culture has ensured that sexual consent is routinely taken into account in early twenty-first-century teen films. However, whether intentionally or not, many of these films simultaneously demonstrate the elusiveness and even the irony of consent as a goal. When tweens seek to obtain consent from an inanimate doll—as the characters in *Good Boys* do—it is evident that consent has not only become the de facto ethical framework but also remains somewhat comically so. In teen films, we are confronted by innumerable problematic aspects of consent in practice—youth say yes when they clearly feel no (such as in *A Girl Like Grace* and *Alex Strangelove*); they insist on a consent and agency adults deem invalid due to their age (such as in *Diary of a Teenage Girl* and *3 Generations*); and they regret their sexual experiences (such as in *Lady Bird* and *Banging Lanie*). Consent, in other words, has not been shown as relieving youth from the complex negotiations and emotions that emerge as one comes of age and embarks on sexual encounters. While consent culture certainly has provided some of the language during these cinematic moments, it is strikingly evident that those words often fall short. Consent, it turns out, has not been the panacea we had hoped—that is, at least, not according to teen films.

NOTES

1. Stupnitsky, quoted in Chuba, "Seth Rogen."
2. Sternin et al., "Sexual Consent," 2.
3. Hurd, "Moral Magic of Consent."
4. Westen, *Logic of Consent*, 2.
5. Ferzan, "Clarifying Consent," 195.
6. Westen, *Logic of Consent*, 3.
7. For more information on how each state defines consent, see RAINN, "How Does Your State Define Consent?"
8. McKenna, Roemer, and Orsillo, "Predictors of Sexual Consent," 1491.
9. Planned Parenthood, "What Is Sexual Consent?"
10. Projanksy, *Watching Rape*, 2–3.

11. Friedman and Valenti, *Yes Means Yes!*, 6.
12. Friedman and Valenti, *Yes Means Yes!*, 7–8.
13. Essays from the 1980s (including Kelly and Norman, "Fusion Process for Productivity Improvement") quote Dr. William Ouchi's 1981 "Theory Z" essay, which defines consent culture as "a community of equals who cooperate with one another to reach common goals." Note that the Google Books Ngram Viewer (which dates back to 1800) registers only a few blips for the phrase "consent culture" before a sharp rise in 2011, and the phrase *consent culture* does not register on Google Trends (which dates back to 2004) until 2012.
14. Dymock, "Towards a Consent Culture." The blog was launched in 2011.
15. Urban Dictionary, s.v., "consent culture."
16. Lukianoff, *Unlearning Liberty*.
17. NPR, "History behind Sexual Consent Policies."
18. Zimmerman, "Campus Sexual Assault."
19. See the Supreme Court cases: *Franklin v. Gwinnett County Public Schools* in 1992 and *Davis v. Monroe County Board of Education* in 1999.
20. Stratford, "U.S. Names Colleges under Investigation."
21. Melnick, "Analyzing the Department of Education's Final Title IX Rules on Sexual Misconduct."
22. Yakas, "This 'Teacher Trial' Rape Sketch."
23. Halley, "Move to Affirmative Consent," 258–63.
24. Halley, "Move to Affirmative Consent," 265.
25. Miller and Wertheimer, *Ethics of Consent*, 10.
26. Halley, "Move to Affirmative Consent," 277.
27. Hardesty et al., "Indiscrete."
28. See Archard, *Sexual Consent*; Hickman and Muehlenhard, "By the Semi-Mystical Appearance of a Condom."
29. Westen, *Logic of Consent*, 247.
30. See Bergelson, "Meaning of Sexual Consent"; Gruber, "Anti-Rape Culture"; Halley, "Move to Affirmative Consent"; Simpson, "Challenging Childhood."
31. Foucault, *Politics, Philosophy, Culture*, 281. From the interview "The Danger of Childhood Sexuality" from 1978 included there.
32. Foucault, *Politics, Philosophy, Culture*, 281. Note that the US Supreme Court case *Lawrence v. Texas* rendered moot laws against sodomy in several US states.
33. Miller and Wertheimer, *Ethics of Consent*, 225.
34. Popova, *Sexual Consent*, 80–81.
35. LD, "What Is 'Sex Critical.'"
36. Scheiner, *Signifying Female Adolescence: Film Representations and Fans*, 3.
37. The restrictions for TV-MA rating seems to depend on platform. Hulu, at https://www.hulu.com/ratings, describes TV-MA as content "specifically designed to be viewed by adults and therefore may be unsuitable for children under 17" and says, "To watch TV-MA content on Hulu, users must be logged in and over the age of 18." Netflix, at https://help.netflix.com/en/node/206, categorizes TV-MA as "For Mature Audiences. May not be suitable for ages 17 and under."
38. Shary, *Teen Movies*, 3.
39. Driscoll, *Teen Film*, 2.
40. Shary, *Teen Movies*, 2.
41. Shary, *Generation Multiplex*, 2.

42. Driscoll, *Teen Film*, 1.
43. Driscoll, *Teen Film*, 90.
44. Lewis, *Father-Daughter Incest*, 2. Emphasis mine.
45. J. Rose, *Case of Peter Pan*, 10.
46. H. Jenkins, "Just a Spoonful of Sugar."
47. Shary, "Course File," 40.
48. I recognize biases inherent in using "America" and "American" to convey the United States of America. As a result, I use either United States or US throughout this text.

ONE

REGULATING ADOLESCENT SEXUALITY IN US CINEMA

From Censorship to Child Pornography Laws

> For over a century, no tactic for stirring up erotic hysteria
> has been as reliable as the appeal to protect children.
>
> —*Gayle Rubin, "Thinking Sex"*[1]

Sex, movies, and youth have been seen as a dangerous combination necessitating regulation since cinema's earliest days. And despite more than a century of increasing acknowledgment that sexual desire and exploration are a normal part of childhood and adolescence, widespread anxiety around the visual depiction of youth sexuality nonetheless persists in the United States. Of course, the presiding concerns of the late 1890s are not the same as today. From the advent of cinema through the Production Code years, calls for censorship revealed widespread apprehension about how films might negatively affect youth behavior. From the late 1970s to the present, however, the urgency has shifted toward ensuring minors are not exploited through child pornography. That is not to say that one fear has completely replaced the other. In fact, teen films continue to be criticized, even by some scholars, for having a negative influence on young people.[2]

By definition, children are a subjugated category of individuals in need of adults' safeguarding, or as Frances Smith has put it, "teenagers continue to be constructed as the vulnerable objects of adult regulation and concern."[3] Ostensibly to protect them, adults have spent over a hundred years debating, legislating, and controlling cinema about and for youth in the United States. As a result, the depiction of adolescent sexuality in US film repeatedly has been transformed by a series of explicit and tacit regulations including censorship, rating systems, and legislation.

Since every representation of sex is also a representation of sexual consent, to chart a history of sexual consent in youth films is also to chart a history of adolescent sex in cinema. And to chart a history of adolescent sex in cinema is to chart a history of its regulation, highlighting not only the visible but the unseen. Allusions to sex take place even in films where sex and romance have little to do with the overall plot, such as *Stand by Me* (1986) and *The Sandlot* (1993). When sex is omitted entirely from a teen film, that too suggests an intentionality. In several eras, adolescent sex appeared nearly dormant, such as during the industry's self-inflicted censorship era of the Production Code, or during the changing sexual ethics of the AIDS epidemic. Certain types of romances have also been both explicitly and tacitly regulated—for example, love stories between people of color and white people were banned by the Production Code until 1956, while homosexual romances were rarely found in US teen films until the 1990s. These exclusions can be as telling as the relationships featured in films released.

In fact, the history of adolescence in US cinema puts into a stark relief how much has been omitted for over a century—and of course that's not just sex. Teen films—like the rest of US cinema—offer a limited view of our diverse cultural past across the spectrums of race, ethnicity, class, ability, gender identity, and sexuality. Due to systemic biases and discrimination in virtually every aspect of the movie industry—from casting to production to distribution to film criticism—the body of films available for historical study consists of mostly those directed by white men about able-bodied, cisgender, heterosexual, white adolescents from middle-class homes. Such biases, alongside the fact that teen films are made by adults, not youth, means that a study of adolescent sexuality in US cinema cannot expose the complex realities of actual adolescents over the past century of filmmaking.

Rather, what such an examination *does* reveal are the culturally dominant concerns of adults that have persisted and shifted through changing times. Fears around sex and class contagion, gender instability, race and relationships, queerness, and promiscuity have manifested in narratives that kept gender roles strictly distinct, upheld ideals of marriage and family, disavowed intermingling across race and class, and concealed the true range of sexual orientations and gender identities. Pushback on any of these fronts often evoked debate and controversy—at times prompting further censorship or court cases. Unsurprisingly, discourse around such representations reveals the urge to protect predominantly or exclusively middle-class white children. While in early cinema such concerns would be overtly stated, today's critiques address them more obliquely. For example, R. Danielle Egan in *Becoming Sexual: A Critical*

Appraisal of the Sexualization of Girls takes aim at the sexualization discourse of the twenty-first century, suggesting it is "not only gendered female, but that its primary focus is on the protection of a small subsection of girls—namely those who are white, heterosexual, and middle class."[4] Looking back over the history of US cinema, it is apparent how the unease regarding youth and sex has transformed dramatically in some cases and simply gone undercover in others.

FROM THE "RIGHT TO LOVE" TO THE "ROAD TO RUIN": USING YOUTH TO BUILD THE CASE FOR CENSORSHIP (1890S–1934)

As soon as there was a commercial film industry, there were calls for film censorship, and unsurprisingly, sex surfaced nearly immediately as a target. Commonly referred to as the first object of government film censorship, Thomas Edison's 1890s short *The Dolorita Passion Dance* attracted lines of customers in Atlantic City for a turn at a single-view Kinetoscope to watch a "peep show" of a young woman dancing. Complaints to the police led officials to request that the Kinetoscope owners cancel the screening, which they did.[5] In other words, from the earliest films, "sex" simultaneously attracted crowds and drew the attention of critics determined to ban them. By 1915, several states and municipalities had formed their own censorship boards to impose local standards of prescribed morality.

Predictably, children's safety was explicitly used as leverage in censorship cases. Chicago's first censor board, created in 1907, classified certain films as for "adults only," even issuing them separate pink permits until authorities realized that "such permits advertised rather than penalized movies with salacious titles and material."[6] Despite resistance, Chicago's censorship of films to "secure decency and morality in the moving picture business" was upheld in the 1909 Illinois Supreme Court case *Block v. Chicago*. In the argument, the city stated that inexpensive prices for film viewings caused them to be "frequented and patronized by a large number of children."[7] Although this case centered on the depiction of crime, not sex, in the films *The James Boys in Missouri* and *Night Riders*, the urgency of protecting youth looms large, as the opinion of the court states that "immoral" representations "would necessarily be attended with evil effects upon youthful spectators."[8] Numerous scholars have noted how youth were seen as uniquely at risk.[9] In the essay "Morality and Entertainment: The Origins of the Motion Picture Production Code," Stephen Vaughn says, "Although no age group was thought to be immune from the seductive power of film, the nation's young seemed especially vulnerable."[10] Georganne Scheiner, in *Signifying Female Adolescence*, takes it a step further arguing that "motion pictures were perceived as being one of the most negative forces on children of the industrial age."[11] News articles, editorials, and letters in the early 1900s about the supposed damaging effects of cinema on children proliferated. Even as one national censorship board boasted of weeding out millions of feet of "objectionable films" in their first two years of operation,[12] religious and conservative organizations accused them of being too "lax."[13]

Simultaneous to cinema becoming an industry, adolescence became seen as a vulnerable and corruptible time of life. In the 1904 book *Adolescence: Its Psychology and Its Relations to Physiology, Anthropology, Sociology, Sex, Crime, Religion and Education*, G. Stanley Hall defined adolescence as a unique phase that warranted supervision and guidance from adults. Hall's detailed volume covered a range of adolescent behaviors and supposed dangers, including sexual desires. He compared adolescents to Adam and Eve who first discover their nakedness and "a special kind of sex shame hitherto unknown."[14] Hall's account reads as both sexist and racist today—he argues that the primary purpose of women is to bear children and suggests that procreation with "savage" races offers "some qualities of body or soul that civilized races lack but sorely need."[15] Despite how offensive the text reads today, in its day, Hall's theories brought about an unprecedented emphasis on the period of adolescence, its perceived risks, and the need for adult control.

Because of the US Constitution's First Amendment right to the freedom of speech, the question of whether government censorship of movies was constitutional ultimately culminated in a US Supreme Court case. The film industry lost. In *Mutual Film Corp. v. Industrial Commission of Ohio* in 1915, the court upheld the right of a US state or municipality to censor and ban films. Significantly, the unanimous decision labeled cinema *outside* the scope of the First Amendment protection to freedom of speech. This blow to cinematic freedom would be maintained for thirty-seven years until the Supreme Court case *Burstyn v. Wilson* in 1952 reversed the decision and deemed films, in fact, under protection of the First Amendment. The impact of this 1915 ruling on cinema for nearly four decades cannot be overstated—it directly led to a prolonged self-regulation by the industry via the Production Code and a corresponding curtailment of visual representations.

The *Mutual v. Ohio* case never directly mentions sex. However, the argument highlights how motion pictures are "capable of evil," and it emphasizes how films might not just be for "amusement" but also for "education." It cites how "a prurient interest may be excited and appealed to" arguing that there are "some things which should not have pictorial representation in public places and to all audiences." Again, the influence on youth is explicitly mentioned, and the case states that the audience for films is not merely adults but also children, which "make them the more insidious in corruption."[16] The argument that youth, seen as uniquely corruptible, were part of the audience had become a primary means for supporting the case for film censorship.

At the same time—as motion picture producers discovered early on—sex sells. Thus, the film industry needed to continue producing content that drew audiences while combating concerns that movies had a negative impact on society and its children. The inevitability of government interference led the film industry to attempt to self-regulate early on. The National Association of the Motion Picture Industry (NAMPI) was founded in 1916, and by 1921, it had instituted the "Thirteen Points" or subjects to be avoided in film, such as themes of "an illicit love affair which tends to make virtue odious and vice attractive" and "scenes which exhibit nakedness or persons scantily dressed, particularly suggestive bedroom and bathroom scenes and scenes of inciting dancing."[17] By 1922, several states had organized official censorship boards, while Hollywood had formed the Motion Picture Producers and Distributors of America (MPPDA), which would later oversee the Motion Picture Production Code, for public relations and self-regulation.[18] In 1927, the MPPDA published "The Don'ts and Be Carefuls," which outlined "topics movie producers should avoid," including "licentious or suggestive nudity," "sex perversion," "miscegenation," "sex hygiene and venereal disease," "actual childbirth," and "children's sex organs."[19] With this list, the industry revealed its priorities. While violence often wound up in the "be careful" category, sexual situations landed on the "don'ts" list. Violence was not the primary concern; sex was.

Scholars have disagreed about how distinctly we might draw a line between pre-Code and post-Code films.[20] In terms of representations of youth before the Code, one of the most notable differences seems to be the representation of girls' forays into premarital sex and their resistance to patriarchal culture. In these films, girls' rebellions often were *not* punished significantly through the plot as later required under the Code. Rather, girls' sexual experiences would sometimes be justified in the story as "true love." For example, the silent short *Her Defiance* (1916), directed by Cleo Madison and Joe King, portrays country girl Adeline Gabler (Madison), who falls in love—and has premarital sex—with the cosmopolitan Frank Warren. We know they've had intercourse in the ellipses since Adeline winds up pregnant. When she mistakenly believes Frank has abandoned her, her brother forces her to accept a marriage proposal from their elderly neighbor, Scapin. At the wedding, however, Adeline runs off before the ceremony. Her brother and Scapin pursue her, but their carriage crashes, killing them both. The film concludes with a scene years later when Adeline (now with her young child) and Frank are reunited after clearing up their misunderstanding. Of course, *Her Defiance* represents what would become a common pattern for adolescent sexuality in Code-era cinema—premarital sex leads to pregnancy, a "problem" resolved through marriage. Nonetheless, this film signifies a daring emphasis on the girl's sexual and romantic desires and antipathies, which run counter to her elders'. Adeline finds her happy ending, while the men who sought to control her wind up dead.

Some of the films of this era represent a near opposite morality to what would be enforced through the Code. In *Untamed* (1929), the main character Alice (Joan Crawford), also known as Bingo, is a free spirit who dances in scanty clothes, swears, picks fights, and kisses her love interest freely. In the story, Bingo is orphaned and left in the care of her father's friends "Uncle" Ben and Howard. Bingo is "untamed" because her father raised her in the jungles of South America while he was prospecting, and he leaves behind a fortune for her. In the opening of the film, she dances for an audience of men—one ogles her and then accosts her, and she fights him off. Although we get the sense that her uninhibited behavior might endanger her, we also see her readiness to defend herself, as she puts it later in the film, "Where I come from, you have to sock them in the nose." Ben and Howard decide to bring her to New York to help her fit into society, and on the ship over, she meets and falls for Andy—a recent graduate with a meager income. In one scene, she saunters uninvited into Andy's cabin and when she insists that she'll find him no matter how big New York is, he calls her a "cute little devil" and kisses her. Immediately, he apologizes saying, "I shouldn't have done that. I'm sorry," to which she responds, "I didn't say anything, did I?" When Uncle Ben finds her there, Bingo has no fears about what others "will say." Her own desires take precedence in the story—and she is rewarded. Despite Uncle Ben's machinations to trick Andy into abandoning her (which leads to Bingo's shooting Andy in the shoulder) and Howard's own romantic interest in her, Andy and Bingo end up happily together at the end. And it is not Bingo who learns to regret and atone for her rebellious ways; rather it is Uncle Ben at the end who admits, "I thought I knew what was best for you.... But I do know now" and pleads for the couple's forgiveness. In fact, Bingo's earlier assertion that she maintains "the right to love who I darn please" might well be the moral of the story. The only consent that matters in the film is the girl's, not her patriarchal guardians'.

Of course, it would be false to imply that girls suffered no consequences for their unruly actions in silent-era and pre-Code films. In his movie plots, prolific and influential early filmmaker D. W. Griffith emphasized that girls who deviated from traditional values either needed to be saved or suffered dire consequences. For example, in *To Save Her Soul* (1909), a freewheeling and successful singer is brought back to conventional society by a minister who, as one of the titles describes, "would kill her that her soul remained pure." And in another Griffith film, *The Painted Lady* (1912), a girl goes mad imagining meetings with her dead lover until her grief finally kills her. Such stories offered an overly simplistic morality for girls who disobeyed their parents', particularly their fathers', wishes. As one scholar noted, an overriding thesis of Griffith's early "women's films" was "that American society is best served by maintaining women in private, family spaces."[21] Even in a film like Griffith's *Broken Blossoms* (1919), where the protagonist Lucy Burrows (Lillian Gish) escapes an abusive father when a Chinese man (played by Caucasian actor Richard Barthelmess) steals her away, her freedom is short-lived. When her father finds out, he brings her back home and kills her. Certainly, the father is no sympathetic character, yet the narrative also implies the futility of the girl's escape from the will and wrath of her father. In Griffith films, in other words, girls tended to be victims, not agents in their stories.

The Production Code, in effect from the 1930s through the 1960s, ultimately institutionalized and nationalized the regulation of such depictions in films. Although a confluence of events led to the adoption of the Code, studies conducted by the Motion Picture Research Council and funded by the Payne Fund over several years in the late 1920s to early 1930s served as a tipping point. The research was summarized in several influential books, including Herbert Blumer's *Movies and Conduct* (1933), Blumer and Philip Hauser's *Movies, Delinquency, and Crime* (1933), and Henry James Forman's *Our Movie Made Children* (1933). These books combine firsthand narratives from youth with statistics to provide what they framed as compelling arguments for censorship. Their key takeaways regarding adolescent sexuality were simplistic: movies incited teenage passions leading to disruptive, regrettable, and illegal behaviors among young people. These behaviors led to the downfall of impressionable youth, brought shame on their families, and jeopardized civil society.

In these studies, girls were often imagined to be in sexual danger, and their transgressions were seen as the greater threat to society. Blumer and Hauser argue that girls themselves "indicated that the movies were a direct contributing influence to their own delinquency," suggesting nearly half of delinquent girls "admit[ted] feeling like having a man make love to them after [seeing] a passionate picture."[22] Similarly, Forman's account is filled with testimonies of girls who blame "love pictures" for seeding their desires for expensive goods, wild parties, romantic adventures, and unconventional lives. In one example,

Forman details how a "typically adolescent love affair" turned into "one of illicit sex relations" due to a movie, which not only "arouses" their "passion" but also offers them "techniques."[23] Forman also describes how movies stirred sexual feelings in young men, leading to rape and sexual assault. Still, according to Forman and others, the dire effects of sex delinquency resided with girls, and thus, girls' deviance from sexual norms came to be seen as the "greatest menace."[24]

Years later such studies would be criticized for their obvious subjectivity since the youth interviewed were largely juveniles in correctional institutions. In other words, the researchers did not seek to discover how films impacted average teenagers; rather, they sought out teens who had been involved in illicit and illegal behavior to provide supposed evidence of cinema's corrupting influences on them. Despite the preposterousness of such reports today, they were taken quite seriously at the time. As Scheiner states, despite being "flawed methodologically," texts like these "seemed to confirm the public's worst fears about the negative influence of this young medium on the youth of America and provided potent ammunition for the pro-censorship forces."[25] Movies, the studies suggested, needed regulation because youth were in danger.

Four films explicitly mentioned in the sexual delinquency chapter of Forman's *Our Movie Made Children*—*Our Dancing Daughters* (1928), *The Pagan* (1929), *Our Modern Maidens* (1929), and *The Right to Love* (1930)—reveal a main source of concern. What unites these films is the way girls' sexual and romantic desires drive the plot and are fulfilled by the conclusion of the film. In *Our Modern Maidens*, Billie Brown (Crawford) and her fiancé, Gil Jordan, both fall in love with other people. At the end of the film, Billie discovers Gil has gotten her friend Kentucky pregnant. So, Billie and Gil's wedding is canceled and both have their happy endings with their actual love interests. *The Right to Love* even demonstrates that premarital sex is nothing new. In the plot, Naomi and Joe have intercourse, and Naomi winds up pregnant. When Joe dies in an accident, Naomi agrees to be married to have a father for her baby. Years later, when Naomi's daughter Brook finds herself in love with a young man who does not meet her father's approval, Naomi urges her daughter to elope and confides in her about her own past. At first Brook is horrified and takes her father's advice to become a missionary in China. There, she meets and falls in love with Eric. Although initially regretful of their romance, she seeks out Eric again upon receiving a message from her since-deceased mother. *The Right to Love*, in other words, suggests girls' desires are worthwhile pursuits and adolescent romance is a routine precursor to marriage—in this case so routine that it spans generations. Even a more conventionally punishing plot in *Our Dancing*

Daughters leaves room for girls' adolescent desires and behaviors. Party girl Diana (Crawford) initially loses her love interest Ben to the more cunning Ann. Later, Ben realizes his love for Diana, who turns out to be more innocent than her freewheeling antics suggest. When Ann falls to her death after getting drunk at a party, Diana and Ben are united. Although the film offers no future for the greedy and conniving Ann, it nevertheless provides a happy ending for the flirting, drinking, and dancing Diana.

The fourth film mentioned by Forman, *The Pagan* (1929), is perhaps most surprising, particularly in how it positions the white Christian patriarch, Henry Slater, as the bad guy in the story. In the film, Slater cares for his ward—a half white/half Pacific Islander orphan girl, Tito (Dorothy Janis).[26] When Slater leaves Tito on his ship while he does business in town, the half white/half Pacific Islander Henry Shoesmith (played by Mexican-born actor Ramon Novarro) hears Tito singing and swims up to the ship to find her. At first, she is shocked and rebukes his repeated advances, hitting him numerous times, although she later falls for him. Slater, however, wants Tito for himself (to make her "*all* white" as he says), and he cheats Shoesmith out of his plantation and marries Tito (in tears) by force. After the wedding, Shoesmith steals her away, and in the fight that ensues, Slater winds up dead, leaving Tito and Shoesmith free to be together in their island hut. Undoubtedly, the girl comes across like a conquest to be won here and the ethnic stereotypes are impossible to ignore, but the film's emphasis on the characters' ambiguous race and their mutual desire out of wedlock is nonetheless significant. And once again, the girl's desires prevail.

Censors during this time not only aimed to maintain gender order but also clearly determined to sustain white supremacy. Hundreds of "race films," made by and about people of color were produced between the 1910s and the 1950s. The fact that most of these films are now lost, even those by prominent directors like Oscar Micheaux, demonstrates the racist practices embedded in film preservation for over a century. Due to this loss, scholars trying to understand this aspect of film history must piece together themes from plot descriptions, advertisements, or reviews. Among the missing films are several that seemed to resist race stereotypes of youth often presented in Hollywood films of the era. For example, *The Realization of a Negro's Ambition* (1916) presented an "alternative embodiment of Black masculinity" with the story of a young Black college graduate who returns to his family farm but then obtains a job in the oil industry after he saves the life of a white executive's daughter. Ultimately, the film ends happily with the protagonist's discovering oil on his property and marrying his hometown romantic interest.[27] Girls, too, found leading roles in

Fig. 1.1. In W. S. Van Dyke's pre-Code film *The Pagan*, Tito (Dorothy Janis) prefers the half white/half Pacific Islander Henry Shoesmith Jr. (Ramon Novarro) over her white Christian guardian.

these films. Micheaux's *The Brute* (1920), another film presumed lost, tells the story of a young woman forced into a marriage after she believes her fiancé has died. Her husband, "the brute," physically beats her, and she ultimately must be rescued by her aunt. By the end, she is reunited happily with her original fiancé. Another groundbreaking film *The Burden of Race* (1921), also lost, presents the story of a Black college student who falls in love with a white woman. However, unlike in Micheaux's film *The Homesteader* (1919), which resolves this plot setup through the discovery of the woman's mixed-race past, *The Burden of Race* instead presents the complex choice between "race pride" and "love."[28] What these films implied specifically about the sexuality of Black youth is difficult to determine without being able to watch them in their entirety.

Race routinely came up in calls for censorship during early cinema. Often citing fears of racial unrest, boards objected to films that promoted racial equality, and movies with protagonists of color or by filmmakers of color seemed to be under a particular scrutiny. In *Fire and Desire: Mixed Race Movies in the Silent Era*, Jane M. Gaines suggests, "One could hypothesize that all race movies had to pass a special white test before they could be exhibited—and this test was erratic and unpredictable, the cuts required differing from city to city."[29] For example, the Virginia Censorship Board in 1927 banned Micheaux's film *The House behind the Cedars*, also presumed lost, about a mixed-race girl who "passes" as white and is "wooed and won by a young white millionaire."[30] The board declared that the film was "so objectionable" that it "necessitate[d] its total rejection,"[31] arguing it was "liable to cause friction between the races" and "incite . . . crime."[32] The board did not conceal its white supremacist agenda, stating that the film "at least indirectly contravenes the spirit of the recently enacted anti-miscegenation law which put Virginia in the forefront as a pioneer in legislation aimed to preserve the integrity of the white race."[33] Despite how other states, in this case, had not required specific cuts to the film, Micheaux indulged the board, making the requested edits, although he also made it clear that "there has been but one picture that incited [people of color] to riot, and that still does . . . *The Birth of a Nation*."[34] Griffith's silent feature *The Birth of a Nation* (1915) represented the antithesis to race films—provoking protests from people of color for its plethora of offensive stereotypes, including Black men in violent pursuit of young white women. The fact that *The Birth of a Nation* has been lauded by film scholars for over a hundred years for its "magnificence" further reveals how depictions of race have been and often continue to be viewed by the industry, critics, and audiences.[35] Both before and during the Code years, fears about racial uprising, integration, and equality motivated explicit censorship. Listed as a "don't" in "The Don'ts and Be Carefuls," in 1927 miscegenation became outright prohibited by the Code.

With the risk of censorship and the advent of sound in motion pictures, producers became more risk averse—due to higher production costs, companies could not afford their films to be banned. While pre-Code films like Dorothy Arzner's *The Wild Party* (1929) or Walter Drake and Dorothy Davenport's *The Red Kimono* (1925) could portray a "wild" girl being misunderstood and ultimately finding her "rightful" place in society, the Code would insist on a "compensating moral value." And even before being officially enforced, the specter of censorship likely altered plots. An apt example is Dorothy Davenport's pre-Code *The Road to Ruin* (1934), a remake of a 1928 silent picture that portrays protagonist Ann, who is tempted away from her sheltered homelife by an aptly named friend, Eve. Ann has never gotten drunk or smoked, but with Eve's encouragement, she does both. She also has never been with a boy, but Eve sets her up with Tommy. Alone in the woods, they have intercourse—and afterward, Ann clearly blames herself. This event sets Ann on the "road to ruin." Soon, she's on to the next boy, and not long after, she's arrested at a party where teens are skinny-dipping. She winds up pregnant, seeks out an illegal abortion, and dies. The heavy-handed moral of the film emphasizes not only the girl's inability to act as a sexual gatekeeper but also the parents' failure to protect and educate their child, specifically about sex. At one point, a detention worker tells Ann's mother, "Our boys and girls today need more than trust. They need the armor of knowledge, of intelligent sex instruction—to protect them." The film's incorporation of adolescent sex merely to outline its dangers foreshadows the "hygiene film," which, starting in the 1940s, used narratives as emotional appeals and warnings for youth.

Filmmakers had learned that if objectionable social behavior, like adolescent sex, was shown, then the characters must undergo sufficient retribution through the storyline—hence the "right to love" had become the "road to ruin." A film that did *not* have dire consequences for sexually active protagonists, including youth, risked calling into question not only the morality of a particular film but also of the industry as a whole.

"MARRIAGE AND THE HOME": SUPPRESSING ADOLESCENT SEXUALITY WITH THE PRODUCTION CODE (1934–50S)

The Production Code was published in 1930, although it would not be adopted widely until 1934—shortly after release of the Payne Film Studies. The Production Code Administration (PCA) then made the code stricter in 1935 due to "increased social and political pressures" and the threat of boycotts from the Roman Catholic Church.[36] Sex featured prominently in the Code—curtailing themes, subject matter, and even specific scenes. It sought to uphold the "sanctity of the institution of marriage and the home" and aimed to prevent "low forms of sex relationship" from being seen as "accepted or common." The Code outlined that adultery and "illicit sex" should not be "justified, or presented attractively" and forbade "excessive and lustful kissing, lustful embraces, suggestive postures and gestures." The Code also specifically banned "miscegenation" from 1930 to 1956. Although the Code did not specifically mention adolescent or premarital sexuality, there was no need, since it was clearly covered by sex that jeopardized respect for "marriage and the home."[37] The original Code also did not explicitly mention abortion, so it was not "technically prohibited" but only because the PCA "believed that studios tacitly understood that this topic was forbidden."[38]

In addition, the Roman Catholic Church created the Legion of Decency in 1933 to provide its own ratings—at first dividing films into three categories: A, morally unobjectionable; B, morally objectionable in part; and C, condemned. It then further divided A ratings to keep children and adolescents from certain films—A-I being "unobjectionable" for general audiences, A-II for adults and adolescents only, and A-III for adults only. Parishioners were often even made to stand and cite the "Pledge of the Legion of Decency" to declare a promise to "condemn" "salacious motion pictures" as "a grave menace to youth, to home life, to country, and to religion."[39]

Unsurprisingly, adolescent sexuality went relatively dormant in films from the 1930s through the 1950s. Child stars like Shirley Temple and Mickey Rooney, who made dozens of popular films, helped the industry promote "an image of children as innocents."[40] Perhaps more importantly, these stars and their films helped the industry project its own image as a benevolent protector of children. Adolescent depictions during the era were epitomized in innocuous teen films like the *Andy Hardy* series (over a dozen films from 1937 to 1958) and *Teen Agers* (eight films between 1946 and 1948). More flirtatious but still sexless themes continued into the 1960s with the beach party genre (1963–66), *Gidget* series (1959–63), and the *Tammy* series (1957–67). During this era, Hollywood largely conformed to "portray[ing] an idealized vision of life . . . unmistakably wedded to an ideology that espoused middle-class views and values."[41] These films displayed "ritualized patterns of courtship" in which the "teenage mating process is clearly designed, regulated, and articulated."[42] In moral comedies, young people found their way in a white heterosexual middle-class suburban world under the tutelage of benevolent and wise parents.

Queer sexualities and trans identities of any sort were never overtly depicted during the Code era, and romances between people of different races were explicitly banned. Even topics or themes not overtly censored drew oversight. As Ellen C. Scott argues in *Cinema Civil Rights: Regulation, Repression, and Race in the Classical Hollywood Era*, films like *Imitation of Life* (1934) featuring a Black and a white woman as heroines and friends (Delilah played by Louise Beavers and Bea played by Claudette Colbert) received considerable pushback from the PCA. Ostensibly the PCA focused on the character of Peola, Delilah's light-skinned daughter, who they argued could have been the "*result* of miscegenation,"[43] although more likely this "angle" was used to censor controversial ideas (such as racial equality).[44] The final film abounds with racial stereotypes, leading one reviewer at the time to label Delilah's relinquishing her business revenue to Bea as "propaganda" designed to disempower people of color.[45] During this era, predominantly Black casts continued to be featured in "race films," and Hollywood studios ventured into the market, seeing an opportunity for expanded audiences and revenue. Few seem to have focused on youth—and sex here was similarly absent. For example, in *Junction 88* (1947), Lolly falls in love with Buster although her father has a more well-off suitor in mind. When Buster's identity is revealed as sought-after songwriter in the church community, all ends well—Lolly gets her guy, and her father approves. Still the film focuses less on the adolescents and more on the music performed throughout. With depictions of youth, sex, and race being so highly regulated in this era, it is unsurprising that it is difficult to find depictions that combine the three.[46]

With adolescent sexuality practically erased, any remaining traces served as warnings to adolescents and their parents. David M. Considine outlines how films of the 1930s and 1940s depicted parents' failure to guide their children as resulting in reform school, imprisonment, and worse. Numerous films also use the transgression of premarital sex as a plot device that leads to an array of miseries for young women—sexual assault in *Stolen Paradise* (1940), estrangement from a child in *To Each His Own* (1946), thoughts of suicide in *Not Wanted* (1949), a regretted adoption in *Unwed Mother* (1958), quest for an illegal abortion in *Blue Denim* (1959), and tragic loss in *Susan Slade* (1961). In case the plots didn't make it obvious enough, a trailer for *Unwed Mother* offers the objective of such films. It begins with the headline: "Every year 20,000 anguished girls live this blistering story!" and through the voiceover suggests it as "the picture every parent and teenager should see—the story of girls who go too far, too fast." Redemption in such films only comes to girls and women deemed to have sufficiently suffered for their actions, and the films' endings invariably affirm the values of marriage and family.

Of course, boys, too, were not-so-subtly warned against adolescent sexuality, as Considine notes, with the message being "good girls don't and neither should the boys."[47] A pattern of sex leading to violence and death for adolescent boys prevails in numerous films in the 1930s and 1940s, as Considine notes, including *All Quiet on the Western Front* (1930), *Are These Our Children?* (1931), *Always in My Heart* (1942), *The Constant Nymph* (1943), and *Youth Runs Wild* (1944). Films depicting adolescent sexual desire in the era nearly always led to tragedy. In *Stolen Paradise*, Richard (Dick) Gordin is a naive teen aiming to become a priest who falls in love with his older, divorced new stepsister, Patricia. As they spend summer days together lazing around the beach, Dick makes a speech that seems to predict *The Blue Lagoon* (1980). He rubs suntan lotion on Pat and muses, "I wouldn't want anything that would make this summer come to an end," adding that the island is "so quiet and far away.... you know I wish we could live here." Of course, Dick's vision is not one that can come to fruition—the deviance of his adolescent desire is exacerbated by his stepsister's being the object of his attraction. Before long, he's swigging alcohol, ogling dancing girls, starting fights, and sexually assaulting a girl. The implied warning for boys is that unbridled sexual desire leads them into increasingly dangerous behavior until they become a perpetrator. And it doesn't end there for Dick. After he impulsively kisses Pat, he leaves to join the Air Force. A subsequent accident leaves him unable to walk, and in the end, he decides to join the priesthood after all. Ultimately, adolescent sexuality in *Stolen Paradise* is portrayed as perverted and incestuous—most certainly *not* an ordinary part of growing up.

In films of the 1930s and 1940s, one of the sources of blame for adolescents' troubles are the parents themselves—specifically an outdated strict form of parenting seen to be ineffective. For example, in *Girls on Probation* (1938), protagonist Connie falls in with a corrupting friend Hilda, leading to Connie's mistakenly being arrested for theft and then later for bank robbery. At the beginning of the film, Connie's father speaks out against Hilda as a "brainless hussy flirting with every man she meets" telling his daughter, "first thing you know you turn out the same as she is," while Connie's mother offers, "the child has to have a few friends her own age." When Connie disobeys her father and attends a party, it leads to a cascade of trouble. But it also leads to her meeting attorney Neil Dillon (Ronald Reagan) who offers a different paternalism. Unlike her father, Neil forgives and trusts Connie, and as such, he is seen as a more effective protector for the girl than her stern and controlling father. Like many films in this era, a key takeaway is that parents cannot protect children by keeping them sheltered. Rather, they must compassionately educate children about dangers awaiting them in the adolescent world.

The focus on parental responsibilities regarding sex education in films during this era points to a tacit admission of youth sexuality. Alan Petigny argues that there existed a "silent" sexual revolution in the 1940s and 1950s, supported by data such as increases in US census numbers of unwed pregnancies and Dr. Spock's popular 1946 child-rearing book, which "advised parents not to become alarmed by their children masturbating."[48] In this same era, Alfred Kinsey's influential reports, *Sexual Behavior in the Human Male* (1948) and *Sexual Behavior in the Human Female* (1953), also postulated that children and adolescents engaged in a wide range of hetero- and homosexual behaviors.[49] In other words, youth—even in the 1940s—were sexually active, and adults knew it.

The cinematic recognition of this fact is evident predominantly through "hygiene films," which experienced a heyday from the late 1940s to the late 1950s. Shown in US classrooms, these films sought to preempt risky behaviors through educational movies and not-so-subtle allegories. As Megan Stemm-Wade in "Careless Girls and Repentant Wives: Gender in Postwar Classroom Films" states, such films emerged out of a belief that the "economic and world political troubles that followed the Roaring Twenties" were the result of the "self-involved, hedonistic youth of the time" (613). Such a view echoes Considine's point that sex in this era was seen as "threatening because it distracted from building for the future."[50] Adolescent sex, in other words, had to be controlled not only because it was believed to endanger individuals but also because it supposedly had the power to destroy the fabric of society. Schools used hygiene films as a means of guiding young people away from drugs, sex, disease, and crime and toward a law-abiding life of work, marriage, and family.

When these films took on the subject of "dating and etiquette," they revealed the key takeaways for girls: "deny your sexual urges; take on all responsibility for keeping boys in line and marriages harmonious; and in all things except sex, be submissive to men."[51] As the adult narrator of the hygiene film *Are You Popular?* (1947) makes clear, "Girls who park in cars are not really popular—not even with the boys they park with." Although such "commandments" were clearly "at stark odds with the shifting and evolving roles of women and girls in the postwar years," these films implied that for youth, particularly girls, the "consequences of making the wrong decisions were dreadful"—including rape, venereal disease, and death.[52] Still, one notable shift is how these films often normalized boys' sexual urges, suggesting "boys will be boys and always, always want to have sex" and reasserting that it was "girl's responsibility to make that 'mature' choice and turn him down in a friendly and appealing way."[53] In short, hygiene films served as propaganda targeted to youth to ensure they conformed to society's archetypes of boys as sexually eager and girls as responsible gatekeepers—foundational roles in the "heterosexual script," as illustrated further in chapter 2. Perhaps most notable in terms of consent, such films cemented the idea that girls should and must prevent sexual situations from occurring.

Studios picked up on the popularity of hygiene films, attempting their own versions with titles like *Mom and Dad* (1945), about a high school girl June who winds up pregnant after her parents refuse to teach her about sex. By integrating a story about teen sex into a heavy-handed educational tale, *Mom and Dad* became "the most successful sex hygiene film in history."[54] The marketing materials capitalized on a tale of "a sweet, innocent girl growing up in this fast-moving age" and emphasized its educational nature by suggesting that if it "saves one girl from unwed motherhood . . . or one boy from the ravages of social disease . . . it will have been well told!"[55] After a night where the couple has intercourse, Jack feels "sorry" and June "ashamed," saying she "feel[s] like a leper, unclean, afraid to associate with her friends" and unable to make eye contact with her parents. Of course, according to the Code, the adolescents must be punished for their indiscretion, and indeed they are—Jack dies in a plane crash, and June winds up pregnant, which leads to her attempting suicide and losing the baby. A similar tale was produced by Universal Studios a few years later. *Bob and Sally* (1948), also known as *Tell Our Parents*, promised a "boldly frank" and "humanely true" story of "the passionate problems of today's youth who forget about consequences and defy conventions."[56] Again in this film, Sally's mother refuses to teach her about sex, which leads to Sally's becoming pregnant by her boyfriend, Bob. The couple resort to an illegal abortion that nearly kills Sally and leaves her infertile, and the police catch Bob pawning his mother's ring to obtain money to pay for the procedure. The film upholds ideals of the era by punishing teens who transgress social boundaries, yet here the plot has a more uplifting resolution with the couple's getting married. However, such a happy ending did not go over well with censors. It was condemned by the Legion of Decency and could not obtain approval from the MPPDA. As a result, *Bob and Sally* never made it to theaters.

The height of the Code era in the late 1930s through the early 1950s might be seen as a nadir for depictions of adolescent sexuality. Despite research indicating that adolescents were sexually active, the rules of the Code ensured adolescent protagonists who dared to have sex suffered a multitude of consequences in the plot. As a result, the era cultivated a prescribed morality—deeming girls sexual gatekeepers; prioritizing family and marriage over love and sex; and implying parents should warn their children about the hazards of sex.

THE CODE CRACKS: EXPLORING ADOLESCENT SEXUALITY (1950S–60S)

The Code didn't officially end until 1968. However, just as the threat of censorship curtailed depictions years before the Code started, so too did suggestions of overturning it allow for more risqué depictions of adolescent sexuality. Additionally, incremental changes in the late 1940s and 1950s caused the Code to become increasingly irrelevant. In 1948, the Supreme Court deemed Hollywood studios in violation of the Sherman Antitrust Act, which forbade monopolistic business practices. As a result, studios ceased to wield complete control over the production, distribution, and exhibition of films, and a more viable path emerged for independent films. In addition, a new cultural emphasis on "teenagers" as a category in the late 1940s caused independent producers to adopt youth as their target market or, as Yannis Tzioumakis argues, their "salvation."[57] Then, in 1952, films became officially protected by First Amendment rights when the Supreme Court case *Burstyn v. Wilson* overturned a 1915 decision. By 1956, independent studios had put enough pressure on Hollywood that the Code was significantly scaled back, removing "all remaining taboos except nudity, sexual perversion, and venereal disease."[58] In *Teenagers and Teenpics*, Thomas Doherty argues that the era gave rise to the "teenpic," or "timely and sensational" films marketed to youth that contrasted with "clean" teen films of the era.[59] Many of these were exploitation films served up as a double bill such as *Sorority Girl* (1957)/*Motorcycle Gang* (1957); *Unwed Mother*/*Joy Ride* (1958); and *Diary of a High School Bride* (1959)/*Ghost of Dragstrip Hollow* (1959).

While the *Andy Hardy* and the *Gidget* series continued to portray teens on a quest for heterosexual young love, other 1950s studio and independent films countered this image—through ambiguous portrayals that often raised more questions than they answered. In the iconic *Rebel without a Cause* (1955), teenager Jim Stark (James Dean) desperately wants his father to be more masculine—early in the film, he wishes his father could "knock down" his mother and declares that he "never want[s] to be like him." But Jim's wish is ultimately exposed as misguided fear and shame. At the start of the story, Jim's parents have been moving town to town to protect him from the consequences of his outbursts—the last arising when boys called Jim "chicken." Now, in his new town, Jim finds himself again in trouble when he's challenged to a game of chicken, which involves racing stolen cars toward a ledge and leaping out just before the car hurtles over the cliff. When Buzz, his competitor in the game, dies in a resulting car crash, Jim bonds with Judy, Buzz's girlfriend, and Plato, a boy who calls Jim his "best friend" despite having met him that day. The film does not overtly depict sex between any of the adolescent characters. However, what it does is perhaps even more transgressive for the time—it calls into question both masculinity and heteronormativity. Numerous scholars and fans have read homosexual desire in Plato's relationship with Jim—Plato's locker contains a pasted-up picture of movie star Alan Ladd, and his quick affection for Jim can easily be viewed as romantic.[60] Ultimately, in the film, Jim's sensitivity is not something he must disavow and be cured from. In a scene between Judy and Jim, she asks him, "What do you think a girl wants?" and he responds, "A man." But Judy already recognizes the answer as more complex, as she says, "Well, yes, but a man who's gentle and sweet and doesn't run away when you want them. Like being Plato's friend when no one else liked him—that's being strong." Jim might not want to be like his father or admire a relationship like his parents, but he also learns that the solution is not some stereotypical illusion of masculinity. As Roger Ebert suggested upon looking back at the film decades later, Jim's character became part of a movement that "decisively altered the way young men could be seen in popular culture. They could be more feminine, sexier, more confused, more ambiguous."[61] And it clearly positioned youth as navigating their own new world in spite of—not with—the adults around them.

The film *Tea and Sympathy* (1956), based on a play by the same name, similarly challenged the values of heterosexual masculine bravado. In the plot, seventeen-year-old Tom would rather sew with the faculty wives than roughhouse with the boys; play tennis over baseball; and sit in the choir room playing music than pursue girls with his peers. As a result, his classmates take to calling him "sister boy." Laura, the school housemaster's wife, takes an interest in Tom because he reminds her of her first husband, a "lonely boy" who was killed in the war "being conspicuously brave. . . . because he was afraid the others thought him a coward." Once Tom is labeled as different (aka queer) by his peers, it cannot be easily shaken off. When his roommate Al tries to help him, they both discover how proving one's masculinity is not clear-cut. As a last resort, Al decides that Tom should take home Ellie Martin, the waitress in the local café who "tells and tells and tells," adding, "Boy, you'd be made!" Through this scene and others, the film suggests there is no clear way to look, talk, or act like a man; the only way to prove one's manhood is to have sex with a woman. So Tom sets up a date with Ellie. However, when she makes her move on him at her apartment, he can't go through with it. Later, Laura consoles him, "You mustn't think . . ." with a dramatic pause for us to fill in the blank ". . . that you're homosexual." Instead, Laura explains, "But you're not in love with Ellie." Tom responds, "But that's not supposed to matter!" and she counters, "Oh, but it does!" Laura then offers herself to Tom saying, "Years from now, when you talk about this, and you will, be kind." They kiss, and the scene ends. Tom is thus relieved of his suspected queerness all due to sex in the ellipses with the adult Laura. At the end, Tom visits his old room years later—he's now married and a published author.

Certainly, if we do read Tom as queer, this vision of the transformative power of heterosexual sex is misleading and damaging. However, because of both a "vacuum of representation that would continue for decades" regarding homosexuality and a scene in the original play that depicted Tom's being "allegedly seen romping naked on a beach" with an accused "fairy," the film has nevertheless often been read queerly.[62] Certainly, the film presents a sustained critique on masculinity, since it is not only Tom's heteronormativity that is called into question but also that of Tom's roommate Al and the school's housemaster (Laura's husband). For example, when Laura discovers Al plans to abandon Tom as a roommate, she threatens, "Al, what if I were to start talking about you tomorrow. . . . the same sort of talk they're making about Tom?" At first, Al laughs it off, saying, "No one would believe it," to which she responds "Why not? Because you're big and brawny and an athlete and what they call a 'top guy' and 'hard hitter'?" Al then realizes that his claim to hetero-masculinity is as tenuous as Tom's, as Laura tells him, "Once I got them believing it, you'd be surprised how quickly your manly virtues would be changed into suspicious characteristics." Her exercise in eliciting empathy from Al works, but it is Laura who cannot comprehend the fear of living with such a feeble claim on one's sexual and gender identity—she is just a "bystander" as Al puts it. If *Tea and Sympathy* is a queer film, then it is not a coming out film—it's a staying in the closet film. Still, it emphasizes gender questioning while depicting a world in which both young and adult men are clinging to a fragile hetero-masculine guise. As such, the ambiguities in *Tea and Sympathy*, like those in *Rebel without a Cause*, prefigure future resistances to gender roles and sexual norms.

Young women too began pushing boundaries before the Code ended, and several films portray girls' discussing sex openly and embarking on premarital (or extramarital) sex. For example, in *The Moon Is Blue* (1953), protagonist Patty flatly asks her older date Donald "Are you going to seduce me?" after he invites her back to his apartment. She tells him that she wants to maintain her "virtue" but doesn't want to "fight" for it. When he agrees to no more than kissing, she says, "Men are usually so bored with virgins. I'm glad you're not." Repeatedly throughout the film, the two older men pursuing Patty find her blunt sexual honesty off-putting yet refreshing—even though her nemesis (the daughter of one of the men) calls her a "professional virgin." When Donald asks her, "Why are you so preoccupied with sex?" she responds, "Don't you think it's better for a girl to be preoccupied with sex than occupied?" Not surprisingly, the film's own preoccupation with sex—despite none taking place in the film—resulted in its failure to earn Code approval. However, director Otto Preminger decided to release the film without it—an "unprecedented move at the time" that paid off—the film became one of the top grossing films of the year, according to *Variety*.[63] Undoubtedly such a successful disavowal helped render the Code obsolete.

One of the most startling presentations of the era is *Baby Doll* (1956), which was the first film that passed the Production Code while also earning a condemned rating by the Legion of Decency. Written by Tennessee Williams and directed by Elia Kazan, the plot of *Baby Doll* itself was salacious—it's the eve of Baby Doll's twentieth birthday, when she must consummate her marriage to Archie Lee as agreed on in a handshake deal Archie made with her father before his death. But as it turns out, Baby Doll has little interest in becoming a conventional wife, and she insults her husband as "a fat old thing" and "not exactly a young girl's dream come true." In the film, Archie represents both a failed father figure and husband—his gruff manner, physical assaults, and ploys to control Baby Doll are futile. Desperate to bring in more money to satisfy Baby Doll, Archie burns down a neighboring cotton gin to attract more business for his own. However, the owner of the burned down gin, Sicilian Silva Vacarro, quickly suspects Archie as the arsonist and decides to take revenge. The film presents nonconsent as embedded in seduction—Vacarro closes in on Baby Doll when she says she wants space, and he follows her into the house when she suggests he wait outside. In one scene, he tickles her with his foot as she cries out in a combination of discomfort and delight. But ultimately when Vacarro heads for the door having obtained her signed affidavit, it is Baby Doll who calls him back to join her for a "nap." Afterward, their mutual passion is clear as they kiss nearly in sight of Archie. Whether the couple ends up together is unclear—the film concludes as Baby Doll waits with her aunt for Vacarro to return after Archie's arrest. But what is clear is that Baby Doll has chosen her own intimate partner out of wedlock, and she is not severely penalized as a result in the plot.[64] *Baby Doll* thus blatantly resists the Code-era value of the "sanctity" of "marriage and the home" and even reverts to the ethos of a girl's "right to love."

Another notable turning point in depictions of teen sexuality in this era appears in *Where the Boys Are* (1960). The film contains the first open manifesto by a teen about sexual activity before marriage. In front of her class, protagonist Merritt critiques an "old fashioned" text that discusses "random dating" and "premature emotional involvement." Merritt challenges her professor saying, "if a girl doesn't make out with a man once in a while, she might as well leave campus because she's considered antisocial." To the teacher's horror, Merritt brings up Kinsey's research and says the more relevant discussion would be "should a girl or should she not under any circumstances play house before marriage?" When the teacher says, "I'm afraid to ask your opinion on the subject," Merritt responds, "Don't be afraid—my opinion is yes." The teacher sends Merritt to the dean.

Of course, the film does not exactly follow through on Merritt's talk—she is clearly more driven toward marriage than sex. According to Merritt, desire is not why girls "play house"; rather, it's necessary for a girl to be considered "social" and keep the attention of a man. When she meets Brown University student Ryder on spring break, she outlines to him how she has learned how to fend off the sexual advances of her dates. Although Ryder thinks Merritt is "sophisticated" saying "experience—that's what separates the girls from the girl scouts," it becomes clear that for Merritt sex before marriage could only happen after an engagement. And her abstinence is rewarded—as a result, Ryder considers her marriageability. On the other hand, Merritt's friend Melanie who *does* take Merritt's classroom speech to heart does not fare well in the plot. On the first night of the trip, Melanie gets drunk and, in the ellipses, has sex with Franklin. Because of her foray into sex, the boys view her as interchangeable. The next night when Melanie thinks she's meeting Franklin at the motel, another boy shows up, and the scene ends with Melanie backing away into the darkened room helplessly repeating, "No. No. No." This time it is rape that happens in the ellipses. Later, Merritt tries to comfort her distraught friend, and she acknowledges that it could have been her. Of course, the fact that Melanie has premarital sex and then winds up sexually assaulted maintains a pattern established in films decades earlier and continued well into subsequent decades. Not until the "no means no" campaigns of the 1980s was there significant pushback on the implication that women and girls who flirted, dressed provocatively, or had sex invited their own sexual assaults. *Where the Boys Are* presents a highly gendered world where boys chase sex and girls pursue marriage, and it becomes clear that consenting girls—those who resist their role as gatekeepers—invite disaster. Still, the openness with which sex is discussed and the overt depiction of acquaintance rape no doubt changed portrayals of adolescent sexuality before the Code had officially ended.

A year later, *Splendor in the Grass* (1961) pushed even further by emphasizing the dangers to girls—not only of having sex, but also of abstaining. Wilma Dean "Deanie" (Natalie Wood) is torn between wanting to please her mother (by avoiding premarital sex) and fulfilling the mutual sexual desire that she has with her boyfriend, Bud (Warren Beatty). The gender double standard is clear here. Bud is able to release his sexual frustration with another girl at school. However, when Deanie tries to pursue sex with Bud, he rebuffs her as a "nice" girl. At a later point, she's nearly raped by a classmate, so that once again, assault is shown as an inevitable risk of sexual desire for girls. However, the difference with *Splendor in the Grass* is that neither the consenting nor the gatekeeping girl quite finds her happy ending. Bud's sister, who has a reputation for promiscuity, gets drunk at a party and is assaulted in a car until Bud rescues her. Deanie, on the other hand, winds up recuperating in a psychiatric institution seemingly due to her sexual frustration. Ultimately, the film makes a damning assertion that there is no safe ground for girls' developing sexuality—she's condemned and assaulted if she does, and she's destined for an asylum if she doesn't.

In 1956, the miscegenation clause was removed from the Code, and depictions of romances across race became more common with films like *Band of Angels* (1957) and *Shadows* (1959). Black actor Sidney Poitier starred in several films that broke new ground. For example, in *A Patch of Blue* (1965), a blind white girl, Selina, falls in love with Gordon (Poitier), who takes pity on her when he finds her helpless and alone in a public park. The two develop a friendship and then romance, although ultimately Gordon helps Selina find a school where she can be educated rather than marrying her as she wishes. The film *Guess Who's Coming to Dinner* (1967) took this plot further with a young white woman, Joanna, who wishes to marry Dr. John Prentice (Poitier), an older Black widower. Although her parents (and his) are initially reluctant, ultimately the couple overcomes their obstacles to be together. These films clearly sought to overturn negative stereotypes that had persisted for many decades—particularly the pattern of Black men as predators of white girls. In one scene in *A Patch of Blue*, Selina's violent and abusive mother tries to take her away from Gordon to no avail despite white passersby who witness the exchange. Perhaps to rewrite the cultural script on race and gender, white girls are given more sexual agency, while the Black characters are shown as gatekeepers in both films. After Selina and Gordon kiss in *A Patch of Blue*, Selina recalls the shame of her prior rape by a white man, which causes Gordon to stop and back away. When she tells him, "I said what I did because I love you so much," he responds, "I know why you said it. I'm glad you said it. You brought me back to earth." She tells him, "I didn't want you to come back to earth. I wanted you to make love with me," and he responds, "I know." Gordon becomes the benevolent Black savior to the abused white girl in this story. So too in *Guess Who's Coming to Dinner* do we get the impression that it is Dr. Prentice who acts as the sexual gatekeeper. In a conversation with her mother, Joanna puts it bluntly, "Do you mean, have we been to bed together? I don't mind your asking me that—we haven't. He wouldn't" at which her mother looks shocked. Here, girls' sexual desire across race lines is viewed as normative despite the apparent incomprehension of an older generation.

Remnants of the prior era's insistence on gender and race boundaries clearly began to be problematized in films of this era. As the Code became increasingly irrelevant in the 1950s and independent movies proliferated, filmmakers began to push the limits of what was acceptable. While much still happened in the ellipses, this era undoubtedly hinted at what was to come—an era marked by more overt acknowledgement of adolescent sexuality.

THE EROTICIZATION OF YOUTH: TEEN SEX COMEDIES, SEXPLOITATION, AND CHILD PORNOGRAPHY (1960S–80S)

As the 1960s continued, adolescent sexuality trickled and then rushed out of the closet. In 1968, the Motion Picture Association of America (MPAA), formerly MPPDA, created a ratings-based system so sexual content was no longer off limits, labeling films as R, restricted, or X, explicit.[65] As a result, the late 1960s brought out everything from teen sexploitation films like *Three in the*

Attic (1968) and *The First Time* (1969) to depictions of sex between youth and adults in *The Graduate* (1967), *Harold and Maude* (1971), and *Pretty Baby* (1978) to more explicit depictions of rape in films like *Last Summer* (1969). The Roman Catholic Church also changed the name of its National Legion of Decency to the National Catholic Office for Motion Pictures in the 1960s. While continuing to condemn films, the church did little to discourage filmmakers from sexual material. By 1969, *The New York Times* reported the number of films meeting the church's A-I rating (acceptable for all) was "the smallest in its 35-year history," while the number of condemned films "set a record at 40."[66] In other words, by the end of the 1960s, controversial material had become the norm.

For teen movies, this trend meant adolescent characters "were no longer confined to monogamous relationships that led automatically to the altar."[67] If one were to point to a heyday of adolescent sexuality in cinema, this era could certainly be it. However, while this period rendered adolescent heterosexuality more visible, it depicted it in ways that were not only realistic but also exploitative such as in the "teen sex comedy," including *Animal House* (1978), *H.O.T.S.* (1979), *Goin' All the Way!* (1981), *Losin' It* (1983), *Spring Break* (1983), *Joy of Sex* (1984), *Hot Moves* (1984), *Revenge of the Nerds* (1984), and *Preppies* (1984), to name but a few. Youth eager to have first sex or "lose their virginity" became a mainstay of the genre—demure teens like Sandy in *Grease* (1978) were anomalies who would come around to being more sexual in the plot.[68] Sex had become so ubiquitous in teen films by the early 1980s that studios criticized writers if there was not enough of it, and directors were routinely instructed to incorporate nudity of young women.[69] Of course, despite a supposedly no-holds-barred sensibility, same-sex desire and gender questioning remained closeted. Rather, stories of adolescent sexuality from the late 1960s to the early 1980s often revolved around sex-crazed white cis heterosexual teen boys who relentlessly pursued girls and women. Of course, not all teen films in this era depicted sex as mindless romps—*The Last Picture Show* (1971) portrayed sex as "an empty experience" as Shary notes; *Smooth Talk* (1985) reiterated sexual dangers awaiting a "wild" girl; and *Last Summer* depicted a group rape that implied that "teenagers cannot handle the responsibilities of sex."[70]

Many films of this era reinforced and rendered more apparent "rape culture"—the prevailing normalization of sexual assault and violation through media depictions and culture. These films routinely relished in a "boys will be boys" mentality, in which teen boys used tactics of persuasion and deception to see girls or women naked and get them to have sex.[71] As the objects of desire, girls and women were routinely objectified, violated, and put on display for masculine characters in the films as well as presumably the audience. As most films depicted white teens, the bulk of the aggressors, too, were white. However, this was not exclusively so—in *Cooley High* (1975) Black protagonist Preach bets his friends a dollar that he will "get" the uppity Brenda into bed, which he does by pretending to like poetry, and a scene in *Fame* (1980) depicted both Black and white boys' spying on naked girls in the locker room.

Of course, there are also notable reversals from the era. For example, *The Graduate* flips the script with Ben, a recent graduate, and Mrs. Robinson, an aggressive married older woman. Although older women are often portrayed as a worthy conquest by adolescent boys in teen films, *The Graduate* complicates this trope by highlighting the coercion involved in their relationship. Mrs. Robinson walks into Ben's room unannounced, convinces him to drive her home, tricks him into staying with her, and then abruptly traps him in a room with her naked as he pleads, "Let me out." Mrs. Robinson takes advantage of both Ben's inexperience and uncertainty, and when he hesitates to consummate their relationship, she persuades him by suggesting it's his "first time" and calling him "inadequate." Other films of the era make girls the aggressors, as in the sexploitation film *Three in the Attic*, in which three college women (one a woman of color) discover their lover sleeping with all of them and decide to lock him in their dorm's attic and repeatedly force him to have sex with them. However, while *The Graduate* portrays the adult woman's coercion negatively, *Three in the Attic* mocks a young man's nonconsent through a depiction of a women-on-man gang rape fantasy.

In the late 1960s through the early 1980s, studios made no pretense about marketing teen sexuality to adults. Adolescent sex comedies typically had R ratings due to explicit situations and nudity, so adults were evidently the target audience. Even sex between teens and adults was seen as less transgressive during this time in films such as *Summer of '42* (1971), *Manhattan* (1979), *Private Lessons* (1981), *Fast Times at Ridgemont High* (1982), *Risky Business* (1983), *Blame It on Rio* (1984), and *Loverboy* (1989). Some of these plots seem especially surprising in retrospect—such as *Loverboy*, in which teen boy Randy (Patrick Dempsey) becomes a prostitute for dissatisfied middle-aged women in the neighborhood; or *Blame It on Rio*, in which two teen girls go on a vacation with their fathers and one of the girls, Jennifer, begins an affair with the other girl's father, Matthew (Michael Caine); or the sex comedy *Private Lessons*, in which a fifteen-year-old boy embarks on a sexual relationship with his adult housekeeper, Nicole. In addition, the film *Manhattan* portrays the forty-something Isaac Davis (Woody Allen) dating and having sex with high school girl, Tracy (Mariel Hemingway). Even *Mystic Pizza* (1988), which depicts the affair between a teen girl and a married man as a heartbreaking mistake, does not suggest the relationship to be transgressive. Although these films normalized adult/teen sex, they also typically showed the relationship as an aberration. Most of the time the teens and adults revert to partners of their own age group by the end of the story. In *Loverboy*, Randy is back with his teenaged girlfriend; in *Manhattan*, Tracy is leaving for a program abroad; and in *Blame It on Rio*, Jennifer winds up finding a new romantic interest closer to her age, while Matthew ends up back with his wife. Since such films present teens who appear mature and at times as sexually experienced as the adults, they blatantly deny problematic aspects of consent. However, as evidence of changing times, the specter of child abuse often remains an unrealized threat in some of the films—in *Manhattan*, Davis says about their sexual relationship, "As long as the cops don't burst in ... I think we're going to break a couple of records," and in the convoluted plot of *Private Lessons*, Nicole is blackmailed by the family chauffeur to avoid being reported as a child molester.

The unleashing of graphic sexual depictions elicited a backlash in the 1970s and 1980s with children as the focus of concern. As one parent put it in a 1971 *New York Times* editorial, "Since the rigidly moralistic Hollywood code of the thirties was abandoned in the more liberal atmosphere of the sixties, adults are no longer limited to seeing only what's suitable for children. The problem is that neither are children."[72] By this time, it was no longer defensible to argue that children would be drawn into unruly behavior by depictions of crime, rebellion, and sexuality. However, this parent's description of bringing a fourteen-year-old daughter to a foreign film that depicts a graphic rape represented a new era's concern for the psychological harm of children. Thus, a new form of education through films emerged. As heavy-handed hygiene films faded out of view, the "after-school special" appeared in the early 1970s. No longer guided so obviously by shaming youth, these TV movies aimed to attract adolescent audiences while tackling topics similar to the former hygiene films—teen pregnancy, STDs, drugs, and alcohol abuse. Although there was more recognition that youth could and would be making sexual and other decisions themselves, the need to protect and instruct youth remained a constant even in this era.

The increase of explicit sexual situations featuring youth in films ultimately galvanized in a widespread debate over the film *Pretty Baby*. Leading up to it were several films that marketed children in sexual situations such as the R-rated film *Nymph* (1973), which advertised a girl in the poster as "a little girl in a woman's body underage and overeager." In addition, Martin Scorsese's film *Taxi Driver* (1976) cast then twelve-year-old Jodie Foster as a child prostitute. Released two years earlier than *Pretty Baby*, *Taxi Driver* provoked more public backlash for its violence than its sexual exploitation. Before the shoot, the Los Angeles welfare board had insisted that Foster undergo a psychiatric evaluation to ensure she was "mentally equipped to handle the part" and that a body double (Foster's twenty-year-old sister, Connie) be hired to play her in the more "sexually suggestive scenes."[73] Still, despite sexual situations involving a preteen girl, *Taxi Driver* and Foster's other film *The Little Girl Who Lived Down the Lane* (1976) did not seem to evoke the same level of concern over child pornography in the initial reviews.[74]

Pretty Baby seemed to change that. The film depicts actress Brooke Shields as Violet, a twelve-year-old prostitute whose virginity is auctioned off at a New Orleans brothel midway through the film. Although the film does not include explicit sex, the film includes several scenes of Shields's naked buttocks and prepubescent chest and places her in sexual and violent situations. Violet's childlike qualities are emphasized so that her consent in the film is obviously questioned—she has been born and raised in a brothel, and she has nowhere else to go. As she's being auctioned, one of the men asks, "How old is she?" to which the madam responds, "Do you want to put me in jail? She's just old enough." By this point, Violet has been so exposed to sex that one of the prostitutes suggests, "This guy is buying a virgin, so she's got to act it right. You've got to give him the idea that you don't know nothing. It should be like a rape." However, Violet does not need to fake innocence when the time comes—the highest bidder gives her a sinister look as she pleads for him to be "gentle," and next we hear her screams behind a closed door. Afterward, Violent jokes about it. Although Violet's immaturity is evident, she develops a mutual sexual relationship outside the brothel with Ernest Bellocq, a photographer. They even marry—an act that becomes nullified when Violet's mother later retrieves her and declares the union to be illegal without her consent.

Whether the film itself—and Shields's mother, who consented for her daughter to be in it—exploited Shields became the subject of a media debate before the film was even released. Several extratextual factors contributed to the perception of the film as pornographic. Reviews, articles, and interviews often commented on prepubescent Shields's "breathtaking" and "extraordinary" beauty as a "pre-pubescent sex symbol";[75] a "Brooke Book" published around the time of the film featured her in adult attire such as a "fur coat and platform shoes, waving a cigarette holder" alongside a quote, "Fur just makes me feel so fantastically sexy. You know what I mean";[76] and *Playboy* published publicity stills of Shields with a cover story. Shields's mother even had authorized photographer Garry Gross to take naked photos of her daughter at age ten for a *Playboy* book years earlier.[77] One of the reasons Shields's performance might have attracted more controversy than Foster's, in other words, were the numerous ways Shields was being marketed as "sexy"—not only via the film but beyond it.

Reviewers often insisted that the film could not be classified as pornography. A reviewer in *The New York Times*, for instance, declared that the film "is neither about child prostitution nor is it pornographic," and Roger Ebert maintained that although the film's premise was "tragically perverted," the film itself is "not a perverted film."[78] Director Louis Malle too was quoted as saying, "Anybody who calls it child pornography has not seen the damn thing."[79] Nevertheless, *Pretty Baby* and Shields herself became apt examples for child rights advocates who critiqued the film for how it depicted Shields without her being old enough to have consented to such a role.

The 1970s and 1980s also exposed the pervasiveness of childhood sexual abuse (CSA). While most assaults were revealed to be perpetrated by parents, relatives, doctors, teachers, priests, and other adults known to the children, public discourse instead focused on pedophiles more broadly. As a result, visual depictions of childhood sexuality became a primary object of concern—child pornography became understood as both a direct result and cause of the sexual exploitation of children. Right-wing conservatives and liberal feminists agreed that photos like the ones of Shields not only violated the child directly but also provided imagery that could be used by and even attract future pedophiles. This atypical unilateral liberal and conservative support for government action led to the rapid development of extensive child pornography laws in the United States beginning in the late 1970s. The Protection of Children Against Sexual Exploitation Act of 1977 became the first large-scale law that "prohibited the use of children to produce child pornography" and outlined punishments for offenders.[80]

In 1982, the Supreme Court labeled child pornography a special category outside of First Amendment protection in *New York v. Ferber*—a stance that continues through the current moment. In the unanimous decision, the justices upheld New York's ban on sexually explicit material of minors (in this case, videos of boys masturbating); however, two of the nine justices wrote specifically about the challenge of protecting artistic, educational, or "clinical pictures of adolescent sexuality."[81] Two years later, the Child Protection Act of 1984 increased the punishments for child pornography and altered the definition of a minor from under age sixteen to under eighteen. As a result, all child pornography is illegal and continues to be defined as "any visual depiction of sexually explicit conduct involving a minor" or a person under age eighteen.[82] The state's age of consent is irrelevant, and the visual depiction does not need to "depict a child engaging in sexual activity" since any "picture of a naked child may constitute illegal child pornography if it is sufficiently sexually suggestive."[83] Unlike adult pornography, child pornography also does not need to

Fig. 1.2. Controversy over the pre-pubescent Brooke Shields in Louis Malle's film *Pretty Baby* helped coalesce the child abuse and child pornography discourses.

be classified as legally "obscene" or work that "appeals to the prurient interest, is patently offensive in light of community standards and lacks serious literary, artistic, political or scientific value."[84] Not surprisingly, such a broad definition of what constitutes child pornography has had a substantial impact on depictions of youth sexuality.

The laws put into effect in that era have held sway ever since—and there seems to be little sign of that changing. In the 1984 essay "Thinking Sex," Gayle Rubin critiques how US laws are "especially ferocious in maintaining the boundary between childhood 'innocence' and 'adult' sexuality."[85] Rubin writes, "Rather than recognizing the sexuality of the young and attempting to provide for it in a caring and responsible manner, our culture denies and punishes erotic interest and activity by anyone under the local age of consent. The amount of law devoted to protecting young people from premature exposure to sexuality is breathtaking."[86] Rubin's words voiced over three decades ago still ring true today. Despite child pornography laws being a "remarkably recent invention," they remain "the least contested area of First Amendment jurisprudence," and they have continued to expand "largely unchecked by critical inquiry."[87] Ostensibly, the goal has been to avoid eroticizing children, but in a Foucauldian sense, the impact might also be the opposite. In *Erotic Innocence: The Culture of Child Molesting*, James R. Kincaid argues that our fascination "with tales of childhood eroticism (molestation, incest, abduction, pornography)" normalizes the "irrepressible allure of children" so that "we no longer question whether adults are drawn to children."[88] Certainly, the overriding sentiment remains that any depiction of child sexuality or nudity is child pornography and that "child pornography *is* child sexual abuse."[89]

Nearly immediately, younger adolescents were no longer depicted in sexual roles, and teen films shifted to stories more about romance than sex. Of course, as sensibilities shift, strange hybrids often emerge. For example, *Little Darlings* (1980) features a sex comedy setup with two girls who aim to lose their virginity at summer camp. However, here both ultimately learn their quest is misguided—Ferris is unable to seduce an adult man counselor, and Angel is ultimately disappointed by first sex with Randy. Similarly, *Fast Times at Ridgemont High* might be known as a teen sex comedy with explicit naked scenes of adolescent intercourse, but the underlying message of the film suggests that girls are happier with romance and love, not sex. In the film, teenager Stacy has two encounters of intercourse. First, she lies about her age and sneaks out of the house to be with an adult man where she has intercourse for the first time in a baseball dugout. Through shots of her expression and the dismal setting, it becomes clear Stacy does not derive much pleasure from the encounter. Later in the film, she also has intercourse with Damone in her pool house. Although Stacy is nude with her breasts exposed, director Amy Heckerling avoids eroticizing the scene. Damone's thrusts and quick orgasm depict sex, for Stacy at least, as anticlimactic. Stacy then winds up pregnant. Although Damone promises to share the cost and take her to the abortion clinic, he fails to do either. Her abortion here is depicted as not much more than an inconvenience, which certainly makes it groundbreaking as far as scenes of abortion are concerned. Still, it follows an unfortunate pattern of punishing girls for their sexual desires and exploits. By the end of the film, Stacy opts for romance with the nerdier and sexually inexperienced Mark Ratner instead. The film even displays a title at the end to clarify that the couple has not yet had intercourse. *Fast Times at Ridgemont High* thus acknowledges girls' adolescent desire, while rendering their sexual pleasure inaccessible through casual sexual encounters. In a chapter "Love's Labor's Lost?," Lisa M. Dresner argues that these films "make their points about not rushing into sex in a way that respects and empowers teenage girls instead of romanticizing or infantilizing them."[90] Still, both films show the pursuit of sex detached from romance or love as unsuccessful for girls. As a result, they uphold traditional values of relationships for girls, epitomizing the move from an era of unbridled adolescent sex into an era of teen romance.

Although talk of sex remained ubiquitous in mid-1980s teen films, visual scenes of adolescent sex in mainstream films changed dramatically. John Hughes's films epitomize this new ethos. In *The Breakfast Club* (1985), both girls, Allison (Ally Sheedy) and Claire (Molly Ringwald), admit to being "virgins," although Allison initially fabricates sexual experience. In *Sixteen Candles* (1984), protagonist Samantha (Ringwald) has no sexual experience and gains little through the film. Instead, sex makes its appearance through the side plot. The "geek" Ted (Anthony Michael Hall) persistently pursues Sam until she finally agrees to give him her underwear to show his friends proof of a sexual conquest that never occurs. Ted does ultimately lose his virginity in the film when Sam's crush, Jake, sends him off with his parent's car and passed-out girlfriend, Caroline, telling him to "have fun." The disconcerting punchline at the end of the film is that Caroline and Ted have had sex, but neither of them remembers it—and the audience never sees it. The couple wakes up disheveled the next morning in the car. Ted asks her, "Did we?" and she says, "I think so," to which he responds, "Did I enjoy it?" Thus, the film retains the formula of the sex comedy through the side plot, while altering the protagonist to someone motivated by and rewarded with a romantic relationship, not sex. It also maintains a distinction between girls who do and girls who don't have sex, continuing the pattern of promiscuous party girls (like Caroline) as being used or violated.

Protagonists' maintaining adolescent innocence amid a world of sexuality was not only true for girls in Hughes's films. In *Weird Science* (1985), two boys magically conjure up a sexualized adult woman, Lisa. Though sex is clearly front of mind for the boys and the plot, the film does not quite fulfill its own strange premise. As one reviewer noted at the time, "real-life situations, sexual or otherwise, are the farthest things from the mind of writer-director John Hughes."[91] Despite sexual innuendo being played for laughs, Lisa ultimately teaches the boys how to attract girls their own age. While many late 1980 teen romances avoided sex, a few, like *Say Anything* (1989), depicted adolescent sex as a normal part of a monogamous relationship. In addition, it seems no accident that two of the more popular mainstream depictions of unabashed teen sexual desire and activity at that time—*Dirty Dancing* (1987) and *Peggy Sue Got Married* (1986)—are set during the 1960s. Teen films, in other words, had begun to express nostalgia for a freer sexual era that seemed to be a thing of the past.

While the late 1960s seemed to bring adolescent sexuality into the mainstream, the late 1980s were marked not only by child pornography legislation but also by the discovery of HIV as a sexually transmitted disease, increased national focus on combating teen pregnancy, and a greater awareness of acquaintance rape. Such a combination of forces made the depiction of freewheeling adolescent sexuality appear problematic and unethical. Hence, bigger budget theatrical films shifted away from stories about sexual conquests to stories about romance. The 1980s might have represented a heyday for teen films, as Shary notes in *Generation Multiplex*, but it also marked the beginning of yet another curtailment of adolescent sexuality.

CONSENT CULTURE: USHERING IN A NEW ETHICS FOR ADOLESCENT SEXUALITY (1990S–2020S)

Among mainstream popular teen films, sexless teen romantic comedies persisted in the 1990s with films like *Clueless* (1995) and *She's All That* (1999), and *Never Been Kissed* (1999), while many other films in the decade depicted adolescent sex with caution or even doom. Larry Clark's controversial *Kids* (1995) depicts girls as young as twelve being "seduced" by the HIV-infected Telly, and *Cruel Intentions* (1999) pits a menacing sexually aggressive cocaine-addicted teen girl (Sarah Michelle Gellar) against a studious and virginal girl (Reese Witherspoon). *The Virgin Suicides* (1999) shows adolescent girl Lux's traumatization upon being abandoned after first sex with Trip on a football field—the experience leads her into a pattern of pleasureless promiscuity and ultimately a suicide pact. The immutable consequences of sex also are raised in Leslie Harris's independent feature *Just Another Girl on the I.R.T.* (1992). The film begins like a girl-driven sex comedy with Chantel as an empowered Black protagonist. However, after she succumbs to pressure by Tyrone to have unprotected intercourse, she winds up pregnant. By the end, she has birthed a child (whom she nearly murders after the birth) and ultimately must make sense of her life as a single parent. Although *Just Another Girl on the I.R.T.* was heralded for its long-awaited prioritization of Black girls' voices, it maintains the patterns of weightier consequences for people of color and a girl's becoming pregnant after a single instance of intercourse. In many ways, films in the 1990s seemed once again to imply a "road to ruin" for sexually active girls.

The 1990s undoubtedly brought with it a diversification of the protagonists of teen films. During the 1980s, there were few teen comedies with protagonists of color. Shary notes that in the 1980s, "African-American youth were shown in films fighting for their lives, under the hegemony of a racist legal and political system, under difficult family and class conditions, and under the influence of the media."[92] These issues did not make for light fare, and films featuring Black teens in this era tend toward the political and dramatic, such as Spike Lee's *School*

Daze (1988) and *Boyz n the Hood* (1991). However, in 1990, *House Party* broke ground as a Black teen comedy about a group of high school students who host a rowdy party while one of their parents are out of town. The immense popularity of the film proved that light-hearted stories about Black teens could command an audience and generate revenue. On a budget of $2.5 million, the film grossed over $26 million and led to numerous sequels—*House Party 2* (1991), *House Party 3* (1994), *House Party 4: Down to the Last Minute* (2001), and *House Party: Tonight's the Night* (2013).[93] Interestingly, *House Party* also reflects the ethos of "safe sex" and consent in the era. When the protagonist Kid discovers he only has one old torn condom, he and Sydney mutually decide to wait to have sex.

In the 1990s, openly lesbian/gay teen comedies also emerged with *Totally F***ed Up* (1993), *The Incredibly True Adventures of Two Girls in Love* (1995), *But I'm a Cheerleader* (1999), and *Edge of Seventeen* (1998). Although each of these films are ostensibly pro-queer, *Edge of Seventeen* still depicts a minefield of consent for queer teens. The protagonist Eric experiences numerous disappointing sexual interactions—a brief encounter with someone he meets at a bar, uncomfortable intercourse with his college-aged coworker Rod, and an awkward heterosexual experience with his friend Maggie that ends their friendship. *The Incredibly True Adventures of Two Girls in Love*, on the other hand, presents a teen romance that culminates in a mutual first sexual experience between two girls—Randy and Evie—who come from different race and socioeconomic backgrounds. Even today, *The Incredibly True Adventures of Two Girls in Love* remains a rare film on many levels due to its depiction of openly queer characters, a Black protagonist who falls in love with a white girl without race being a plot issue, and its emphasis on unambiguous mutual consent.

In fact, the film industry's increased focus on adolescent girls as an audience in the late 1980s and since has helped usher in an era of consent. In a *New York Times* piece, Peggy Orenstein labeled 1996 the "year of the teen-age girl" noting how girls were not used merely as "plot devices" but rather shown "in charge of their own fates, active rather than reactive" in movies "about girls' relationships to one another rather than to boys, that tackle the big themes of teen-age life, like anger, sexuality, alienation and displacement."[94] She specifically cites *Manny & Lo* (1996), *Foxfire* (1996), *Girls Town* (1996), and *Welcome to the Dollhouse* (1995). Linked to the "rape revenge" genre, both *Foxfire* (based on the Joyce Carol Oates novel) and *Girls Town* feature protagonists who explicitly seek revenge for sexual harassment, assault, and rape—demonstrating girls' rage over assault. *Welcome to the Dollhouse* takes a more subtle approach. In the film, Dawn's classmate Brandon threatens to "rape" her after school. Rather than avoiding him, Dawn appears to wait for him not once but twice after school. The first day, Brandon threatens Dawn at knifepoint and his insistence that she "strip" is only interrupted when the janitor comes out, provoking Dawn to run off. But in their next meeting, he asks when she needs to be home, and when she starts to strip, he says, "Wait, there's something I want you to do for me first." Brandon apparently has no intention of raping Dawn. Rather, he uses this as a combined tactic to scare her and to express his romantic interest in her. They go to an abandoned junkyard. As it turns out, Brandon was hurt that she used the word *retard* because his brother is disabled—Dawn apologizes, and the two mutually kiss. Dawn asks if he's still planning on raping her, and he responds "Nah, there's not enough time." Although it's disturbing how rape is conjured here, the point seems to be that rape culture is so prevalent that it is embedded in the seduction habits of preteens who have no clue what it means—and in fact, actress Heather Matarazzo states in an interview years later that she did not know what it meant when she acted in the film.[95]

Films with adolescent sex in this era often depict ambiguous consent negotiations. In *Cruel Intentions*, the malicious Kathryn wants to ruin Cecile's reputation and convinces her brother, Sebastian, to seduce her. In the resulting scene, Sebastian threatens to call her mother unless she allows him to kiss her, but "not on her lips." When Cecile reports the act to Kathryn the next day, she says that "something awful" happened, adding, "He took advantage of me." Kathryn asks if he forced intercourse on her or made her give him a "blow job." Cecile then whispers what happened, and Kathryn says, "He went down on you" and then asks, "Did you like it?" Cecile at first responds, "No," but after Kathryn's disbelief adds, "Well, I don't know. It was weird. At first it felt icky and then it was sort of OK. And then, and then I started getting really hot and then I started shaking and then, I don't know, it was weird. It just felt like an explosion! But a good one." Of course, nonconsent and sexual pleasure are not mutually exclusive. Like the scene in *Welcome to the Dollhouse*, this scene in *Cruel Intentions* shows coercion uncomfortably embedded in intimate interactions.

The 1990s also represented an era of negotiation over whether girls were automatically victims in stories with adult men or not. The *Poison Ivy* series embodies the era's transformation—while the original 1992 film featured Ivy (Drew Barrymore) as a predatory high school student ruthlessly in pursuit of her friend's father, the fourth film in the series *Poison Ivy: The Secret Society* in 2008 portrays college student Danielle "Daisy" being drawn into a secret society of college girls. Not only did the later film move away from a primary focus on the adult man/young woman relationship, but it also sets the story in college and emphasizes a sex trafficking angle. One could argue the turning point as Adrian Lyne's *Lolita* (1997). While the 1962 Stanley Kubrick adaptation of Nabokov's novel did not even depict Lolita and Humbert's kissing,

Lyne's version rendered explicit intimate scenes between the twelve-year-old Lolita (played by fourteen-year-old Dominique Swain) and her adult stepfather Humbert Humbert (Jeremy Irons). Since Swain was a minor, the film provoked accusations of child pornography. *Lolita* was reedited, but Lyne nevertheless struggled to secure a distributor for over a year. In 1998, Showtime acquired the film and released it on cable, making it the most expensive film at the time to premiere directly on television.[96] Lyne's *Lolita* served as a tacit warning—and to this day filmmakers avoid placing actual minors in any romantic or sexual roles. Even a first kiss as depicted between preteens Sam and Suzy in *Moonrise Kingdom* (2012) or Max and Brixlee in *Good Boys* (2019) remains rare. In contemporary films, the onset of romantic and sexual exploration is generally depicted during later teen years, which places stories safely above US states' age of consent (sixteen to eighteen). And youth depicted in sexual situations routinely are cast with adult actors.

Between 1996 and 2002, child pornography laws became so strict that they called into question *any* depiction of sex in a teen film—even ones acted by adults. In 1996, Congress passed the Child Pornography Prevention Act (CPAA) to prohibit "virtual" child pornography. The law banned the creation and distribution of images or movies that contained either computer-generated children or adults who "look like minors."[97] This meant that child pornography need not have *actual* minors—just the suggestion of them. Although ostensibly designed to curtail internet pornography, it was initially unclear what this far-reaching legislation meant for fictional films. The 1996 CPAA was ultimately struck down in 2002 when the Supreme Court ruled 6–3 in *Ashcroft v. Free Speech Coalition* that it violated the First Amendment. In the opinion by the court, the justices acknowledged specifically that "teenage sexual activity and the sexual abuse of children ... have inspired countless literary works" and that "teenagers engaging in sexual activity ... is a fact of modern society and has been a theme in art and literature for centuries."[98] This ruling, thus, redirected the court's intent for child pornography laws to protect actual children harmed during the production of child pornography as opposed to policing fictional depictions that might arouse pedophilic adults. The specific mention to "art" in this case clarified that cinematic portrayals that do not feature actual minors within them would not be read by the court as child pornography, once again paving the way for works made *about* minors but *without* them.

Of course, like most shifts, there is not exactly a clean distinction between films prior to 2002 and after. The independent feature *Slums of Beverly Hills* (1998) depicted a girl protagonist exploring masturbation and first sex. In 1999, *American Pie* brought back the teen sex comedy—and its enormous popularity (and lack of any substantial backlash) paved the way to bringing adolescent sex back into the genre with consent being taken into greater account. At the same time, during the aughts, many films continued to omit adolescent sexuality. In the book *Abstinence Cinema*, Casey R. Kelly posits that the aughts led to a sex negative backlash during which "popular cinema contribute[d] to the ideological salience of a growing neo-conservative movement that seeks to reestablish abstinence until marriage as a social and political imperative."[99] Kelly locates this conservative trend of abstinence in both films like *Thirteen* (2003), which presents tragic consequences for girls' sexuality, and sex comedies like *Superbad* (2007), which omits sex for the two protagonists. Still, a handful of popular teen films in the era include adolescent sex as part of a relationship, such as *Love and Basketball* (2000), *Save the Last Dance* (2001), and *Juno* (2007), and the teen sex comedy continued with independent films like *Coming Soon* (1999), *The Girl Next Door* (2004), and *Sex Drive* (2008).

Since the 2010s, sex appears to have returned more consistently for adolescents in teen films—with consent as a guiding principle. In current films, boys routinely seek some verbal permission before initiating an intimate act with a girl. In *The To Do List* (2013), Rusty asks Brandy, "Can I kiss you?" Brandy, at first corrects him, telling him, "I know you *can* kiss me, but *may* you kiss me?" When he doesn't get it, she says, "Forget it. Yes, you can definitely kiss me," and they kiss. Queer teens too are shown making consent more explicit. In *Unpregnant* (2020), Kira asks Bailey, "Would it be OK if I kissed you?" Bailey's hesitance causes Kira to apologize, but Bailey admits, "I'm just warning you that I might be like kind of bad at it. I've never really done it before." Bailey smiles and says, "It's OK," and they kiss. In the more recent *Sex Appeal* (2022), consent is seen as being needed more than once. The teens use an app one of them built which asks, "Do you both consent?" and when they both say, "Yes," the app replies, "Foreplay may begin." The app presents the same question before they have intercourse. Both girls and boys are also shown confirming consent or demonstrating their respect for nos from girls, with dialogue such as "Are you sure?" (*The To Do List*); "We don't have to . . ." (*The Kissing Booth*); or "Tell me when to stop." (*The Miseducation of Cameron Post*). While the specter of teen boy sexual assaulters appears in several films, such as in *American Pie: Girls' Rules* (2020) and *Moxie* (2021), there is no longer tolerance for explicit sexual assault and harassment against girls as the punchline of a joke. Distancing from their prior gatekeeping role, girls now often drive sexual exploits for love, pleasure, and edification, although this sometimes comes at the expense of their not obtaining consent from teen boys.

Of course, subtleties have not disappeared. In the film *Premature* (2019), Ayanna looks uncomfortable, covering her body with her hands until Isaiah takes his shirt off and she then takes her bra off. In *The To Do List*, Rusty finds Brandy in a bedroom, thinks she's his girlfriend, and begins kissing her before he realizes his mistake. In *Booksmart* (2019), Amy doesn't ask Hope for consent before kissing her quickly in the bathroom. But Hope's smile and mutual kiss back implies consent. During their encounter, Amy then puts her finger in the "wrong hole," which makes for an awkward sexual encounter. And even films that show teens employing a "contract" show its futility. In *To All the Boys I've Loved Before* (2018), the couple mutually agrees to terms for a pretended relationship, but after falling in love, they decide to scrap the contract and "trust." And in *Sex Appeal*, despite the app she built to obtain clear consent and create a positive sexual experience, Avery finds her first experience of intercourse disappointing. Recent films also problematize a youth's agency as distinct from adults'—*Unpregnant* and *Never Rarely Sometimes Always* (2020) depict the problem of teen girls who seek abortions in states that require parental consent; the film *3 Generations* (2015) depicts a trans teen who must obtain consent from his parents before treatment; and films like *The Tale* (2018) and *The Diary of a Teenage Girl* present girls' desires and choices within childhood sexual abuse.[100]

Consent is undoubtedly a guiding ethos in contemporary teen films—but there is much that remains unseen in the genre, even today. Restrictions on what can be shown have not vanished; rather, they have morphed over time, guided by the ways that mainstream US society believes that youth sexuality should be controlled or at least hidden from adults' sight. In the book *Screening Sex*, author Linda Williams describes how the history of sex in US cinema demonstrates "the remarkable degree to which acts once considered ob-scene (literally, off scene) because they had the capacity to arouse have come 'on/scene.'"[101] Although Williams does not focus on youth sexuality, much has changed throughout cinema in that regard as well—the type of adolescent sexual exploration now commonplace in teen films, for example, would have been unthinkable in the Code era. However, to suggest that there is no longer censorship of youth sexuality in cinema would be untrue. Even an NC-17 film is subject to laws against child pornography in the US today. Teen films, undoubtedly, have adapted accordingly—emphasizing consent, avoiding sexual depictions of younger children/teens, and more carefully navigating depictions between adults and youth.

NOTES

1. Rubin, "Thinking Sex," 141.
2. For examples, see Callister et al., "Evaluation of Sexual Content in Teen-Centered Films" and Behm-Morawitz and Mastro, "Mean Girls?"

3. Smith, *Rethinking the Hollywood Teen Movie*, 12.
4. Egan, *Becoming Sexual*, 18.
5. I have not included the exact year here, since various sources report this happening as early as 1894 or as late as 1897. However, the film is often cited as the first example of censorship by the local police in Atlantic City, in response to public complaints.
6. Encyclopedia of Chicago, s.v., "Film Censorship."
7. Encyclopedia of Chicago, s.v., "Film Censorship."
8. Illinois Supreme Court, Block v. City of Chicago.
9. Considine, *The Cinema of Adolescence* and Scheiner, *Signifying Female Adolescence*.
10. Vaughn, "Morality and Entertainment," 41.
11. Scheiner, *Signifying Female Adolescence*, 8.
12. The National Board of Censorship of Motion Pictures makes this claim. See "Censors Destroyed Evil Picture Films; National Board Weeded Out 2,000,000 Feet of Objectionable Motion Scenes," *New York Times*, May 11, 1911, https://nyti.ms/3B08tnA.
13. "Say Motion-Picture Censorship Is Lax; Board Which Passes on Films Paid by Manufacturers, Women Investigators Declare," *New York Times*, November 8, 1911, https://nyti.ms/3zjDdUW.
14. Hall, *Adolescence*, 97.
15. Hall, *Adolescence*, 722.
16. US Supreme Court, Mutual Film Corporation, Appt., v. Industrial Commission of Ohio et al.
17. Young, *Motion Pictures*, 13–14.
18. Vaughn, "Morality and Entertainment," 42. The MPPDA has since been renamed to the Motion Picture Association.
19. Thalberg, Allen, and Wurtzel, "Don'ts and Be Carefuls."
20. Mayer, "Parallel Universe."
21. Simmon, "Female of the Species' D. W. Griffith," 10.
22. Blumer and Hauser, *Movies, Delinquency, and Crime*, 80–81.
23. Forman, *Our Movie Made Children*, 229.
24. Scheiner, *Signifying Female Adolescence*, 29.
25. Scheiner, *Signifying Female Adolescence*, 8.
26. Some reports list Janis as half Cherokee or "Native American," but numerous sources suggest her heritage was never confirmed.
27. Massood, "African-Americans and Silent Films."
28. Butters, "Capitalizing on Race," 114.
29. Gaines, *Fire & Desire*, 234.
30. Gaines, *Fire & Desire*, 157.
31. Geltzer, *Film Censorship in America*, 187.
32. Smith, *Managing White Supremacy*, 101.
33. Smith, *Managing White Supremacy*, 101.
34. Smith, *Managing White Supremacy*, 102.
35. Brook, "Birth of a Nation."
36. Sandler, *Naked Truth*, 23.
37. Leff and Simmons, "Appendix."
38. Kirby, "Regulating Cinematic Stories about Reproduction."
39. Catholic News Archive, "Pledge of the Legion of Decency."

40. Leff and Simmons, "Appendix," 223.
41. Considine, *Cinema of Adolescence*, 216.
42. Considine, *Cinema of Adolescence*, 215.
43. Courtney, *Hollywood Fantasies*, 144. Courtney clarifies in the text that "none of the extant versions of *Imitation of Life* (the 1933 novel, the 1934 film, and the 1959 film) ever specifies if, when, or by whom any interracial sex took place" so that the "PCA reads Peola's light skin and her eventual passing as signifiers of 'miscegenation.'"
44. Scott, *Cinema Civil Rights*, 22.
45. Scott, *Cinema Civil Rights*, 151.
46. In seeking "race films" I looked to Horak's "Preserving Race Films" and descriptions outlined in Mary Baldwin University's "Race Films: Getting Started" guide.
47. Considine, *Cinema of Adolescence*, 216.
48. Petigny, "'Silent' Sexual Revolution." For a more detailed understanding of this era, see Petigny's 2009 book *The Permissive Society: America, 1941–1965*.
49. The Kinsey reports have been criticized for their methodology; however, their impact on the understanding of sexuality in US society was significant.
50. Considine, *Cinema of Adolescence*, 216.
51. Stemm-Wade, "Careless Girls and Repentant Wives," 612.
52. Stemm-Wade, "Careless Girls and Repentant Wives," 612–16.
53. Stemm-Wade, "Careless Girls and Repentant Wives," 615.
54. Schaefer, "No False Modesty," 197.
55. Schaefer, "No False Modesty," 199.
56. Internet Movie Database, *Bob and Sally* movie poster.
57. Tzioumakis, *American Independent Cinema*, 125.
58. Leff and Simmons, "Appendix," 224–25.
59. Doherty, *Teenagers and Teenpics*, 7, emphasis in original removed, and Doherty, *Teenagers and Teenpics*, 158.
60. Jeffery P. Dennis in *Queering Teen Culture* argues that "the homoeroticism of *Rebel* is so integral to plot and characters that to call it a subtext is a misnomer" (39).
61. Ebert, "Young and the Restless."
62. Koresky, "Queer & Now & Then."
63. Turner Classic Movies, "Ben Mankiewicz Intro."
64. Palmer, "Baby Doll."
65. The MPAA has since been renamed the MPA. Numerous scholars and critics have pointed out alleged biases and secrecy of the MPA ratings. For a broad understanding of some of these issues, see Kirby Dick's documentary *This Film Is Not Yet Rated* (2006).
66. Weiler, "'69 a Bad Year for Good Films."
67. Considine, *Cinema of Adolescence*, 246.
68. "Losing virginity" is often conjured in teen films to signify having heterosexual intercourse for the first time, although I recognize the problems inherent to the phrase. For more, see McDonald, *Virgin Territory*.
69. In an interview, Martha Coolidge discusses the requirement of nudity in *Valley Girl*—see Meek, *Independent Female Filmmakers*. In addition, Heckerling released a 2021 director's cut of *Fast Times at Ridgemont High* that includes full-frontal male nudity of Robert Romanus (Damone), which Heckerling was not allowed to include in the original cut since it would have meant an X-rating.

70. Shary, *Teen Movies*, 43–44.
71. There are numerous examples from tricking a popular girl into sex through a disguise in *Revenge of the Nerds* to handing over one's girlfriend for another teen to lose his virginity in *Sixteen Candles*.
72. R. Kramer, "What Every Parent Needs to Know."
73. Klemesrud, "Jodie Foster's Rise."
74. As J. Paul Constabile summarized about censorship of *Pretty Baby* in Canada, "if this film is to be condemned for its treatment of Brooke Shields, where was the board's vigilance when it passed, without cuts, *Taxi Driver*, in which Jodie Foster was prominent as a 12-year-old-hooker?" Rather, Foster's early films were used after *Pretty Baby* to further the case of the exploitation of girl children.
75. Canby, "Film"; Davis, "Pre-pubescent Superstar." Ebert calls Shields "an extraordinarily beautiful child" (see Ebert, "Pretty Baby").
76. Erb, "Jodie Foster and Brooke Shields," 90.
77. Yardley, "Sugar and Spice."
78. Ebert, "Pretty Baby."
79. McMurran, "Pretty Brooke."
80. United States Sentencing Commission, "History of the Child Pornography Guidelines," 8–9.
81. US Supreme Court, New York v. Ferber.
82. United States Department of Justice, "Citizen's Guide."
83. United States Department of Justice, "Citizen's Guide."
84. "Excerpts from Opinions in Ruling on the Child Pornography Prevention Act," *New York Times*, April 17, 2002, https://www.nytimes.com/2002/04/17/us/excerpts-from-opinions-in-ruling-on-the-child-pornography-prevention-act.html. See also Miller v. California.
85. Rubin, "Thinking Sex," 163.
86. Rubin, "Thinking Sex," 161.
87. Adler, "Perverse Law of Child Pornography," 210–11.
88. Kincaid, *Erotic Innocence*, 13.
89. Adler, "Perverse Law of Child Pornography," 215–16.
90. Dresner, "Love's Labor's Lost?," 174.
91. Boyar, "Frantic 'Weird Science.'"
92. Shary, *Teen Movies*, 82.
93. In addition, a remake of the original House Party is slated for 2023.
94. Orenstein, "Movies Discover the Teen-Age Girl."
95. Independent Film Channel, "Indie Sex: Teens."
96. Carter, "Lolita Reaches a U.S. Audience."
97. "Excerpts from Opinions."
98. Legal Information Institute, "Ashcroft V. Free Speech Coalition."
99. C. R. Kelly, *Abstinence Cinema*, 5.
100. Another film, *Plan B* (2021), also depicts an adult pharmacist preventing a teen from receiving an abortion pill, but it does not seem to be the state law in that film.
101. Williams, *Screening Sex*, 7.

TWO

FLIPPING THE HETEROSEXUAL SCRIPT AND RACE-BASED SEXUAL STEREOTYPES IN TEEN COMEDIES OF THE 2010S AND 2020S

I could get a piece of ass anytime I want. Shit, I got Caroline in the bedroom passed out cold. I could violate her ten different ways if I wanted to.

—Jake in *Sixteen Candles* (1984)

Penises are not for looking at. They're for use—they're like plungers.

—Kayla in *Blockers* (2018)

In an April 6, 2018 essay in *The New Yorker*, actress Molly Ringwald reflects on the 1980s John Hughes films that made her famous. Specifically, she revisits their depiction of sexual consent and finds that the films do not hold up well under consent culture scrutiny. She recalls in *The Breakfast Club* (1985) how Bender and Claire (Ringwald) become a couple after Bender "sexually harasses Claire throughout the film," including a scene in which he crawls under her desk to peek up her skirt, and in *Sixteen Candles* (1984), Samantha (Ringwald) is repeatedly sexually harassed by Ted while the film's heartthrob Jake brags about how he could "violate" his intoxicated girlfriend in numerous ways if he chose.[1] Consent culture has since forced a reckoning with how such scenarios fail to take young women's consent into account. As a result, contemporary teen films now typically show boys' respecting a girl's no and obtaining a clear yes before sexual interactions. However, the opposite is not always true. As writers, filmmakers, and producers have sought to reimagine the "heterosexual script," they often simply swap the roles, converting girls— often girls of color—into the drivers of romances and sexual exploits who then fail to obtain clear and informed consent from unsuspecting boys they pursue.

This pattern demonstrates the resiliency of the narrative structure of coercive seduction and exposes a key criticism of affirmative consent: namely, its being a highly gendered discourse meant to protect girls and women but not always boys and men. Looking at several twenty-first-century heterosexual cisgender girl-driven sex comedies—including *The To Do List* (2013), *Blockers* (2018), *Yes, God, Yes* (2019), *Banging Lanie* (2020), *American Pie Presents Girls' Rules* (2020), and *Sex Appeal* (2022)—and teen romances, such as *To All the Boys I've Loved Before* (2018), *Sierra Burgess Is a Loser* (2018), and *The Half of It* (2020), reveals how the long-standing heterosexual script of seduction is alive and well—just in reverse.

THE "HETEROSEXUAL SCRIPT"

Most contemporary sex researchers start with the premise that human sexuality is developed through and guided by "sexual scripts." Known as sexual script theory (SST), this framework offers a way of understanding how individuals navigate sexual consent, behavior, and interactions. In "Sexual Script Theory: Past, Present, and Future," Michael W. Wiederman describes that sexual scripts are "the mental representations individuals construct and then use to make sense of their experience, including their own and others' behavior."[2] SST is broken down into three components: *cultural scenarios*, or shared norms and values developed via media and other societal influences and institutions; *interpersonal scripts*, or the adaptation of cultural scenarios through interactions; and *intrapsychic scripts*, or the development and understanding of one's own sexual motives and desires.[3] Wiederman explains that "cultural scenarios lay out the playing field of sexuality" such as "what is deemed desirable and undesirable, and where the broad boundaries lie between appropriate and inappropriate sexual conduct." Interpersonal scripts are then formed by adapting cultural scenarios via specific and varied situations and conversations with others, while intrapsychic scripts include "fantasies, memories, and mental rehearsals."[4] While both cultural scenarios and interpersonal scripts are primarily narrative in nature, intrapsychic scripts can be more visual or even emotional.

Film and television wield significant influence in creating, perpetuating, and transforming these scripts. As sex researchers note, "movies may offer particularly salient cultural scenarios,"[5] and "a viewer's own sexual decision-making may be shaped, in part, by viewing these types of portrayals."[6] Movies and television present a unique means to impact what we deem normal regarding sexual acts and interactions—and what we don't. For instance, as movies depict which sexual acts teens perform, who makes the first move, and what is off limits, viewers develop an idea of "normal" adolescent sexuality. Still, as influential as cultural scenarios within media are, as Wiederman notes, they are not "synonymous with sexual behavior."[7] Youth take additional cues from social media, schools, parents, and peers. Furthermore, since teen films are crafted by adults, they represent only what adults believe about normative adolescent behavior. In practice, youth, like adults, formulate cultural norms from movies and television, but they also watch critically, shaping their own interpersonal and intrapsychic scripts in response.

Numerous researchers note the ubiquity of our "culture's dominant courtship script," a cisgender and heteronormative script, which presumes "submissive behavior" for girls and women and "dominant behavior and sexual agency" for boys and men in sexual situations.[8] Known as the "heterosexual script," this pervasive scenario "socialize[s]" men to be the "aggressor and pursuer during sexual encounters" and women to "remain passive and to communicate indirectly."[9] In other words, in sexual situations, the cultural presumption is that a man or boy would desire and initiate a sexual encounter, while a woman or girl would respond subtly to that desire as the gatekeeper. In studies, researchers often mention the persistence of sexual double standards that correspond with this script, such as men being more desirous, women seeking relationships as opposed to casual sex, and promiscuous sexual behavior as being more socially acceptable for men.

Sexual scripts are further complicated by race-based stereotypes, or "implicit beliefs and expectations of sexual encounters that are dependent on the partner's race/ethnicity."[10] These deeply embedded assumptions can perpetuate damaging ideas about an individual's sexual desirability, availability, and agency based on their race or ethnicity. For example, Black women have historically been portrayed in media as "hypersexual" and "emasculating," which compounds pressure on them to conform to a heterosexual script.[11] Due to such "stigmatizing" race-based sexual stereotypes, young Black women report feeling "less empowered within intimate relationships and more likely to jeopardize their sexual well-being."[12] Race and ethnicity thus can be factors in the presumptions and actions of individuals and their partners during sexual consent negotiations.

A social norm that expects men and boys to be sexually assertive and women and girls to respond indirectly causes consent to remain fraught. Unsurprisingly, many researchers report that "sexual coercion and rape are likely an outcome of sexist and heteronormative sexual scripts."[13] Such scripts normalize masculine aggression and violence while diminishing feminine sexual desire and agency. Men can misread women's indirect signals, causing men, as one study phrased it, to be "fairly inaccurate at gauging women's sexual interest."[14] As a result of these misperceptions, nonconsensual sex is not only frequent but can be difficult to recognize—even by victims. In a study with college-aged women, Lynn M. Phillips shows that while nearly all of them had been coerced into sex, few saw themselves as victims of coercion. Instead, the young women viewed themselves as complicit. Phillips suggests that they misinterpreted their own experiences because of the normalization of coercion and the false belief that "abuse is uncomplicated."[15] When men's aggression and women's passivity are the tenets of the dominant cultural script, it becomes more challenging to identify and root out unwanted sexual interactions.

Sex researchers note how sexual double standards are changing. While mainstream media still tends to perpetuate a heterosexual script, individuals themselves nonetheless can deviate from expectations. For instance, some researchers note that although "the way people talk about sexuality" might be "in line with gendered stereotypes," individuals' personal "sexual experiences and relationships do not necessarily match these cultural scenarios."[16] Many men and women, in fact, do not support sexual double standards and wish to see them change.[17] As a result, the current era presents an opportunity to rewrite cultural, interpersonal, and intrapsychic sexual scripts to be "more egalitarian" and to "challenge the sexual power disadvantage of women."[18] In this light, it makes sense that writers and directors of teen comedies have sought to reverse the long-standing narrative trend of the heterosexual script. In one study of more recent tween, teen, and young adult television, researchers even found that girl characters were more likely than boys to "initiate casual sex," causing them to hypothesize that perhaps "when repeatedly exposed to the televised casual sexual experience script, viewers will eventually adapt such scripts in real life."[19] Of course, it would be hard to know precisely what changed first—youth's behavior or the media's representations of their behavior. Such shifts come about in a dispersed way as youth assimilate cultural scripts and rewrite their own interactively.

Films, TV, and other media not only perpetuate but also revise these sexual scripts. As J. Hillis Miller describes, "narratives reinforce the dominant culture and put it in question, both at the same time."[20] While certainly the typical teen romance and sex story of the twenty-first century remains centered on a heterosexual cisgender couple, disruptions to this convention have been long in the making as independent and major studios practice more inclusive casting and create more queer stories. As Popova suggests, changing our sexual scripts does not mean simply altering ideas about "what is and is not romantic" but also what we mean by "sex" itself,[21] adding that "we have to stop assuming that we know what sex looks like."²² Part of how we might reimagine what sex looks like is through narratives that disrupt the traditional heterosexual script and more accurately reflect diverse experiences.

THE PERSISTENCE OF RAPE CULTURE WITHIN CONSENT CULTURE: *THE KISSING BOOTH*

Before delving into how the heterosexual script has been flipped in contemporary teen films, it's important to note how, in many instances, traditional cultural scripts also remain in effect. Despite consent culture, nonconsent is still often a fundamental facet of teen film plots. For example, even though *Good Boys* (2019) clearly takes consent into account, the premise of the plot relies on nonconsent—a group of preteen boys steal a drone to spy on the teenage girls next door. And boys are still shown as using deception to attain sex with girls— for example in *Lady Bird* (2017), Kyle misleads Lady Bird into thinking he too is a "virgin." After they have intercourse, he denies having lied to her, criticizes her for being "upset," and asserts, "You're going to have so much unspecial sex in your life." Director Greta Gerwig highlights Kyle's coercive tactics in this scene, pointing out a key problem of consent—Lady Bird might initiate the sexual encounter, but she is also tricked and disappointed by it.²³

However, not all films seem to be depicting shortcomings of affirmative consent intentionally. For example, *The Kissing Booth* (2018), adapted from the 2012 young adult novel by Beth Reekles and, according to Netflix at the time, "one of the most-watched movies in the country, and maybe in the world"²⁴ clearly minimizes the coercive behavior of the love interest. In the film, protagonist Elle harbors a secret crush on her best friend Lee's older brother, Noah. A junior in high school, Elle believes that boys do not like her because she has never been asked out on a date. What she does not know is that Noah has warned all the boys at school to stay away from her. And Noah's threats are taken seriously because he has a violent streak that leads him repeatedly to engage in physical fights with other boys. Through this narrative structure, *The Kissing Booth* perpetuates a pattern of mistaking violent and controlling behavior for romantic interest. In one scene, Elle comes to school wearing a uniform skirt short enough to reveal her underwear. She attracts the shocked attention of boys and girls alike, and one of the boys, Tuppen, grabs her buttocks as she passes. Her friend Lee comes to her defense, but just as he is about to be punched by Tuppen, Noah steps in and punches Tuppen first. All three of them (Tuppen, Noah, and Elle) wind up in detention, where Tuppen begins flirting with Elle, tossing her a note across the room which says, "What do I have to do to get your number?" Elle smiles and writes back, while Noah shakes his head in disapproval. Elle's romantic choice, in other words, is between a boy who has physically assaulted her and a boy with violent tendencies who exhibits domineering behavior toward her. Noah's controlling behavior is thus depicted as a protective intervention due to her inability to make wise choices herself.

A similar setup is presented again later in the film when one of Elle's classmates, Warren, tells her at a party that she needs a "hot tub," and although she says no twice, he grabs her hand and starts dragging her away as she protests saying, "I'm not feeling well." Noah arrives to intercept and shouts, "She said no, Warren!" Noah, of course, is ready for another physical fight, but Elle pleads with him to take her home. But when Warren makes a comment, Noah takes the bait and punches him anyway. Elle runs away, and Noah chases her, yelling, "Elle, wait. Just get in the car, Elle. Just get in the car, Elle." When he catches up with her, he says it a third time while slamming his hand down on the car roof so hard that she jumps and stops in her tracks, looking afraid. He then says, "Please," and we see her expression waver and soften. In the next scene, she is in the passenger seat of his car. She soon realizes that "this isn't the way home," and he tells her that he wants to show her something. He drives her to an isolated lookout to view the city from behind the Hollywood sign, and it is here that they first have sex.

Clearly, their sexual encounter occurs as the result of Noah's trickery and abuse. He has ensured that no other boy (except abusers) will pursue Elle; he threatens and then pleads with her to get into his car; and he then drives her to a make-out spot instead of her home, as she had asked. So what does it mean when she consents now? Although she calls him out on his "player" moves, she nonetheless thinks to herself, "He's good." She then lays out a set of rules—no more fighting, no more telling her what to do, and "if we do this, nobody can know, at least until I can figure out a way to tell Lee." He humors her on her terms, and then they kiss. When he starts to unbutton her shirt, he pauses and says, "Um, you know we don't have to." She responds by unbuttoning *his* shirt. Noah will not proceed to have sex with Elle unless she consents, which she does. Clearly, we are meant to believe that Noah is a "good" guy who does the "right" thing by obtaining affirmative consent—that he is nothing like characters like Tuppen and Warren, who physically assault girls. But Noah and Elle's scene of intimacy only works as ethical if we accept that all his coercive and violent behaviors leading up to this moment are part of a well-intentioned romantic seduction. Elle's consent might be perfectly valid—she has long harbored a sexual attraction to Noah, so her desire for him has been clearly established—but it is difficult to watch this scene without feeling that something has gone horribly wrong. While *The Kissing Booth* clearly shows how "no means no," it simultaneously reinforces an all too familiar trope of masculine dominance and seduction—with one brief affirmative consent moment sprinkled in to make it supposedly acceptable.

Anne Barnhill, in a 2010 chapter titled "Just Pushy Enough," attempts to draw a line between egregious assaults and supposed "strategic and morally permissible" romantic pursuits. While acknowledging such scenes "are influenced by regrettable gender norms and retrograde romantic notions" in which "we find it romantic and fitting for the man to violate the woman's boundaries, despite her protests," Barnhill ultimately argues, "How does John Cusack always get the girl? It's not by scrupulously respecting her boundaries. It's by violating her boundaries."[25] Barnhill defends "these particular boundary violations" as "unproblematic" because the young men "are acting like boundaries don't exist, in the hope that the boundaries will cease to exist."[26] Barnhill's position does not align with current thinking on consent, but the essay represents an argument that underpins *The Kissing Booth*—and films with similar patterns such as *Twilight* (2008) and *Fifty Shades of Gray* (2015). Noah's boundary crossings are seen as romantic and normative masculine behavior. However, consent is not moot because young men want long-term relationships, and there is nothing morally permissible about pursuing girls against their will, despite the fact that it certainly might be strategic. In other words, as we shift to examining how contemporary teen films often render boys' consent irrelevant, it's important to recognize that current films also demonstrate that affirmative consent might not be as protective as we think for girls either.

REVISING THE TEEN SEX COMEDY: *AMERICAN PIE* AND *SUPERBAD*

In the initial emergence of the teen sex comedy in the 1970s and 1980s, adolescent boys were routinely depicted using any means possible, including alcohol, drugs, deception, and coercion, to seduce girls, and they were typically rewarded for their efforts. Not all, but many of these films represented the heterosexual script at its worst. Numerous films, such as *Animal House* (1978) and *Revenge of the Nerds* (1984), showed girls being spied on, manhandled, harassed, and assaulted. Such actions were not depicted as aggressive breaches of consent. Rather, they were shown as a normal part of teen life—"boys will be boys" so to speak—and girls and women were objects to be used and conquests to be made. This pattern even ran through many of the teen romantic comedies targeted to younger audiences in the 1980s. In light of the emergence of consent culture, however, these films now seem fraught with inappropriate and unethical boundary transgressions.

The changing ethos of the late 1980s was marked by AIDS awareness, teen pregnancy prevention, and child pornography legislation, all of which made stories of rampant adolescent sex appear problematic. The teen sex comedy largely disappeared from the mainstream for over a decade until 1999 when *American Pie* reinvigorated the genre.[27] With a budget of $11 million, the film earned over $230 million at the box office and launched a series of films that has continued for over two decades.[28] In many ways, the original *American Pie* keeps many of its predecessors' tropes through its gross-out humor and narrative structure about four adolescent boys who make a pact to lose their virginity by prom night. However, *American Pie* also shifts some conventions in characters and plot that indicate girls' consent had gone from a moot point to a necessary consideration.

While the story perpetuates the idea that boys use persuasion and even deception, girls had become more complicated adversaries. In one of the storylines, Kevin tries to persuade his girlfriend, Vicky, to have intercourse with him, but she sees through his attempts and breaks it off with him. He renews his efforts with a different tactic—finding a carefully passed-down and handwritten sex "bible," he learns about the "tongue tornado," a cunnilingus technique that becomes the key to pleasuring her and winning her back. Although Kevin ultimately does succeed in losing his virginity to her on prom night, Vicky breaks up with him immediately after explaining they both should have the freedom to date other people in college. Jim is similarly both successful and foiled in his efforts. At one point, he sets up a webcam in his room to spy on an exchange student, Nadia, as she undresses, and it winds up accidentally being broadcast to the whole school. When he returns to the room while Nadia is masturbating, Jim becomes the object of ridicule when he accidentally broadcasts their interaction to his classmates who witness him prematurely ejaculate twice from touching Nadia's leg and breast. Undoubtedly such a scenario remains problematic in an era of consent culture, especially since Nadia is sent back to her home country after the incident. Still, the film subverts the previously accepted idea that an adolescent boy's sexual conquest could ethically come from subterfuge. After being outcast at school, Jim instead invites the band geek Michelle to the prom. It turns out that Michelle has had her share of sexual exploits at band camp and only accepted Jim's invitation because she thought he was a "sure thing." She seduces him. The morning after, Jim wakes up alone to the revelation, "Oh my god, she used me. I was used. . . . I was used—cool." While Jim failed at "using" Nadia, he was pleased to be "used" by

Michelle. In reviving the sex comedy, in other words, directors Paul and Chris Weitz, fused an old premise with revised social mores.

The 2007 film *Superbad* takes this disruption a step further. At the beginning of the film, Seth tries to convince his friend Evan that they should get girls drunk to have sex with them. Seth says, "You know when you hear girls saying 'Aw, I was so shitfaced last night. I shouldn't have fucked that guy,'—We could be that mistake!" But part of the humor of this scene is that Seth's point of view is untenable and wrong, and in this way, the film simultaneously spouts the tenets of rape culture while condemning them. Unlike in earlier films where the adolescent boys succeed in such a quest for sex, neither Seth nor Evan loses his virginity in the film. As it turns out, Jules (the girl Seth likes) doesn't drink, and Becca (the girl Evan likes) gets so intoxicated at the party that she winds up vomiting all over the bed as they make out. Even before the plan goes so awry, it is evident Evan does not want to have sex with Becca while they are both intoxicated. When they kiss, he stops her saying, "Becca, I don't think you want to do this. You're really drunk." Although she insists that she is fine and even shames him by calling him a "little bitch," Evan stops them before she throws up. So although *Superbad* initially presents the familiar setup of boys' pursuing sex with girls, it also disrupts this plot arc via the character of Evan, who embarks on the quest reluctantly and does not want to see it to its culmination. As a result, the boys "get" the girls, but they don't get the sex. In other words, in both *American Pie* and *Superbad*, writers and directors had already begun to adapt their storylines in response to consent culture—pushing against boys' coercion and incorporating girls' sexual agency.

GIRLS RULE: FEMALE-DRIVEN SEX COMEDIES

Gender role reversals have long been a trope in romantic comedies. In *The Unruly Woman: Gender and the Genres of Laughter*, Kathleen Rowe suggests that "unruly women" have been a constant throughout Western cultural history and notes how Shakespearian comedies often portrayed a strong or "unruly" woman (at times disguised in men's clothing) who ultimately would be "tamed" through domestication. Certainly, film plots too from their earliest days drew from this long-standing pattern of gender role reversals. In *Romantic Comedy: Boy Meets Girl Meets Genre*, Tamar Jeffers McDonald notes that while the "basic plot of all mainstream romantic comedies is boy meets, loses, regains, girl," a main theme in film sex comedies over the last century has been "reversions" or "inversions of the 'natural order.'"[29] McDonald explains how in *Bringing Up Baby* (1938) for example, protagonist Susan Vance (Katharine Hepburn) uses deception, diversion, and bribery in pursuit of her love interest

David Huxley (Cary Grant). McDonald describes that the comedy of such an inversion "lies in the incongruity of the events, the reversal which creates the man's passivity and the woman's action, because, it is assumed, men are not passive, and women are not in charge."[30] In other words, such reversals can be played for their humor because they are not believed to be common. The joke lies in the swapping of normative gender behavior—such premises are only funny because the heterosexual script remains the presumed norm.

The teen sex comedies of the 2010s and 2020s that present girl protagonists' driving the plot and initiating sexual interactions are not the first to do so. *Little Darlings* (1980) tells the story of fifteen-year-old girls Angel and Ferris who make a bet to see who can be the first to lose their virginity, and *Joy of Sex* (1984) depicts high school senior Leslie, who, thinking she only has a few weeks left to live, embarks on a furious quest to lose her virginity. Despite how it was marketed, *Fast Times at Ridgemont High* (1982) also could be characterized as a girl-driven sex comedy since Stacy, a fifteen-year-old "virgin," seeks out sexual interactions, hoping to catch up with her supposedly more sexually experienced friend Linda. However, none of these comedies depict sex in the freewheeling way that the masculine-driven sex comedies of their era did. For many of the girls who achieve their goals, such as Stacy and Angel, sex turns out to be a disappointing experience—nothing like the ecstatic romps boys experience in sex comedies like *Risky Business* (1983) or the Canadian film *Porky's* (1981), which was heavily marketed in the United States. For girls, the moral often suggests a relationship, not sex, is a more worthwhile and gratifying goal.

The same year as *American Pie*, Colette Burson's teen sex comedy *Coming Soon* (1999) was also released. The film remained relatively under the radar and has received mixed reviews. However, the plot offers a fresh take on the genre. Here, protagonist Stream does not just want to lose her virginity—she wants to orgasm. In other words, Stream has no trouble finding a sexual partner, but it turns out that an attentive sexual partner interested in pleasing her is harder to come by. She makes her way through several unpleasant—and coercive—encounters with her boyfriend, who seems to only have his own sexual satisfaction in mind. In one scene, they kiss on his couch, and he pushes her head down to give him fellatio—and after resisting twice, she relents. In the docuseries episode "Indie Sex: Teens," the director of *But I'm a Cheerleader* (1999), Jamie Babbit, describes this scene, stating, "I think all girls can relate to that scene. . . . because they've all been through it. I mean it's like, hello? Can you put *your* head down?" Babbit suggests it was no accident that *Coming Soon* neither found widespread distribution nor received acceptance into major film festivals, stating that "the culture wasn't quite ready to deal with" a movie about girls who just "want to come, they want to come, they don't want to just be fucked, they want to come." *Coming Soon* might have remained in the fringe, but it epitomizes some of the concerns coming into the twenty-first century—young women's sexual desire, pleasure, and agency.

More recent girls' teen sex comedies have swung further in this direction, depicting girls as not only sexually eager but forceful. In an obvious nod to girls' sexual empowerment, these films intentionally shift young women into the role of initiator of sexual encounters instead of placing them in their more traditional gatekeeping role. On the surface, this change feels like a consent culture win, and in many ways it is—it has become more conventional to show girls' embodying feminist tenets of sexual equality. Girls in teen films are shown routinely making the first move and believing themselves entitled to sexual agency and pleasure.

However, rather than creating a story of mutual exploration and desire, many of these films simply flip the heterosexual script—imagining girls as aggressors who pursue boys without considering boys' consent. For example, in *The To Do List*, straight-A student Brandy Klark creates a sexual "to do list" to complete before college. Brandy lusts after the older Rusty Waters, and believing an attempt to be with him failed partly due to her inexperience, she decides to pursue other boys for sexual experience, checking items off her list along the way. In one scene, Brandy's friends encourage her to tackle the "hand job" next, and the film cuts to Brandy and Cameron in a movie theater. Without asking, she takes his popcorn from him and unzips his pants. He asks, "What are you doing?" to which she responds, "What do you think I'm doing?" She begins touching him, but then abruptly stops after she discovers something unexpected about his penis. He asks, "Why'd you stop?" and she doesn't answer but gets up, goes to the lobby, and calls her mom. Instead, she reaches her older sister, who gives her advice on how to handle an uncircumcised penis. She returns to her seat after getting a handful of butter from the popcorn stand. Cameron asks her, "Is everything OK? Did I do something wrong? Are you sure?" She then unzips his pants again and starts touching him, at which point he asks, "Do you want me to touch you?" As he climaxes, he yells out, "I love you!" and he leans his head on her shoulder while she examines the semen in her hand. Cameron clearly has more than a sexual interest in Brandy—he appears to want a relationship with her—but to her, he is simply a convenient prop to check an item off her list. As such, it would be difficult to imagine a contemporary teen film depicting this comedic scene with the genders reversed. The abruptness of Brandy's actions also directly contrasts with the way Cameron obtains consent from her in an earlier scene. While they kiss on the couch, she tells him, "I'm so wet. Touch me," and then getting impatient, she demands, "Finger me already" at which point he admits to being confused by her skort—"Are these shorts or a skirt?"—and asks, "Over or under?" When she says, "Under," he again confirms her consent, asking, "Are you sure?" and she says, impatiently, "Yes!" Only then does he proceed. Despite how carefully Cameron is depicted as checking for Brandy's consent to touch her, she neither asks nor tells him before she touches him. As a result, *The To Do List* perpetuates the false idea that men and boys are always already consenting.

Blockers, too, pairs an ambivalent teen boy with an aggressive teen girl for a comedic effect. Along with her friends, Kayla has vowed to lose her virginity the evening of prom. When her date Connor offers her alcohol, she says, "Before I do drink this, though, I just want to let you know that I am fully planning on having sex tonight—with you." He says, "Wherever the wind blows us," to which she responds, "Well the wind's going to blow us there." Again, he expresses hesitance, saying, "Wherever the night takes us," and she says, "It's going to take your penis into my vagina." He then says, "OK, if the universe wills it," to which she responds, "And the universe *will* will it," to which he finally concludes, "Thanks for letting me know, I guess." In another film *Yes, God, Yes*, sex-obsessed Alice actually physically attacks the strait-laced Chris. At a religious retreat, the older Chris comes to check on her, and Alice slowly touches his arm. Clearly, Chris is not consenting to additional touching based on the confused look on his face, but Alice abruptly kisses him, climbs on top of him, and proceeds to hump him. At first, he kisses her back but then gets up abruptly and stammers, "W-w-what are you doing?" and when he sees her staring at his crotch, he pushes down his erection, saying, "You know that I get turned on like a microwave," reiterating a line from their abstinence workshop. These moments depict an exaggerated form of girls' sexual empowerment for comedic effect, but they seem to rely on an assumption that young men cannot be harmed by nonconsensual sexual behavior. Such scenes simply would not work amid consent culture with the genders swapped because it would no longer be acceptable to make a similar joke about girls' nonconsent. Both Chris's and Connor's consent is a nonissue. Kayla even seems to suggest it is only *her* affirmative consent that needs to be addressed, which is why she states in advance of drinking that she consents to future sexual intercourse even if she gets drunk later (although, ethically intoxication could invalidate her consent). While these scenes of girls' sexual aggression seem meant to embody feminist ideals, they demonstrate that affirmative consent is perceived as only necessary for boys and men to obtain from girls and women, not the other way around. Later in *Blockers*, the joke culminates with a scene in their hotel room: Kayla

Fig. 2.1. In Kay Cannon's *Blockers*, Kayla (Geraldine Viswanathan) insists to her date Connor (Miles Robbins) that they will have intercourse after prom.

and Connor decide mutually not to have intercourse. However, Kayla says that she is "still down for pleasure," as she points to where he should direct his attention. He smiles, kisses her, and then the shot cuts away as he begins to move his head down, presumably to perform cunnilingus on her. As we understand it later, no other sexual act besides this one occurs between them that night. But one cannot help but wonder how this scene would be viewed if the roles were reversed. Even if we do not read this scene as nonconsensual, Kayla's forceful demeanor and their subsequent one-sided sexual interaction make light of a troubling dynamic that has existed in films for decades, albeit with the genders reversed.

The film *American Pie: Girls' Rules* also depicts aggressive girls in an obvious swap of the original. In the film, released over twenty years after *American Pie*, four teen girls make a mutual pact. Rather than the goal being for them to lose their virginity (two of them are already sexually active), they discuss how each needs something different "in the romance area"—Kayla needs someone "less emotional" who "likes to fuck"; Michelle needs "someone smart" and a "little kinky"; Steph needs "a nice guy"; and Annie needs to "have sex with the man" she loves. They agree to achieve their goals by MORP, prom spelled backward and the name of the homecoming dance. The wrinkle in their plan comes when they all fall for the same guy, Grant, who is new to the school. Several girls engage in aggressive behavior from the onset of the plot. When the story begins, Annie is determined to lose her virginity to her boyfriend, Jason, before he leaves for college the following day. So, after she drops him off at home, she climbs over his backyard fence, over the roof, and through Jason's bedroom window. We are then introduced to Kayla, who rifles through her boyfriend Tim's phone. When he walks in, he says, "Again?" which suggests she frequently violates his privacy. Each of these scenes seem designed to demonstrate girls' empowerment, but in doing so they also simply flip the script of climbing through windows and acting possessive from boys to girls. Such a switch continues in both individual scenes and the overall plot. For example, in one scene, girl lacrosse players spot Grant across the field and objectify him, calling him a "snack" and "fresh meat." One of them yells, "Nice dick!" at him. Stephanie then bets the two other players twenty dollars that she can hit him with a ball to get his attention, and she does. She goes to check on him, and as he walks away afterward, Stephanie mutters, "You will be mine." To imagine such a scene being played for its humor today with boys acting this way with girls feels impossible. Such aggression follows through several of the girls' storylines. Stephanie pays Grant's friend Emmett a hundred dollars to learn about him so she can seduce him. Kayla, too, is routinely depicted as overstepping boundaries—she hacks her boyfriend's phone, lies about him to his cousin, and enters and searches Grant's room without his permission. Although Tim initially breaks up with her because of her egregious behavior, she tricks him into restarting a relationship. By the end, they are reunited, as he says, "I don't want you violating my trust, but I do want you." Although their plot concludes on this note where she must change her ways, the story still excuses much of Kayla's boundary-crossing behavior in the name of love and passion—much in the way teen movies routinely have done for boys in the past.

Not all the current films in this genre show such behavior as unproblematic. The teen boys in *The To Do List*, *Banging Lanie*, and *Sex Appeal* all express feeling exploited after the girl protagonists use them to acquire sexual experience. In *The To Do List*, after Cameron finds Brandy's list, he says to her, "You gave me a hand job. Doesn't that mean anything to you?" to which Brandy responds, "No, it's a hand job." He says, "Brandy, I told you that I love you," and she asks, "You meant that?" Cameron is clearly affected, and he ends up crying on her bed and finally storming out telling her, "I hope you get AIDS." Later, when Brandy recounts the scene to friends saying, "He was crying. I think I really hurt him," one of her friends says, "He's just being a little baby. Guys mess around all the time, and girls just have to put up with it. It's bullshit." In fact, *The To Do List* also shows how numerous boys leverage Brandy's "list." When Cameron's friends discover Brandy's sexual agenda, they make themselves conveniently available to her—as a result, Duffy "dry humps" her and Derrick performs cunnilingus on Brandy without her ever realizing they are wise to her plan. It is only Cameron who feels used, and Brandy does come to regret how she treated him. Ultimately, *The To Do List* resolves their relationship in the film's conclusion when they meet up again later at college. Both have since had sex with other people, and they agree that "sometimes sex is just sex." They then have intercourse, which leads to Brandy's having her first partnered orgasm.

In other films, the repercussions of girls' actions are shown as irreparable. In *Banging Lanie*, protagonist Lanie pursues a crush (Jordan) after learning that sex is a "basic human need" on Maslow's hierarchy. And in *Sex Appeal*, the girl protagonist Avery recruits her childhood friend Larson to help her practice sexual behaviors as part of her research for an app she's building and as preparation for sex with her long-distance boyfriend. Although the girls act as the sexual initiators, Lanie and Avery (like Brandy) are straight-A students who initially have little time or interest in romance or sex. Sexual desire or curiosity is not actually the prime motivator of the girls' actions. Rather, each decides to pursue sex only after learning that sex represents knowledge they "should" acquire and a skill worth mastering. While during intimate moments, consent is taken clearly into account in both *Banging Lanie* and *Sex Appeal*, the moments of perfunctory sexual intimacy throughout are played for their humor, and the films' overarching plots imply the girls' belief in the irrelevance of boys' consent. When Jordan eventually discovers Lanie's checklist of their sexual activity after they've had intercourse, he confronts her. Lanie explains, "I wanted to have sex, OK?" to which Jordan responds, "You don't get sex by lying to people," as he holds back tears. She apologies and tries to convince him that she was simply "withholding the truth," but he is clearly hurt as he says, "It's too late for apologies" and "Just stop—don't talk to me anymore" as he walks away. Similarly, in *Sex Appeal*, Larson attributes more meaning to their sexual interactions because of his own romantic and sexual feelings for Avery (which she does not seem to reciprocate). While he proceeds with the intimate encounters with the understanding that Avery is only using him, he suggests nonconsent when he breaks it off later telling her, "You sucked me back in with this thing that I didn't want to do." In both films, the relationships are irrecoverable from the resulting harm. Avery, having lost Larson as a friend, secretly sets him up with another girl he had a crush on, and Lanie embarks on a new relationship with another boy at the end. *Banging Lanie* even overtly acknowledges the problem of ignoring boys' consent in one scene. When Lanie seeks the advice of her gay guy friend, she asks, "Don't guys want to have sex all the time?" to which he replies, "That's a terrible stereotype that needs to die." In this way, films like *Banging Lanie* and *Sex Appeal* might signal a growing awareness that boys' consent matters too.

Many of these films, including *Girls' Rules*, epitomize a growing emphasis on representations of girls' sexuality—and some depictions are quite affirming. Several depict mutual first sexual experiences—such as Julie and her boyfriend Austin in *Blockers* and Annie and Grant in *Girls' Rules*. Furthermore, a girl's sexual drive is often normalized—in *Girls' Rules*, one of the friends, Michelle, is shown masturbating in the film and has an array of sex toys. She then convinces Annie to give them a try, and at a sex shop, the girls get a rundown of options from another woman customer, who turns out to be their new principal. The storylines of these films often suggest girls should and can embrace their sexuality openly. And quite plainly, many also demonstrate an intolerance for sexual harassment and assault against girls. Early in *Girls' Rules*, we are introduced to McCormick, who tells Stephanie at the party, "You've got the reputation of being the bang of the century. Feels like I'm missing out." Stephanie responds, "You know, that's a real panty-dropper, McCormick. I'll tell you what. Not today. Not tomorrow. Not if you were the last man on Earth. Not if I even loved the reek of Axe body spray. Not if I didn't already know you have an itty-bitty little dick." As she walks away, she says, "Just don't throw up anywhere or do any nonconsensual groping. That's your job for today. I believe in you." McCormick's presence in the plot suggests that while masculine behaviors like demeaning and assaulting girls continue, they have become intolerable. Sexual assault, including "nonconsensual groping" can no longer be given a pass in teen films with "boys will be boys."

Yet, the vengeance of girls against masculine perpetrators at times is extreme. In Stephanie's first scene, she has set up a sexual trap for an abusive principal—he thinks he's come for kinky sex, but instead she blackmails him into early retirement. After recording him, she leaves, telling him he has the weekend to think about it, giving the impression that she is leaving him tied up for days. At the end of the film, when McCormick starts berating Stephanie and lying about them having slept together, Stephanie turns to him and says, "Hey, asshole." She grabs him by the crotch and says, "I don't like bullies, and I don't like misogynistic douchebags drinking my liquor and disrespecting me in my own house. And I don't like you, McCormick," dealing him a punch that knocks him down. These scenes are depicted as satisfying feminist come-uppances to masculine characters who do harm. But they also imply that the antidote to sexual violence is more violence. It offers no imaginable path for girls who do not have the nerve or the physical training to oppose perpetrators in this way. While empowering girls, characters like Stephanie come across as cartoonish feminist superheroes who take down assaulters in an absurdly violent manner.

AGGRESSIVE GIRLS IN TEEN ROMANCES FOR YOUNGER AUDIENCES

Just as the pattern of teen boys' coercion that existed in 1980s teen sex comedies was mirrored in romances for younger audiences, so too has the recent trend of girls' aggression found its way into seemingly innocuous films targeted to tweens. Without the explicit sexual encounters of R-rated films like *American Pie: Girls' Rules*, *The To Do List*, and *Blockers*, films like *Sierra Burgess Is a Loser* and *The Half of It* obtained PG-13 ratings and *To All the Boys I've Loved Before* received a TV-14 rating. Yet even in these films, boys' consent is overlooked, and deception is a frequent component of the plot.

For instance, in *To All the Boys I've Loved Before*, high school student Lara Jean Covey has never had a date, but she's had lots of crushes and has written them each a love letter she keeps hidden in her closet. When her younger sister sends them out without her consent, the complications of the plot begin. Lara Jean is approached on the high school running track by one of her former crushes, Peter, who tells her, "I just want to say, I appreciate it, but it's never going to happen." Lara Jean has no idea what he's talking about until she spots the letter in his hand. She faints as Peter says, "It's just Gen and I . . ." talking about his ex-girlfriend. When she awakens, Peter is leaning over her asking if he can get her some water. She then spots Josh, her older sister's ex-boyfriend, heading toward her—also with one of her letters in his hand. To avoid a confrontation with Josh, she immediately grabs Peter, turns him over, lays him on the ground, leans on top of him, and kisses him until a coach stops them. In their next meeting, Peter says, "I just want to be super clear. I'm flattered. I am. But Gen and I just broke up." She asks, "Are you trying to reject me right now?" and he answers, "Well, yeah, because it doesn't really seem like it took the first time." She admits that she was only using him to prevent someone else from thinking she liked him. Even though she kissed Peter against his will and used him as a diversion, Peter does not seem upset. Later Lara Jean says, "I'm sorry for the whole jumping you thing," and he responds, "Could've been worse, right?" Peter's nonconsent, in other words, is not something we are meant to take too seriously.

Still, *To All the Boys I've Loved Before* emphasizes consent negotiations in their relationship. After this incident, Peter suggests they can pretend to date to confuse Josh and make his ex-girlfriend, Gen, jealous. When Lara Jean asks, "So you want to use me as your pawn?" he replies, "Technically you used me as your pawn first when you jumped me." After thinking it over, Lara Jean decides to go along with the ploy. When she meets him on the field to tell him, he kisses her. As a result, Lara Jean suggests a "contract so they are on the same page about the rules," one of which is that Peter cannot kiss her. Although Peter tries to argue against the idea of the "contract," saying, "You really know how to zap the fun out of a situation," and arguing, "You kissed me first," Lara Jean nonetheless responds, "This is nonnegotiable." In other words, Peter didn't consent for Lara Jean to kiss him on the field, and she didn't consent to be kissed by him as her "fake" boyfriend. However, while the breach to Peter is laughed off, the one to Lara Jean necessitates a contract. Of course, this fake relationship causes them to both fall in love with each other, a fact that supposedly excuses any of the boundary breaches in their initial interactions. In their contract, they agree on a few other terms, and Lara Jean is surprised when Peter insists, "You're coming with me on the ski trip," an annual trip "infamous" for where "more students lost their virginity than senior week and prom combined." She consents only because she thinks to herself, "I'm certain that by the time the ski trip comes around, Peter and I will be ancient history." Certainly, this explicitly drawn "contract" suggests the pervasiveness of consent culture where the terms should be clear and both people should agree. But the film also demonstrates the futility of a contract's protecting one from harm in a relationship. At the end, when Lara Jean admits her true feelings for Peter, she says, "How do we do this?. . . . What do we put into a contract for a real relationship?" he laughs and says, "Nothing. You gotta trust." In other words, while *To All the Boys I've Loved Before* obviously resides within consent culture, it also suggests that in a relationship, clear terms might be harder to define than we'd like to admit.

Other teen romances like *The Half of It* and *Sierra Burgess Is a Loser* use the Cyrano de Bergerac trope, so romantic deception is embedded in the plot. In *The Half of It*, protagonist Ellie Chu is hired by jock Paul to woo Aster Flores, who already has a boyfriend she seems resigned to marry despite her hesitation. Ellie sends texts and letters on Paul's behalf which pique Aster's interest in him. Complicating matters, Ellie too harbors a crush on Aster, while Paul begins to develop a romantic interest in Ellie to form an irreconcilable love triangle, or as Ellie's voiceover in the beginning states, "This is not a love story."

Fig. 2.2. In *To All the Boys I've Loved Before*, Lara Jean (Lana Condor) and Peter (Noah Centineo) shake hands to signal agreement to the contract for their pretended relationship.

Or not one where anyone gets what they want." Eventually, their deceit is so effective that Aster agrees to meet Paul, but his nervousness renders him unable to communicate effectively. Ellie, watching them from the car, tries to redeem the date by texting Aster from Paul's phone, messaging her that, "I get nervous when you're close." Even Paul doesn't seem to consent to this nerve-wracking scenario, as Ellie plays them both like puppets. It works, and eventually Ellie drives off so Paul and Aster can spend the remainder of the evening together. The next day, Paul tells Ellie that they kissed. Surprised and jealous, Ellie asks, "How do you know she wants to be kissed?" and Paul says, "She gives you a look." Later, when the two girls are alone together, Ellie asks about Paul, and Aster says, "He's confusing. When I'm with him, I feel, I feel... safe. He's a sweet guy. But then it's like he writes these things that feel... not safe." The fact that Aster feels "not safe" by the texts that Ellie is secretly sending on Paul's behalf suggests the darker side to their actions. Eventually, the house of cards comes crumbling down—Paul tries to kiss Ellie, but she pushes him away; Aster witnesses it; and Ellie ultimately confesses her love for Aster and kisses her herself. The film does not depict anyone as being traumatized by all of these lies and in fact minimizes them when Ellie later apologizes and Aster acknowledges the thought of them being together had crossed her mind and says, "Deep down I probably knew the truth." Neither of them end up with Aster, but the film still perpetuates the problematic idea that purposeful deception can be easily excused when it is done for love.

The film *Sierra Burgess Is a Loser* takes the concealed identity plot even further. It starts when Jamey approaches popular girl Veronica in a café and asks for her number, and as a joke, she gives him the unpopular Sierra's number instead. When Jamey texts Sierra (thinking she's Veronica), Sierra goes along with the charade. Sierra then connives a mutually beneficial relationship with Veronica to keep the deception going: in exchange for coaching Veronica on philosophy and literature to impress her college boyfriend, Veronica pretends to be the physical embodiment of Sierra's texts with Jamey. As part of this arrangement, Jamey and Sierra develop a relationship together via texts, but when pressed, they use Veronica's selfie in response to his selfie, and it's Veronica who shows up on camera for a video call. This ruse gets taken quite far—Sierra even convinces Veronica to go out on a date with Jamey and secretly tags along. At one point, Veronica insists Jamey close his eyes before a kiss, and she pulls in Sierra to kiss him instead. Undoubtedly, the "positive" message of the film is that it's what's inside, not outside, that matters, and thus, by the end Jamey and Sierra do get together. But it nonetheless is disturbing that Sierra stands in for a kiss that Jamey thinks he has with Veronica. Again, to imagine a gender role reversal here in a contemporary film is nearly impossible. The egregiousness of this action is minimized in the film—at the end when Sierra and Jamey kiss, he asks her jokingly, "Have we done that before?" Making light of nonconsent in this way again highlights that the only difference here is that boys' consent does not seem to matter.

Whereas in 1980s films, it was tacitly suggested that girls were not assaulted because they didn't see themselves as assaulted, we seem to be getting a similar message about boys in contemporary teen films. Certainly, we cannot expect teen films always to model ideal behavior, and Driscoll points out that scholars "tend to judge films in the genre as good or bad in terms of a responsibility to represent adolescence in ways that would be *good for* adolescents."[31] Still, what is troubling about some of these more recent teen romances and sex comedies is how they seem to espouse feminist ideals of girls' sexual agency at the expense of boys' consent. While these films might not intentionally depict nonconsent as moot or a joke, they reveal how filmmakers and writers have unwittingly adopted the tenets of a consent culture that prioritizes affirmative consent from girls and women but not from boys and men.

DISRUPTING RACE-BASED SEXUAL STEREOTYPES IN TEEN FILMS

As casts of teen films have become more diverse, many of the protagonists and supporting roles are girls of color. This shift to more inclusive casting has been a welcome change after a long history of omitting people of color—or including them as racist stereotypes. Perhaps it is merely coincidental that many of the girls playing aggressors are multiethnic—Aubrey Plaza (*The To Do List*) is Puerto Rican American; Leah Lewis (*The Half of It*) is Chinese American; Lana Condor (*To All the Boys I've Loved Before*) is Vietnamese American; Piper Curda (*American Pie: Girls' Rules*) is Korean American; Madison Pettis (*American Pie: Girls' Rules*) is Black American; and Geraldine Viswanathan (*Blockers*) is Indian Swiss.[32] However, if it is intentional, then putting girls of color into aggressive roles might work doubly to undermine both the heterosexual script and race-based sexual stereotypes by affirming they too can assert their sexual desires and interests. At the same time, such depictions might also run the risk of perpetuating race-based sexual stereotypes such as girls of color being more sexually available or aggressive. Or it could be that the "humor" of their empowerment becomes heightened when it is a girl of color—the tacit message might be, how could *she* actually be a threat?

Still, many of these films are written and/or directed by women of color who emphasize their goals of disrupting not only stories about gender but also race. For example, Jenny Han, author of the *To All the Boys I've Loved Before* book series, wrote a *New York Times* editorial titled "An Asian-American Teen Idol Onscreen, Finally" detailing how production companies that sought to adapt her novels into movies wanted to change the main character to a Caucasian girl. As Han puts it, "One producer said to me, as long as the actress captures the spirit of the character, age and race don't matter. I said, well, her spirit is Asian-American. That was the end of that."[33] Han picked the *only* company who agreed to keep the teen protagonist Asian American. Her determination stemmed from her own childhood watching films and seeking someone who looked like her, which she only found in supporting roles. She ponders, "What would it have meant for me back then to see a girl who looked like me star in a movie?" answering, "Everything. There is power in seeing a face that looks like yours do something, be someone. There is power in moving from the sidelines to the center."[34] This sentiment is echoed by other actors, writers, and directors. For instance, Chinese American actress Lauren Tsai (*Moxie*) notes that seeing characters like oneself continually relegated to supporting roles can be damaging. As she puts it, "you start to feel that way in your own life as well;

you start to feel like your life may be a side piece to someone else, or that you are not so much who's the voice of power, or you're not someone who people are going to think is beautiful, or attractive in some way."[35] Undoubtedly, Lara Jean as an Asian American girl protagonist having romantic adventures is a groundbreaking depiction. The success of the film—and that of the two sequels in the trilogy, *To All the Boys I've Loved Before: P.S. I Still Love You* (2020) and *To All the Boys: Always and Forever* (2021)—cemented the fact that Lara Jean's ethnicity was no detriment to the film.

Writer/director of *The Half of It*, Alice Wu, has expressed a similar interest in presenting Asian American stories. Her first feature, *Saving Face* (2004), became the "first movie wholly about Chinese-Americans bankrolled by Hollywood" since *The Joy Luck Club* (1993).[36] After taking time off to raise a child, Wu came back about a decade later with her teen film *The Half of It*. In interviews, Wu talks about her intersectional identity as a queer Asian woman, which her films reflect. For *The Half of It*, she also set the story in a small conservative, religious, and predominantly white town intentionally because, as she describes, "In towns that are majority white, there's always one immigrant family, or there's always one POC family. So maybe this movie will make people think about that, or that one kid who's a bit different, whether they're coming out as queer, or whether it's coming out as something else."[37] Wu and Han emphasize both how movies provide visibility for girls like themselves and how stories can transform how others see minoritized individuals. Having released directly to Netflix during the COVID-19 pandemic, *The Half of It* quickly garnered praise from critics and attracted an extensive fan base. *The Half of It* and the *To All the Boys* trilogy represent a new era of films marketed to mainstream audiences that move teens of color from the sidelines into the leading roles.

However, some fans critique the continuation of the pattern to omit Asian American teen boys—even in stories with Asian American girl protagonists.[38] The argument is that although the film *seems* progressive, in fact, it perpetuates white masculine fantasy by reducing romantic interest in Asian American characters only to girls and women. It does appear that in *To All the Boys I've Loved Before*, Lara Jean writes five love letters and none of them are to ostensibly Asian American boys. However, two are persons of color. Lucas, who tells Lara Jean that he's gay, is played by Rwanda-born actor Trezzo Mahoro. In addition, the character of John Ambrose, who was originally Caucasian in both the books and the first film, is replaced in the second film by multiracial actor Jordan Fisher, who has articulated his background as Nigerian, English, Tahitian, Italian, Greek, and Scandinavian.[39] This casting switch might have been prompted by fan criticism, although Netflix offered no reason.[40] Playing Lara

Jean's primary love interest, Peter, Noah Centineo has expressed his heritage by saying, "I'm Italian, Native American. I believe I have a bit of Puerto Rican in me, and I'm Dutch."[41] Some viewers have criticized his claims, suggesting he masquerades as Latinx to get parts. A fan site that delves into celebrities' ethnicities using public records found that he is half Italian and half German,[42] and in one interview he suggests that he might have faked being Puerto Rican to get roles.[43] In that interview, Centineo suggests he could do 23andMe genetic testing to "set the record straight," although he has not since released any results. As a result, Centineo has received backlash—after over a century of exclusion and white actors' playing people of color, fans want to see their ancestries and ethnicities authentically represented in films.

Undoubtedly, race-based sexual stereotypes impact teen films too—and yet already there are signs of pushback, not just in the casting choices but through some of the plots. For example, while Erwin (played by Hayden Szeto, a Canadian actor of Hong Kong descent) in *Edge of Seventeen* (2016) plays a somewhat tepid love interest for Nadine, Seth (played by Japanese American actor Nico Hiraga) in *Moxie* (2021) is nothing of the sort. After the summer, Vivian almost doesn't recognize Seth on the first day of class—she tells him, "You look different," and he shows her that he grew three inches over the summer. Later, outside at lunch, Vivian notices Seth again and says to her friend Claudia, "Have you ever noticed Seth Acosta is just like nice to everybody?" Claudia says, "Seth, the shrimp?" And Vivian says, "Oh he's not a shrimp anymore—he grew like a foot over the summer." They look over at Seth as he exposes his bare chest while using his shirt to wipe his mouth (in slow motion for emphasis), and Claudia says, "Whoa, you're right. Seth the shrimp is going to need a new nickname." They then both admire him as he skateboards by. Although we understand through this conversation that Seth would have been undesirable as a "shrimp," their reevaluation of him seems to reflect a reevaluation of the Asian American teen boy love interest. Seth's character completely counters the Asian race-based sexual stereotype of "passive, emasculated boys lacking sex appeal and a voice."[44] Instead, Seth's sensitivity and masculinity coexist unproblematically.

Moxie, directed by Amy Poehler, does not simply flip this script by turning the Asian American teen boy into an aggressive "bad boy" character. Instead, Seth's appeal grows as he aligns himself with the feminist cause Moxie that Vivian has secretly started. In one of her pamphlets, she calls for everyone to draw stars and hearts on their hands to show feminist solidarity. When Vivian and her friend Lucy spot Seth coming into class and notice his hand has a heart and star drawn on it, the girls watch him in another slow motion scene. As he walks away, Lucy says, "That's hot." Again later, when Moxie calls for everyone to wear tank tops, Seth too participates, spotting Vivian in the hall and commenting, "We both went with blue—tank top twinsies." Seth recognizes how feminist causes can be furthered by boys, and thus he looks to find ways to show his support. For instance, when he accidentally discovers Vivian's the one behind Moxie, he offers to put some of the pamphlets in the boys' bathroom saying, "Totally get it if they're just for the girls. I just thought all the boys here could use all the help they could get." Ultimately, the film depicts how Seth's attractiveness manifests through his feminist allyship.

Although the film shows Vivian as an empowered girl and sexual initiator in the story, it doesn't fall into the trap of making Seth's consent irrelevant. Although it's clear that the two like each other, on their first date, neither wants to make the first move, leading to an awkward moment in the car when he drops her off. After she gets out and walks away, he runs after her and admits, "I like you—a lot. I do. I don't know. I got all in my head about it. I mean, I started worrying that I shouldn't come off too strong, I mean you're this super powerful feminist and not just a cute girl. I mean you are a cute girl..." She interrupts him with a kiss. In other words, we see Vivian make the first move toward physical intimacy after she has a clear verbal indication from Seth of his feelings. Another scene also shows Vivian as more physically assertive, without making Seth passive. When they make out in the car, Seth says, "Um, Vivian, I feel like I should tell you. I haven't... I never..." She says "I haven't either" as she keeps kissing him. He says, "OK, OK, but I kind of wanted it to be special." She stops and pulls back, and says, "Oh. Oh, OK, I'm sorry." He then clarifies, "No, no, no, wait I'm sorry. I want it one hundred percent to be with you. I just don't know if we should hurry up and do it before a football game." Their mutual uncertainty in this scene is evident—both want to be together, but they also want to find the balance between acting on their impulses and planning something special. Throughout the film, Seth never backs away from expressing his emotions, and he embraces his own "femininity"—he tells Vivian in one scene how he had his hair routinely braided as a child and knows all the names of the American Girl dolls because of his three older sisters.

While Seth is not a pushover, he also allows his vulnerability to show, making him a groundbreaking teen boy character—a consent culture version of the John Cusack characters. Later in the film, Vivian feels guilty about not admitting her role in Moxie to the principal, causing her friend Claudia to take the blame and get suspended. As a result, she misdirects her anger, causing a scene at a dinner with Seth, her mom, and her mom's new boyfriend. When Seth tries to calm Vivian down, she lashes out saying, "Forget hearts and stars on my arm, why don't I just write your name on my arm and tell everybody that

I'm your property or something?" She then says, "Fuck the patriarchy!" as she leaves the table. Later when she sees Seth at school, she asks if he's mad at her. In responding, he says, "I've done nothing but support you. I don't deserve to be your punching bag." Although we understand Vivian's behavior as wrong—and it certainly might be hard to accept a teen boy character behaving as she has—Seth nonetheless asserts himself simply and clearly. Although he likes and supports her, he also expresses that he will not be her "punching bag." After a student reaches out to say she's been raped and wants Moxie's help, Vivian is inspired to graffiti the steps of the school, launch a protest, and admit she started the movement. At the resulting rally, Vivian mouths "I'm sorry" across the crowd to Seth, at which he lifts up his shirt sleeve where he's written, "Vivian." Seth's action shows how he seeks to flip the heterosexual script. But the film itself ultimately subverts both the heterosexual script and its simplistic reversal, instead opting for a more nuanced story where the characters both assert themselves and allow themselves to be vulnerable.

The cast of *Moxie* is purposefully diverse, including Lucy (played by Dominican American actress Alycia Pascual-Pena), Claudia (played by Chinese American actress Lauren Tsai), Amaya (played by Black American actress Anjelika Washington), and CJ (played by trans actor Josie Totah). Although it's impossible not to notice that the girls of color and trans girl in the film are supporting characters while Vivian, the protagonist, is cis and white, the film models how youth take up a feminist cause in a more inclusive way all while acknowledging how race, sexuality, and gender identity impacts each of their lives uniquely. According to the actors, Poehler sought to embody these same ideals on set. As Tsai puts it, as both the director and owner of the production company Poehler, "create[s] a set where everyone feels safe, empowered, and seen, and comfortable."[45] Similarly, Totah explains how the cast and crew had discussions on set that were "reflective of the conversations we were having in our movie," adding, "We talked about race, socio-economic status, class, gender identity, like we got into it. . . . I think what was so incredible about it [was] we were all willing to learn and we all recognize that there are certain blind spots in all of our lives because of our different identities and experiences we all have faced but the fact that we're all willing to learn and engage in those conversations is really what creates change and generates growth in the world."[46] In several scenes, each of the girls contributes how they have been silenced, mistreated, or judged due to their sex, gender identity, race, and appearance—and they empower each other to make a difference.

Like many other teen films, *Moxie* shows the continued threat of masculine sexual abuse—not through the main love interest, Seth, but through a side character, star athlete Mitchell. After several interactions with Mitchell, including one in which he spits in her soda, Lucy reports him to their woman principal saying, "Mitchell Wilson is harassing me, and I don't feel safe." Through humor, this scene demonstrates how authorities tolerate and perpetuate abuse. The principal comedically winces, correcting her, "He's *bothering* you." Lucy repeats, "He's *harassing* me," to which the principal says, "Ooh. There's that word. If you use that word, it means I have to do a bunch of stuff, but if he's *bothering* you—and that's what it sounds like to me—then we can actually have a conversation." Despite her protests, Lucy gets nowhere. The woman principal (also a flipped script) is no ally to consent culture.

Lucy's character epitomizes a girl of color who refuses to be abused and ignored—and it is she who inspires Vivian to start Moxie. Early in the film, Vivian stops Lucy on the school stairs to advise her, "Look I just wanted to say, ignore Mitchell." Lucy responds, "Why should I have to ignore him? Why can't he just not be a dick?" Vivian explains, "He's an idiot—he has been since the second grade." While Vivian suggests that he's not "dangerous" but merely "annoying," Lucy insists that "you know that annoying can be more than just annoying, like it can be code for worse stuff." In fact, Lucy's instincts here are justified later when Mitchell is exposed for rape. Again, Vivian tries to offer her advice saying, "If you keep your head down, he'll move on and bother somebody else," to which Lucy responds, "Thanks for the advice, but I'm going to keep my head up—high." The visual cues of the scene emphasize Lucy's empowerment via a low angle shot that shows Lucy standing high versus Vivian, who looks small in comparison, as if she doesn't even realize how she has been put down. In other words, it's not just the adults who have normalized Mitchell's behavior—Vivian too has mistaken Mitchell's actions for harmless "boys will be boys" outbursts. Lucy's outrage for the status quo ultimately enables Vivian to see her environment through new eyes. Mitchell and his friend put out their annual list (Best Rack, Most Bangable) adding a new "c word" category for Lucy, and again the principal does nothing. At that point, Vivian, enraged, takes matters into her own hands to launch Moxie.

Significantly, *Moxie* offers empowerment in a way that doesn't insist on boys' consent being moot. Despite the ineptitude of teachers and principals and the complacency of students, girls and boys come together to fight mistreatment, bias, and assault. *Moxie* is by no means a "perfect" teen film—likely there is no such thing. However, considering the pervasiveness of recycled narrative patterns in teen romantic comedies, *Moxie* stands out as a welcome shift among the recent cluster of girl-driven teen films. It embodies an intersectional perspective via casting, and it resists repeating a plot structure where the obstacle to romance/sex is also the object of desire. In this way, it clearly contrasts with other films in its category that suggest that being "empowered" for girls means boys' consent doesn't matter and instead offers a way forward for youth across the range of sexualities, ethnicities, and gender identities to work together toward social justice.

NOTES

1. Ringwald, "What about 'The Breakfast Club'?"
2. Wiederman, "Sexual Script Theory," 7.
3. Klein et al., "Perceptions of Sexual Script."
4. Wiederman, "Sexual Script Theory," 8.
5. S. Smith, "Scripting Sexual Desire," 327.
6. Coyne et al., "Contributions of Mainstream Sexual Media Exposure," 434.
7. Wiederman, "Sexual Script Theory," 8.
8. Klein et al., "Perceptions of Sexual Script."
9. Newstrom, Harris, and Miner, "Sexual Consent," 455.
10. Bond et al., "Race-Based Sexual Stereotypes," 296.
11. Bond et al., "Race-Based Sexual Stereotypes," 296.
12. Bond et al., "Race-Based Sexual Stereotypes," 301.
13. Rossetto and Tollison, "Feminist Agency," 69.
14. Sternin et al., "Sexual Consent," 3.
15. Phillips, *Flirting with Danger*, 158.
16. Klein et al., "Perceptions of Sexual Script," 632.
17. Timmermans and Van den Bulck, "Casual Sexual Scripts on the Screen."
18. Klein et al., "Perceptions of Sexual Script."
19. Timmermans and Van den Bulck, "Casual Sexual Scripts on the Screen," 1492.
20. J. H. Miller, "Narrative," 70.
21. Popova, *Sexual Consent*, 83.
22. Popova, *Sexual Consent*, 41.
23. I delve into this film further in the essay "Exposing Flaws."
24. Adalian, "Inside Netflix's TV-Swallowing, Market-Dominating Binge Factory."
25. Barnhill, "Just Pushy Enough," 91, 99.
26. Barnhill, "Just Pushy Enough," 91, 92.
27. As Shary notes in *Generation Multiplex*, there were a small handful of fringe teen sex comedies in this era, including *The Big Bet* (1987) and *Virgin High* (1991).
28. Kaplan, "'American Pie' at 20."
29. McDonald, *Romantic Comedy*, 12 and 44.
30. McDonald, *Romantic Comedy*, 49.
31. Driscoll, *Teen Film*, 4. Italics in original.
32. Geraldine Viswanathan is an Australian actress who is often identified in interviews as having Indian and Swiss heritage.
33. Han, "Asian-American Teen Idol Onscreen."
34. Han, "Asian-American Teen Idol Onscreen."
35. Valentine, "Lauren Tsai on 'Moxie.'"

36. Leibowitz, "Kissing Vivian Shing."
37. Ramos, "'The Half of It.'"
38. Lee, "Kissing Vivian Shing."
39. "Where Is Jordan Fisher From?" PopBuzz, December 3, 2020, https://www.popbuzz.com/tv-film/features/jordan-fisher/ethnicity-where-from/.
40. Dumaraog, "Why John Ambrose Was Recast."
41. "Noah Centineo: 27 Facts You about the to All the Boys Actor You Need to Know," PopBuzz, February 11, 2021, https://www.popbuzz.com/tv-film/features/noah-centineo/.
42. Madman, "Noah Centineo," Ethnicity of Celebs | What Nationality Ancestry Race, April 10, 2021, https://ethnicelebs.com/noah-centineo.
43. See @Euphocity, "Fuck Noah Centineo for pretending to be a Latino to get a Latin role," Twitter, September 22, 2020, https://twitter.com/Euphocity/status/1308475436360298498.
44. Kung, "Desexualization of the Asian American Male."
45. Valentine, "Lauren Tsai on 'Moxie.'"
46. Hullender, Tatiana. "Sydney Park, Anjelika Washington & Josie Totah Interview: Moxie." Screen Rant. February 25, 2021. https://screenrant.com/sydney-park-anjelika-washington-josie-totah-interview-moxie/.

THREE

QUEERING CONSENT

Navigating Performative and Subjective Consent in Queer Teen Films

I have a totally perfectly normal life—although I have one huge ass secret.

—Simon in *Love, Simon*

When *Love, Simon* hit theaters in 2018, *USA Today* ran a story with the headline "Why Did It Take So Long for Hollywood to Make a Gay Teen Story?"[1] Certainly, by 2018, the plot of a teen's coming out felt long overdue. For over a century, Hollywood directors and producers omitted or concealed queer desire. Hence, *Love, Simon* marked a considerable US milestone as the first mainstream queer teen film backed by a $17 million budget and released to over 2,400 theaters.[2] This chapter charts the long-awaited emergence of queer youth in cinema and investigates how independent and Hollywood teen films of the early twenty-first century often continue to reflect queer marginalization. Films that depict teens struggling to accept their sexuality such as *Love, Simon*, *Alex Strangelove* (2018), *Blockers* (2018), and *A Girl Like Grace* (2015) portray adolescents who face formidable obstacles to coming out. In fact, a teen's queer sexuality often is emphasized as a unique "problem" in the film—for their peers, their families, their partners, and even themselves. As a result, queer youth are often depicted in the genre as not initially accepting their own desires—a sentiment that appears to put them at risk for moments of problematic consent and even violent assault in these narratives. This pattern becomes further heightened in two films, *Boy Erased* (2018) and *The Miseducation of Cameron Post* (2018), in which teens legally consent to a conversion therapy program despite their obvious lack of desire to do so. Ultimately, these narratives expose a key flaw of affirmative consent—namely, how a focus on verbal assent might mask a lack of desire.

In *New Queer Cinema*, B. Ruby Rich argues that there was "no such thing" as "'gay and lesbian' theatrical movies" in the United States prior to 1969 but rather "just a scattering of gay and lesbian directors, often closeted, making films that were masquerading as mass-market heterosexual fare, albeit with the occasional gay or lesbian actor or subtle wink." The dearth of representations led viewers to look for "connotative homosexuality" or depictions that "implied that a character might be queer, through subtle mannerisms, costuming, or speech patterns" such as an "overly effeminate" man or masculine woman.[3] Of course, this technique also led to filmmakers' and audiences' perpetuation of queer stereotypes. During the era of the film industry's Production Code, in effect from 1934 through the 1960s, explicit scenes and inferences of "sex perversion," which tacitly included homosexuality, bisexuality, trans identities, and any other non–cis heteronormative sexuality or identity, were prohibited. This moratorium significantly curtailed depictions of queerness during the era. Even when plays with queer themes such as *The Children's Hour* or *Tea and Sympathy* were adapted into the films *These Three* in 1936 and *Tea and Sympathy* in 1956, any overt references to sexuality were removed from the plot. Films at this time could only hint at homosexuality, and as Rich argues, not only scholars but also audiences became accustomed "to reading between the frames." Not surprisingly, as a result "queer film scholarship has always been attentive to practices of not showing,"[4] and scholars have resorted to "a wide range of interpretive strategies to recuperate a history of homosexual images from the censored screen."[5] The authors of *Queer Images: A History of Gay and Lesbian Film in America*, Harry M. Benshoff and Sean Griffin, for example, define a "queer film" by locating queerness among characters, authorship, audiences, and genres.[6] Such variability in how scholars read queerness in films allows for the inclusion of a larger body of work, but it also means that "sometimes films are queer in certain contexts and not in others."[7]

If locating queerness in film has been slippery, so too is the notion of queerness itself. The term *queer* is often used "as an umbrella term chiefly associated with non-normative sexual practices and desires but is also sometimes used to refer to gender non-normativity."[8] While *queer* can be understood as a way of being and seeing that questions and subverts norms, exactly what it encompasses shifts over time. For example, a group of scholars and members of the Society for Cinema and Media Studies in the 1990s founded the Lesbian and Gay Caucus, later renamed the Lesbian/Gay/Bisexual Caucus, then the Queer Caucus, and now the Queer and Trans Caucus.[9] These modifications over time demonstrate how the meaning of *queer* has transformed in the field, currently understood to represent a variety of sexualities but not necessarily gender identities. While GLAAD recognizes the term *queer* broadly as an "adjective used by some people, particularly younger people, whose sexual orientation is not exclusively heterosexual," it also suggests that "those who identify as queer" often find "the terms lesbian, gay, and bisexual.... to be too limiting and/or fraught with cultural connotations."[10] However, numerous activists and scholars have begun to resist *queer* as an umbrella term, suggesting that it prioritizes gay and lesbian embodiments of queerness while rendering less visible trans, bisexual, pansexual, asexual, and other ways of being queer.[11] This pushback has caused scholars to express the need to define the term before using it, such as the authors of *Queer Cinema in the World*, who note, "A minoritizing discourse reminds us of the need for specificity."[12] Nonetheless, even they forgo a "neat definition of queer cinema," instead opting for a "radically promiscuous approach," stating that they are "unwilling to relinquish the category of queer to charges that openness equals conceptual looseness and a dissipation of power."[13] There's no doubt that any definition of queerness can be easily disrupted and disputed, which perhaps accounts for why the authors seek a specificity of meaning and yet then resist providing a precise and limiting definition. For the purposes of this chapter, I take queer to mean any *sexualities* other than heterosexuality. Note I have not grouped *gender identities* such as trans under this queer umbrella since numerous trans studies scholars and activists deny the usefulness of such a classification. For this reason, I address the representation of trans teens' identities and sexualities separately in chapter 5.

As other scholars have noted, throughout film history, queer characters have often been depicted as tragic, evil, or silly.[14] Benshoff and Griffin point to the 1950s when "slightly more overt queer characters" appeared in Hollywood films, although "their existence was tempered with a 'compensating moral value': the films punish their queer characters by killing them often in quite brutal ways."[15] Queerness—particularly homosexuality—also often found its way into films as the punchline of a joke, as Benshoff and Griffin state, "the possibility of a homosexual relationship is raised, only to be disavowed by laughter."[16] These long-standing trends clearly have been challenging to undo, and fans and critics today continue to call out films that rely on a "bury your gays" trope where queer characters are murdered or die of suicide. Even in supposedly affirming queer teen films today, queer youth are routinely depicted as an anomaly, a disappointment, or a shock to family and friends.

In adolescent films, queerness initially appeared in veiled or peripheral portrayals such as in *The Wild Party* (1929), *Rebel without a Cause* (1955), *Tea and Sympathy*, and *Suddenly, Last Summer* (1959). As the Code was phased out and sexuality became more blatantly depicted in the 1960s and 1970s, homosexuality became more openly, although not always positively, depicted. One example is *Norman, Is That You?* (1976) about a man Ben Chambers (Redd Foxx) who shows up on the doorstep of his son Norman after having problems with his wife only to discover his son is living with another man. Although the film suggests some cultural normalization of queerness with Ben's discovery that one in six individuals are homosexual, it simultaneously demonstrates its unacceptability as Ben seeks to change his son's sexuality. In *The Celluloid Closet*, author Vito Russo describes the film as perhaps the "first pro-gay fag joke."[17] While the film conveys a clear message that some people are indeed gay, it nonetheless suggests that parents would not want their own children to fall into such a category.

Rich deems 1985 "as close to [a] defining moment as any" for the beginning of New Queer Cinema.[18] For adolescent films, more openly affirming queer youth stories emerged first in Europe with titles like *Du er ikke alene / You Are Not Alone* (1978). Meanwhile in the United States in the mid- to late 1980s, John Hughes dominated the box office with films in which the "words 'fag' and faggot' are tossed around with abandon,"[19] and teen films typically only mentioned or hinted at homosexuality to ostracize or reject it. For example, Russo recalls a scene from *Teen Wolf* (1985) in which the lead character reveals himself to his best friend. His friend asks, "You're not going to tell me you're a faggot, are you?" When he tells him, no, he's a werewolf, "his friend is greatly relieved. Better a werewolf than a faggot."[20] Representations of queer youth in the 1980s, in other words, remained relegated to the "sad, frustrated, lone gay student" in *Fame* (1980) or deviant villains such as a gay vampire in *Once Bitten* (1985).[21]

However, the 1990s brought youth decidedly out of the closet with independent films such as *Totally F***ed Up* (1993), *The Incredibly True Adventures of Two Girls in Love* (1995), *The Basketball Diaries* (1995), *All Over Me* (1997), and *Edge of Seventeen* (1998). Meanwhile, Hollywood more cautiously ventured out with the "gay best friend" trope in the 1990s and early twenty-first-century teen films like *Clueless* (1995), *Mean Girls* (2004), and *Easy A* (2010). John E. Conklin in the book *Campus Life in the Movies: A Critical Survey from the Silent Era to the Present* quantifies the number of queer characters in college films, suggesting that only seven college films between 1966 and 1992 featured a gay, lesbian, or bisexual character, while from 1993 to 2006 there were twenty-six.[22]

Homosexuality in the twenty-first century has become more part of the mainstream. Queer media and TV representations have proliferated, and states approved same-sex marriages and civil unions, culminating in the 2015 Supreme Court decision *Obergefell v. Hodges* granting same-sex couples the right to marriage across the United States. Yet still, even now, as Eve Ng puts it, "Queer media marketed to the mainstream remains shadowed by fears of being too niche."[23] Perhaps for this reason, independent studios have continued to produce most contemporary queer teen films such as *The Curiosity of Chance* (2006), *Pariah* (2011), and *Booksmart* (2019), while VOD platforms like Netflix picked up and even produced several of these recent titles including *Alex Strangelove*, *The Half of It* (2020), and *The Prom* (2020). In offering the reason why it took so long for a movie like *Love, Simon* to be made, director Greg Berlanti echoes this risk of "being too niche," as he states, "My sense is that [Hollywood] make[s] fewer and fewer movies these days, and they're more reliant on pre-existing things and want more sure bets."[24] Undoubtedly the default for the genre has been heteronormativity, as Katherine Hughes suggests, "it is widely agreed that teen film is a genre that has largely been understood as taking heterosexuality as one of its central tenets."[25] Some minoritization appears to be systemic. For example, scholars and critics argue that the Motion Picture Association (MPA) "discriminates by holding queer content to a higher ratings standard than content in other films."[26] In a study in the *Journal of Homosexuality*, Bruce E. Drushel found that while 52 percent of films on movie lists featuring heterosexual teens receive a G, PG, or PG-13 rating, only 17 percent of films featuring queer youth do. Drushel proposes that since queer teen films are largely produced by independent studios, they tend not to be rated by the MPA. However, in addition, filmmakers and activists have criticized the MPA for more direct bias—via opaque guidelines that rate homosexual stories as more mature.

Still there are signs of industry change. In a 2021 GLAAD study, researchers found that 22.7 percent of the 44 films from major studios in 2020 featured LGBTQ characters—up 4.1 percent from the previous year.[27] Furthermore, three of the five Outstanding Film–Wide Release category of the GLAAD Media Awards in 2018 included gay or lesbian teens. The films (*Love, Simon*, *Blockers*, and *Deadpool 2*) performed well at the box office, earning more than 3.5 times their production costs.[28] Studios and VOD platforms have taken note of such success and have sought to capitalize on it—for example the film *Three Months* (2022) about a teen boy Caleb (played by Troye Sivan) who awaits HIV test results after an exposure was produced by MTV Studios and is distributed by Paramount+.

STILL QUEER TO BE QUEER

Undoubtedly, minoritizing and pathologizing homosexuality and queerness in film for one hundred plus years has had a tremendous impact on all cinema, including teen movies. While contemporary teen films often affirm queerness through their underlying messages, many focus on homosexual protagonists' tumultuous coming out stories within a world that is not always as accepting as the presumed audience. Coming-of-age films even in the early twenty-first century—including *Love, Simon*—routinely highlight how queer teens feel or are seen as abnormal by their friends, families, or communities. Plots centering on queer protagonists nearly always emphasize a teen's ostracization for being queer (e.g., *Prom, Freak Show, Boy Erased, Speech & Debate, Moonlight, The Miseducation of Cameron Post*) or their queerness as a secret to be exposed through the resolution of the film (e.g., *The Half of It, The Truth about Jane, Alex Strangelove, Blockers, Pariah, The Perks of Being a Wallflower, Easy A, Geography Club, Henry Gamble's Birthday Party*). In a study titled "Teen Lesbian Desires and Identities in International Cinema: 1931–2007," Rebecca Beirne also found teen tragedy still figured prominently in more recent lesbian films such as *Loving Annabelle* (2006). Several teen dramas such as *Bully* (2001), *Wrecked* (2009), *As You Are* (2016), and *Beach Rats* (2017) pathologize young men's homosexuality by connecting it to violence, drugs, and misery. Queerness is called "nasty" (*We the Animals*), "messed up" (*The Miseducation of Cameron Post*), and "weird" (*A Girl Like Grace*), and many teen films depict youth who are tormented, beaten, ostracized, and punished for their sexuality.

Queer protagonists of color—who are even more rare in the genre—are often shown to face additional obstacles to coming out. In one of the most celebrated contemporary queer films, *Moonlight* (2016), the Black protagonist, Chiron, struggles to come to terms with his homosexuality amid a world of drugs and violence. At the end of the film, we learn that Chiron's first homosexual interaction with Kevin as a teen has been his only one, and the film ends with Chiron as an adult still in the closet. In *Three Months*, the Caucasian protagonist finds acceptance from his grandmother while his love interest, Estha, who is Indian American, never comes out to his family in the film. And in *A Girl Like Grace*, the Black girl protagonist's queer status remains ambiguous even through the film's ending. Although numerous reviewers call Grace "queer" and "gay," she never comes out officially as lesbian or bisexual in the film.[29] Like many films about Black teens, *A Girl Like Grace* offers a much bleaker portrait of youth than its Caucasian counterparts. Grace is Haitian American, and she contends with living in poverty with her single mother in addition to homophobia at school and home. The film chronicles Grace's senior year of high school after her best friend Andrea died of suicide after being outed as lesbian. By the film's end, Mary, a closeted lesbian (also a person of color) who rules over the mean girls, becomes revealed as the cause of Andrea's suicide. In other words, self-hating lesbian teens of color are both the victim and the perpetrator here. Not surprisingly, the film has not sat well with fans, who have posted, "as a lesbian, i'm tired of these movies never having a happy ending"[30] or "i just wanted to watch a nice movie about a young black lesbian with a happy ending. guess that's asking too much?"[31] The film *Pariah* offers perhaps one of the more optimistic conclusions for a queer Black teen, but even here Black protagonist Alike ultimately must come to terms with *not* gaining the acceptance of one's mother. In their last encounter in the film, Alike says, "I love you," followed by a long pause until Alike's mother responds finally, "I'll be praying for you," while Alike cries. However, the film does depict Alike as having the support of queer friends. Ultimately, Alike determines to leave home to attend college early, declaring, "I'm not running. I'm choosing. I'm not going back home." Films like *Pariah, Three Months, A Girl Like Grace,* and *Moonlight* portray intersectional identities as a further hindrance to coming out and achieving acceptance.

Of course, the point here is not that teen films fail to present positive depictions for queer youth but rather how evident it is through this body of films how it remains queer to be queer—even in the early twenty-first century. In fact, queerness is still shown as so transgressive in these films that youth often appear to not consent to their own sexual desires. Numerous plots concern queer teens who actively stifle or deny their sexual impulses (*Alex Strangelove, Blockers, Beach Rats, The Miseducation of Cameron Post, Boy Erased, A Girl Like Grace*). As if to epitomize this issue, in the film *Geography Club*, when protagonist Russell ultimately embraces his homosexuality, his boyfriend, Kevin, refuses, telling Russell, "I don't want to be gay. . . . I just want to be normal." In other words, as queerness becomes more integrated in adolescent stories of the twenty-first century, it nonetheless continues to be shown as significantly "other" in the world of teen films—a cause for disapproval from parents, teachers, friends, communities, and the characters themselves—even in independent films marketed as pro-queer.

A teen's announcement of their sexuality to parents and even peers is frequently depicted as filled with trepidation. The protagonist's coming out often even serves as the focus of the plot with turning points centering on an untimely exposure and ultimate acceptance. *Love, Simon* follows this pattern neatly—in the beginning of the film, Simon's sexuality is a secret. In the opening sequence, Simon describes in voice over that "I'm just like you. For the most part my life is totally normal." After a montage of Simon's suburban life showcasing his home, loving parents, sister, and friends (Leah, Nick, and Abby), he concludes, "Like I said, I'm just like you. I have a totally perfectly normal life—although I have one huge ass secret." It cuts to Simon's peeking out his window to catch a glimpse at a muscular man doing yardwork at his house. The plot of the film propels forward when one of Simon's classmates anonymously comes out of the closet in an online letter signed "Blue." Simon then begins an anonymous correspondence with Blue signing his own letters as Jacques. When a classmate, Martin, discovers their correspondence, he uses it to blackmail Simon—Martin will keep the emails a secret only if Simon helps him win over Simon's friend Abby. Not ready for his sexuality to be public, Simon agrees. Thus, Simon goes to great lengths to keep his "huge ass secret" in the closet and indulge Martin, a choice that jeopardizes Simon's closest friendships.

Clearly, *Love, Simon* suggests a pro-queer stance and that in itself is significant seeing how long it had been awaited in Hollywood teen films. The affirmation that comes through the film's resolution is resounding—Simon's parents, sister, friends, principal, and classmates (except for two homophobic peers who are quickly shut down) all accept Simon's homosexuality—and the conclusion of the film depicts Simon's classmates' cheering him and "Blue" (now revealed as Bram) for their first kiss on a Ferris wheel. In its pro-gay stance, the film highlights the precarious balance of affirming Simon's coming out story and emphasizing his marginalization. In one letter to Blue, Simon pinpoints this irony of growing up queer when he bemoans the necessity of coming out. He writes, "It doesn't seem fair that only gay people need to come out. Why is straight the default?" His question is followed by a comedic montage of teen characters in the film breaking the news to their parents that they're straight—for example, one teen states, "I'm heterosexual," as her mother bursts into tears crying, "Oh god, help me Jesus!" Yet even as the film ridicules the idea of coming out being such a monumental life announcement, it nonetheless emphasizes it as exactly that since Simon himself worries that his coming out will "change everything."

Depicting the fact of queerness as such a weighty proclamation begs the question—how accepting is the world of *Love, Simon*? The film's setup implies that Simon's secret—the fact that he's gay—is what sets him apart and makes his otherwise "perfectly normal life" *not* normal. His queerness is depicted as something to hide—something Simon believes is undesirable or shameful. At one point in the film, Simon writes to Blue about how he first realized he was gay. In a flashback scene, Simon recalls that it all started with "this one recurring dream" about Daniel Radcliffe—and the shot depicts young Simon waking up abruptly and seeing his poster of Radcliffe on his bedroom wall. He then proceeds to have this dream for a month, as the scene depicts young Simon repeatedly waking up looking frightened until he finally gets up and tears the poster off the wall. The discovery of his homosexuality is thus portrayed as a disturbance, or even a recurring nightmare.

Simon's otherness is further emphasized by the pervasive presumption of heterosexuality in the world of the film. Simon's parents obviously do not see it coming—throughout the film his dad makes jokes about Simon's masturbating to lingeried women, and at one point, his dad pokes fun of the star of *The Bachelor* episode for seeming "fruity" as Simon silently winces. Later in the film, Simon's mom acknowledges that she suspected Simon had a secret because he used to be "carefree" until the last few years when it seemed he was "holding [his] breath." In a tearful scene between the two, his mom tells him "being gay is your thing, and there are parts of it you have to go through alone. I hate that." She adds, "As soon as you came out, you said, 'I'm still me.' I need you to hear this—you are still you, Simon. . . . the same son who I love to tease and who your father depends on for just about everything." Her speech offers a touching acknowledgment of Simon's not being different for being gay. Yet the gravitas of the scene feels burdensome—as if she is desperately trying to convince herself and him that nothing has changed—when they both know everything has. Perhaps most blatantly unfortunate is Simon's principal's reaction—he too reads the rumor board and learns Simon has been outed. When Simon arrives at school the next day, the scene proceeds in slow motion with all his peers turning to look at him. As he reaches the principal, it reverts to normal speed as the principal asks Simon, "You alright?" to which Simon responds, "Hanging in there." The principal then states, "For the, uh, record, when I was saying that we have a lot in common, I wasn't really . . . that's not what I was talking about." Simon nods and says, "Gotcha" as he walks off. The principal does not want to be mistaken as gay—and therein lies the joke, if we can call it that. Simon has been relegated to an undesirable category—and his new ostracized status is emphasized by both the curious looks of his peers and the distancing of an authority figure. Even in the affirming world of *Love, Simon*, in other words, it is still queer to be queer.

However, not everyone in the film responds to Simon's news with shock. When he tells his friend Abby that he's gay, she expresses little surprise, simply smiling and saying, "Oh." He asks her, "You surprised?" and she says, "No." He then asks her, "So you knew?" to which she also answers, "No." She asks him, "Do you want me to be surprised?" and he replies, "I don't know." She says, "Well I love you," and he says, "Love you too." Abby's reaction to Simon's declaration is a simple acknowledgment—to her, his being gay is not monumental and changes nothing. She accepts it as a simple fact that she didn't previously know. But hers is the *only* nonchalant reaction in the film, and thus this scene presents us with a more ideal but, at least in the world of the film, rare reaction to Simon's announcement.

HETEROSEXUALITY FIRST IN QUEER TEEN FILMS

Even in queer teen films, heterosexuality nearly always comes first. Queer adolescents are often depicted as trying out heterosexual experiences—as if that had to be ruled out *before* acknowledging one's homosexuality. Such a pattern is not new in queer teen films—in the 1999 film *But I'm a Cheerleader*, the protagonist Megan consents to kissing her boyfriend despite her obvious disgust, ameliorated only by imagining her fellow cheerleaders leaping in slow motion. However, such scenes carry a new significance amid consent culture. Whether intentionally or not, they depict queer teens in precarious romantic and sexual situations where they clearly lack desire (i.e., "subjective" consent) even when they provide "performative" consent.

In *Love, Simon*, this "ruling out heterosexuality" scene is short and innocuous—through a flashback he recalls being at a dance with "his first girlfriend" who tells him, "I think I'm falling in love with you," at which Simon rushes to the bathroom to hide and phones his mom to pick him up. In teen films marketed for more mature audiences, these scenes become more explicit and more problematic. Although the queer teen might appear to consent to heterosexual interactions, it is evident from the narrative that such experiences are unwanted and unpleasant. For example, in *Blockers*, three teen girls—Julie, Kayla, and Sam—make a pact to lose their virginity on prom night. Sam, who has kept her homosexual desires to herself, attends with the nerdy Chad but then connives a way to run into her real crush, the out lesbian Angelica. While Sam nervously shovels food from the buffet into her mouth, she learns that Angelica recently has broken up with her girlfriend who is "still a little confused." Sam asks, "How do you think one becomes *not* confused?" Angelica acknowledges that "it's probably different for everybody" but says she personally "suspected" it when she first kissed a boy and adds, "Then last year when I touched Ash Lowenstein's dick, I was like fuck no. It was like holding a dead snake." Sam shakes her head in disgust, and Angelica says, "But I guess you never know until you try." Angelica's position suggests that one must test out heterosexuality before embarking on homosexuality. Although we might presume Angelica consented to touch Ash's "dick," we also recognize that this was an undesirable intimate encounter. Sam, who clearly seems to realize her own lesbian desire, similarly, does not experiment that night with homosexuality with Angelica but rather proceeds to test out being heterosexual with Chad. She gets drunk, and they go to a hotel room where the scene starts with them already naked under the covers. When he asks, "You sure you want to do this?" She responds, "Yeah.

Yes. Fuck, yes. You're going to penis me. First, I'm just going to touch it." He consents, and when she does, Chad exclaims with delight, saying, "Wow. OK. That is like the greatest feeling I've ever had in my entire life." Sam is surprised and responds clinically, "Really? It doesn't just feel like a super dry hand of a friend?" When he asks, "OK, do you want to put it in?" Sam shakes her head and says, "No. I can't." As Chad is accepting her no, saying, "Look we don't have to . . . ," he accidentally climaxes and then apologizes repeatedly while Sam laughs. Sam by no means appears to be traumatized by this experience, and she is shown as being able to draw the lines between what she would and would not do—even changing her mind about intercourse. Still, her evident lack of desire is played for its humor, particularly in contrast to Chad's abruptly orgasmic experience.

In *Alex Strangelove,* Alex goes as far as having intercourse with his girlfriend to convince himself that he's heterosexual. In the film, high school couple Alex and Claire plan to have intercourse for the first time together, but what Claire does not realize is that Alex has been struggling to come to terms with his homosexuality. At one point in the film, Claire, drunk, attacks Alex with kisses and jokes, "Get in the tub bitch!" He complies but the pair are ultimately thwarted by Alex's best friend, who arrives in the bathroom and vomits all over them in the tub. Later in the film, the couple rents a hotel room to complete the act more privately and soberly. There, Claire performs fellatio on Alex, who says, "OK, OK, this ain't so bad." Claire doesn't hear him. When he puts a condom on, Alex is unable to stay erect until he fantasizes about a boy he met, Elliot, while Claire kisses his neck. They then successfully begin having intercourse. During the act, Alex says, "It's kind of weird having sex with your best friend," and Claire stops abruptly insisting on knowing what exactly is "weird" about having sex with one's girlfriend. Alex, afraid to tell Claire about his sexual questioning, blurts out that he likes someone else. Their sexual interaction immediately becomes a source of hurt and regret, as they both finally face that the intimate experience they have been building toward has been a sham and a disappointment. Claire has had sex under false pretenses: she thought Alex wanted to have sex with her, and Alex has had intercourse with Claire despite his obvious lack of desire.

This is not Alex's only unpleasant heterosexual intercourse encounter. After his breakup with Claire, Alex's friends surprise him one night to drag him to a party, which his friend Dell says will have "booze and slutty girls, booze and slutty girls," telling Alex, "And you're going to let your little constipated hair down and enjoy yourself." When Alex resists saying that he's "sick and tired of this, 'Let's get you laid, Alex.' I'm not into it," Dell says, "Who said anything about getting you laid—clearly that's impossible. In fact, I never want to hear about your flaccid little micro-penis ever again. I don't give a shit if you get laid or you don't get laid or you're a bisexual, asexual, pansexual, or if you join fucking NAMBLA!" Dell's prompting feels contradictory—while Dell suggests he doesn't care what Alex's sexuality is, he also attacks Alex for his lack of virility and ultimately associates him with pedophilia by conjuring up the North American Man/Boy Love Association (NAMBLA). Alex succumbs to his friends' pressure, and on their way into the party states, "Claire has been holding me back. I can't be with one girl for the rest of my senior year. I should be playing the field with the ladies—plural." When Alex gets a text from Elliot, he ignores it. We next see him chugging beers. It isn't long before he's intoxicated and making his way up to a bedroom with one of the girls at the party—which again leads to Alex's inability to maintain an erection while the girl demands, "Fuck me. Come on mister class president." While Alex tries to talk himself into heterosexual sex, the girl becomes agitated and ultimately pushes him off. Although these scenes might not demonstrate nonconsent, they certainly suggest how complicated consent can be in practice, with queer teens who demonstrate "performative" but not "subjective" consent and their heterosexual partners who are not fully informed of their lack of desire.

Also notable in most of these films is how heterosexual interactions are more visible than queer sex. For example, *Alex Strangelove* includes two explicit scenes of Alex's heterosexual intercourse while keeping his homosexual encounters decidedly subdued. In fact, the only intimate scenes between Alex and Elliot are one where Alex abruptly kisses Elliot on the bed and then jumps back in horror at his own action saying he was just "giving [Elliot] what he wanted" and the final scene in which Alex finally comes out publicly by kissing Elliot on the dance floor. Like *Love, Simon* and *Blockers*, queer teen sex here is relegated to a brief kiss at the conclusion of *Alex Strangelove*, thus keeping explicit queer teen sex in the closet in more popular teen films. Considering that more explicit gay teen scenes occurred in *Edge of Seventeen* over two decades earlier, the omission seems particularly surprising.

Even more disturbing are sexual interactions in the drama *A Girl Like Grace*. Grace's same-sex desire is apparent in flashbacks with her deceased friend, Andrea, and scenes with Andrea's older sister, Share. In one scene, Grace tells her date Jason that Share makes her feel "alive again." When he asks how *he* makes her feel, she tells him that's still to be determined. Nevertheless, Grace has intercourse with Jason on a beach later that night. In a subsequent flashback scene, Andrea tells Grace that she had heterosexual sex but didn't like it, adding, "I wish I did." She then suggests to Grace, "Maybe you should try it." Once Grace does, it seems she shares Andrea's distaste, and yet she proceeds

Fig. 3.1. In Craig Johnson's *Alex Strangelove*, scenes of teen homosexuality between Alex (Daniel Doheny) and Elliot (Antonio Marziale) are less sexually explicit than heterosexual scenes.

to spiral downward with Share's prodding into a world of drugs, alcohol, and heterosexual sex. Her descent ultimately leads to tragedy. When Grace goes to a hotel room with a guy one night, she winds up gang-raped by him and his friends. Not only does this scene perpetuate the stereotype of sexually active girls' inviting rape but it also presents one of the most disturbing outcomes for a queer teen testing out heterosexual sex.[32]

Although many of these films are lauded as pro-queer, they still follow a pattern of adolescents forcing themselves into heterosexual encounters. Perhaps inadvertently, such scenes expose a major flaw of consent culture and the affirmative consent framework. Although the teens appear to consent to these heterosexual interactions, it is evident through the plots, dialogue, and characters' body language that these sexual encounters are not desired. These scenes are complicated by the fact that the teens appear to not fully accept their own hidden impulses—forcing themselves into sexual situations they believe are more socially acceptable. Ultimately, these moments suggest perplexities of consent—how can one possibly consent to an unwanted sexual interaction that runs counter to one's sexual preferences? If any of these characters were later asked in a survey whether they had experienced unwanted sexual contact, their answer certainly could be yes, meaning that by definition such scenes could be classified as assault. At the same time, the films do not seem to suggest teens are assaulted in these moments. Recognizing such a discrepancy might enable us to admit that the delineation between consent and nonconsent is sometimes blurrier than we like to admit and that what we consider consensual sex might still be rife with unethical and regrettable behavior, unpleasant and perplexing feelings, shame, disappointment, or even disgust.[33] These moments underscore the flaws of a framework that prioritizes "performative" over "subjective" consent or presumes the two automatically align. While the characters' verbal consent is often prioritized, their states of mind are more complex. In such scenes, queer teens want to want heterosexuality (hence, why they consent), but in fact, their bodies belie their actual queer desires.

SHAME AND CONSENT IN HOMOSEXUAL TEENS' CONVERSION THERAPY STORIES

Homosexuality for teens in films is often depicted as a shameful secret even when the world of the film is socially progressive like in *Alex Strangelove*, *Blockers*, and *Love, Simon*. When the film takes place within a highly religious and conservative world, as in *Boy Erased* and *The Miseducation of Cameron Post*, this struggle is exacerbated. Here, homosexuality is perceived as a terrible sin that one must learn to resist, and teens are sent to conversion therapy programs to change their sexuality. A topic that was once fodder for comedy nearly two decades earlier in *But I'm a Cheerleader* in these films becomes the basis for dramatic stories of injustice, abuse, and harm. Incredibly, conversion therapy programs remain in legal operation in the United States in 2022. Although the American Psychiatric Association declassified homosexuality as a "psychiatric disorder" in 1973,[34] some health care professionals and other religious organizations have continued the practice of attempting to "cure" queer teens of their sexuality. The UCLA Williams Institute has estimated in a 2019 study that 350,000 LGBTQ+ adults have been subjected to conversion therapy as minors.[35] And, as of July 2022, only twenty US states and the District of Columbia have banned the practice on minors.[36]

The films *Boy Erased* and *The Miseducation of Cameron Post*, adaptations of books with the same titles, chart how teens navigate through and out of their oppressive religious upbringings. With their sexuality initially a source of disgrace, both main characters experience disturbing sexual encounters. In *Boy Erased*, eighteen-year-old Jared recalls being sexually assaulted through flashbacks. At college, he meets Henry. The two share a love of running, and at one point, Henry challenges Jared to a race to see who gets to attend the other's church. One night after a run, Henry catches Jared eyeing him. Later, the two boys play video games in Jared's room, and Jared invites Henry to stay since his roommate is away. Henry initially goes to the top bunk to sleep, but then jumps down to join Jared on the bottom bunk. Henry makes a move toward Jared, and at first, Jared signals consent, leaning into Henry, but then when Henry climbs on top of him, Jared says, "Hey wait." Henry then covers Jared's mouth and holds him down, while Jared repeatedly says "Stop-stop-stop-stop." Henry proceeds to rape Jared who cries in pain. Immediately afterward, Henry feels guilty, getting off the bed, crying and slapping himself as he says, "What the hell is wrong with me. I'm so sorry. I'm gonna be in so much trouble. I need to confess. I need to confess. Will you hear me? Please." Jared, who has just been attacked and raped by Henry, appears completely stunned and mumbles, "uh huh." Henry then confides to Jared that "something pretty bad" happened with a kid they saw earlier in church, and then he tells Jared, "You wouldn't dare tell anyone would you? Please. Keep it between us." Jared nods almost imperceptibly. In this interaction, Jared's homosexual desire turns against him in a violent and traumatizing manner. In the next scene, Jared cries alone in the bathroom after Henry has left. Following that is a sequence depicting Jared as out of sorts—sitting in a lecture hall long after class has ended, walking through a crowded hallway in slow motion, and hiding from Henry who awaits him for their routine run.

This rare depiction of a young man's homosexual rape is an important acknowledgment that rape does not only happen to girls and women. In the autobiographical book *Boy Erased*, on which the film is based, Garrard Conley writes about how the "shame" of this experience haunted him afterward, stating, "For the longest time, I wouldn't allow myself to admit that it was rape at all. Like many victims, I was embarrassed. How could I have let this happen? What kind of man let another man do this to him?"[37] Since rape is more commonly perpetrated against women—a 2015 CDC study showed 21.3 percent of women surveyed reported completed or attempted rape compared with 2.6 percent of men[38]—it remains highly stigmatized in men. As such, this portrayal draws attention to an important and often unacknowledged issue. In the film, Jared's shame remains below the surface, showing subtly what the book explicitly states—how "extremely difficult" it was for Conley after the experience "to consider gay sex as anything other than rape."[39]

The combined experiences of Jared's sexual assault and religious upbringing confuse his sexual desires. In fact, the rape is the *only* sexual interaction we witness for Jared in the film. Jared has an intimate—although completely nonsexual—encounter with a boy, Xavier. In a flashback, Jared recalls the two of them going back to Xavier's apartment. There, Xavier tells him, "Stay with me. Nothing needs to happen, I swear. I'll prove to you that God won't strike you down." Xavier walks into his room, and Jared follows. The scene completes at a later point with a repeat of Xavier's offer. This time, we see the conclusion with Jared and Xavier lying in bed together—Jared touches Xavier's face, and Xavier touches Jared's. They then spend the night holding hands. Certainly, this scene provides a calming contrast to the violence depicted with Henry, but the scene with Xavier is not sexual. At the end of the film, we learn that years later Jared is in a relationship with a man—we see them hosting a party as Jared comes up behind him and kisses his neck. But the film still does not depict any consensual homosexual encounters—and in that way, it only renders visible nonconsensual homosexuality. Perhaps this omission would not seem so noticeable if it were not for the fact that so many teen films continue to steer clear of explicit depictions of queer sex—especially among teen boys. This persistent absence—not just in *Boy Erased*, but in numerous queer teen films—calls to mind David M. Considine's comment that "in the cinema of adolescence, one of the crucial determinants is not simply what we see but what we choose not to see."[40] Consensual queer teen sexual behavior remains rare in teen movies—even in explicitly queer films.

Sex in *The Miseducation of Cameron Post* is more visible but with more ambiguous consent. The film begins with two girls, Cameron and Coley, being lectured during religious education—Cameron appears uninterested and Coley, amused. Immediately after, they go to Cameron's house, and finding no one home, they rush to Cameron's room where they immediately begin to kiss. In the next scene, Cameron is preparing for the homecoming dance. Both girls bring teen boys as dates, but the girls sneak off to the car to get high and make out. Consent is certainly implied in these scenes, although it is never as explicit as affirmative consent. In the backseat of the car, the girls, presumably high, move toward each other to kiss. Then Coley gets on top and says, "I want to try something" as she pulls down Cameron's underwear. Coley begins to touch Cameron nearly to the point of climax until one of the boys abruptly opens the door. Although the world around them disapproves (the boy who catches them exclaims, "This is so messed up"), it initially seems these scenes of Cameron and Coley's sexual interactions are reciprocal explorations.

Cameron's perception of her relationship with Coley as mutual, however, becomes upended later in the film. While at the camp, Cameron receives a letter from Coley who accuses her of coercing her into lesbianism. Coley writes,

"I'm very angry at you for taking advantage of our friendship. You already had this thing in you, but I didn't. And I think of how long it took me to gain the strength to tell my mom." Cameron realizes then that she was not outed by the boy who caught them but rather by Coley herself. Suddenly Cameron finds herself in a moral quandary. She brings the letter to her friends Adam and Jane, asking them, "What if she's right? You know, like I took complete advantage of our friendship, and I wasn't even aware I was doing it." Adam hesitates, but Jane immediately responds by tearing up the letter and declaring, "No. Pink stationery does not get to fuck with you. This girl is spineless. Let's say what you did was fucked up and you infected her or whatever. It was a shit move to rat you out." Cameron's discovery leads her into a deeper shame over her sexuality, and she replies, "She was just trying to help me. . . . She's better than all of us. And I hurt her. What if this really is our only chance and we're blowing it? I'm tired of feeling disgusted with myself." But Jane responds flatly, "Maybe you're supposed to feel disgusted with yourself when you're a teenager." Cameron's self "disgust" over her homosexuality becomes compounded by the revelation that she might have been an aggressor or assaulter.

Ultimately, there is no comforting resolution to Cameron's doubts—even while defending her, Jane suggests that Cameron might have done something "fucked up" and "infected" Coley. On a closer look, this idea of coercion is hinted at in an earlier flashback. Coley and Cameron are watching the lesbian film *Desert Hearts* together—in it, one of the characters says to the other, "I want you to put your clothes on and leave," and the other woman says, "No you don't." She says, "Yes, I do," and the other woman replies again, "No you don't." Cameron interrupts the film's dialogue to say, "This movie's weird." Coley says, "You knew that was going to happen," and Cameron replies, "No I didn't. . . . I really didn't know what was going to happen." Coley playfully kicks her and says, "Yes you did." They go back and forth like this, echoing the dialogue of the film within the film—a world where no sometimes means yes. Cameron turns to Coley to kiss her, and Coley leans in to kiss back. Cameron then climbs on top of Coley and unbuttons Coley's shirt and then starts to unbutton her pants, saying, "Tell me when to stop." The scene ends there as Cameron's memory is halted abruptly by the flashlight for night checks at the conversion therapy camp. Although Coley seems to be also enjoying their sexual interaction in this memory, there is no verbal consent, and Cameron drives the physical milestones—initiating the first kiss and then unbuttoning Coley's shirt and her pants. Rather than asking for yes, Cameron acknowledges that she will accept a no when she says, "Tell me when to stop." If Coley does feel violated by these interactions, there is no observable indication of it in these scenes, other than the fact that Coley seems to believe that Cameron picked the film purposely for its lesbian theme. Whether Coley felt coerced in the moment or regret later remains unresolved in the film.

Affirmative consent is only possible when both parties are open and aware—and *The Miseducation of Cameron Post* shows how that system breaks down when sex is laced with secrecy and shame. The only other sexual encounter in the film occurs between Cameron and her camp roommate, Erin. One night, Cameron dreams about a woman teacher kissing her during a test, and she is awakened abruptly by Erin in her bed. When Cameron says, "What the fuck," Erin hushes her, saying, "You were making a lot of noise." Erin desperately wants to know what Cameron's dream was about and does not believe Cameron when she insists that she does not remember but says only that "it was scary." Erin says, "Those weren't scary noises." Cameron replies, "This is ridiculous. Go back to bed," but Erin insists, "I heard you." Cameron then turns away, and Erin leans down and kisses her. Both then sit up in bed kissing, and although it is not explicitly shown, it is implied that Erin manually pleasures Cameron, as they rock back and forth until Cameron reaches orgasm. Immediately after, Erin exhibits regret. Cameron tries to pull her back into a kiss, and Erin says, "No, it's OK, I'm good." When Cameron tries again, Erin says forcefully, "Get off" to which Cameron responds, "Are you serious?" Erin returns to her own bed and tells Cameron not to tell anyone, saying, "I really do want to get past this," and "I knew this would happen." When Cameron admits, "I didn't," Erin responds, "Because you don't think of me that way." In other words, their sexual interaction not only lacks clear verbal consent but is also marked by the characters' ambivalence of desire. What does it mean to consent to a sexual encounter one wishes to repress or to consent to sex with someone who is not the object of sexual attraction? Although she is certainly craving a homosexual encounter, Cameron is not attracted to Erin. And although Erin makes the first move by kissing Cameron, her regret afterward is clear. Their encounter is the result of an impulsive decision, even a mistake—consensual perhaps but nevertheless mixed with regret and shame.

In both films, the protagonists' lack of access to clear consent is further emphasized through their experiences in conversion therapy programs. While both teens themselves sign consent forms to enter programs, their actual desire to be treated is repeatedly called into question through the narratives. After being outed, Cameron spies her aunt in the living room talking on the phone and sitting with a woman and the leader of her religious education group. Although we don't hear what is said in that scene, we know that the outcome is Cameron's being sent to God's Promise. Upon arrival, Reverend

Rick rifles through Cameron's bags for contraband (he finds and confiscates a Breeders cassette), and he explains how she will likely receive room decorating and mail privileges in a few weeks, adding, "It's all spelled out in the contract." Once he's done with the bag search, he asks her, "You take a look at the contract?" She responds, "Yeah," and he says with a smile, "All that's left is your signature, and we're good to go." A long pause ensues in which Cameron looks back and forth between him and her aunt who finally breaks the silence saying, "I think you're going to do really well here, Cammy." Cameron then signs the contract. Thus, she becomes, as Rick says, "officially a disciple of God's Promise." In the next shot, Cameron stands outside in the parking lot watching her aunt drive away and says, "Fuck." Cameron's consent, in other words, appears constrained at best. Although technically both her aunt and Reverend Rick require her signature to enter her into the program, Cameron has little choice in the matter. This lack of subjective consent despite performative consent is emphasized later in the film when Cameron tells fellow disciple Jane, "You don't seem like the type of person who would be here," and Jane responds, "I didn't have a choice. Did you?" Cameron pauses and then shakes her head mouthing no. Although some of the teens seem earnest in their quest to be "cured," several appear not to be there of their own volition but rather at the forceful direction of their parents or guardians. Adam, who is Two Spirit, attends because their father became a politician and converted to Christianity, meaning, as Adam puts it, "me being like this fucks his image." Jane attends because her mother married an evangelical man. And Cameron, who has lost both her parents, is there at her aunt's bidding.

For these teens, there initially is no other imaginable option than to consent to the program. When Adam, Jane, and Cameron go for a hike, Cameron asks, "Couldn't we just walk off?" to which Jane responds, "And go where?" Adam adds sarcastically, "Should we go directly to Times Square to turn tricks or would you rather try break dancing first?" while Jane adds, "What's worse, karaoke night or living on the streets?" Initially, the three cannot envision what simply walking off would mean—Where would they go? How would they support themselves? Are they prepared to give up the safety of their familiar world—even as awful as it is? The film depicts how even the most skeptical adolescents cannot easily picture their lives without the protection of their parents, guardians, and the other adults around them.

In *Boy Erased*, Jared too signs a document (after his mother signs) upon arrival at the program Love in Action. However, neither seems to have read the terms carefully, since immediately Jared's mother asks if she can see the place (she's not allowed) and offers for Jared to call her if he needs her (cell phones are confiscated). The actual details of the program Love in Action are, in fact, meant to be kept secret from both the adolescents and their parents. At one point, Jared discovers that what he thought was a complete program of a few weeks is only an "assessment" to determine if he will be transferred to long-term residency. Parents too remain in the dark about many details. At one point, Jared, fed up, lays out the hypocrisy for his mom, "You know the whole thing you and dad are paying for here is all about how messed up we are by our parents. They want to know all about *you*, that's why you can't know all about *it*, because then they wouldn't get their money out of you." Despite being eighteen, Jared's "choice" to attend is portrayed as considerably forced. The decision to send him to Love in Action is made by a cabal of religious men gathered by Jared's dad in the middle of the night after Jared's admission of homosexuality. Although acknowledging they don't have "all the answers," his father says to him, "Your mother and I, we cannot see a way that you can live under this roof, attend service, and work at the dealership if you're going to fundamentally go against the grain of our beliefs—and against God himself." He then asks his son, "In your heart, do you want to change?" Jared pauses as a slow zoom closes in on him. The shot then goes back and forth between Jared and his mother, who tearfully anticipates his response. He breathes deeply and then nods and says, "Yes. Yes, I want to change." Although Jared offers this clear yes, we soon learn that he is deeply doubtful that he can or even wants to change. In this decisive moment, Jared is offered a false choice—give up your entire world (loving parents, a nice home, support for college, and "God himself") or change your sexuality. Thus, a consent framework here offers no protection for a queer teen facing such an impossible choice.

Some of the teens in these films do earnestly attempt to change because they believe in the dichotomy these programs suggest, perhaps best outlined by a white board scene in *Boy Erased* where the "choice" is written out with heterosexuality equaling "marriage, family supporting, caring and acceptance" and homosexuality defined as "rape, abuse, promiscuity, AIDS." Jared and Cameron both agree to attend the programs not only due to fears of leaving their worlds behind but also because of a belief that adults know best so their sexuality is something they can and should change. Both programs are run by supposedly "recovered" homosexuals, giving the teens false belief that such a program "works." And both teens urgently want to please their parents/guardian who love them. Jared's parents and Cameron's aunt in these films are not depicted as vilified enemies forcing their children to attend, unlike in another conversion therapy film, *Trapped: The Alex Cooper Story* (2019), based on a true story. There, Alex's parents sign over her custody to another family against her will and then refuse to release her despite clear evidence of the physical and emotional abuse she endures. Instead in *Boy Erased* and *The Miseducation of Cameron Post*, the teens are convinced to stay in the program by guardians who mistakenly believe they have their children's best interests in mind. In such a way, the teens initially think this is what they too want. When Cameron sneaks off to call her aunt, she asks, "If I told you I was unhappy and wanted to come home, would you let me?" Her aunt replies, "Come on. You have to give it a chance. You know I'm doing this because I love you. Don't you want to have a family someday?" Her aunt then starts to cry, saying, "I love you, Cammy," and Cameron replies, "I love you too." Cameron cries, hangs up the phone, and stays. Jared too reaches the point where he asks to be released from the program. He tells his father on the phone, "I don't want to be here anymore.... I don't feel good here.... I'm not sure I feel any different," and his father has an answer to each statement, suggesting, "Son, you're not even halfway through." He asks his father, "Why didn't you tell me how long I might stay for?" His dad says, "The devil's not going to ask you once. He's going to ask you over and over again, son, and you have got to find the strength and commitment inside you. You can get through this, OK?" and Jared then replies, "All right." Although not exactly forced to stay against their will, the teens are nonetheless convinced to stay by loving but seriously misguided adults. Ultimately, the youth have as little opportunity to revoke their consent to stay in the program as they had to enter it in the first place.

Both films chart how the protagonists become increasingly wise to the fallibility of adults. Jared's first clue comes early in the film when his parents send him to a doctor to test his testosterone levels. The doctor tells him, "I'm a religious woman... but I have also been to medical school." She tells him that she will take his blood as his parents requested, but she already knows it will show that Jared is a "perfectly normal very healthy teenage boy." She tells Jared, "It's not my place to tell you that your parents are wrong, but let's say that they are wrong. I understand that your father signed you up for a program next month. Whatever happens next, it is still your choice. It may not feel that way, but it is. You're eighteen." This speech carries significance throughout the film as Jared struggles to decide whether his parents are wrong and whether he is in fact a "perfectly normal very healthy teenage boy." When one evening Jared leaves the program visibly frustrated, one of his peers, Gary, asks him, "Starting to see this place for what it really is?" Gary offers Jared his advice: "Play the part. Show them it's working. You're getting better," he says sarcastically and laughs. He adds, "Fake it until you make it, right?" adding that he has "heard the stories" about the long-term programs and "they're not good." Gary tells him, "Then once you're home, you've got to figure out what to do next. If it comes down to it, you may have to walk away from everything. Everyone." Jared, however, is unwilling to fake it, and he does not want to leave his family behind.

Eventually, Jared can no longer contain his outrage or his empathy for the other adolescents abused in the program. In the climax of the film, program leader Victor Sykes demands Jared roleplay his supposed anger toward his father with an empty chair. Jared becomes increasingly irritated during this exercise, standing up abruptly when Sykes suggests, "Tell him how much you hate him." Jared asks, "Why do I have to be angry?" and adds "I don't see how it is going to help picking someone to blame or hate." Sykes asks him, "If you don't hate anyone, then where is all this anger coming from?" Jared responds, "Because *you're* making me angry. I'm not going to pretend I hate my father. I don't hate my father." Sykes insists, "You do." Jared then yells, "You don't know me!" and he storms off the stage and out of the room, yelling, "You're all crazy. All of you. *You're* in my chair. There you go. I hate *you*! But how does that help?" Jared's outburst turns into a no-going-back moment. Through a series of shots, he breaks into the office, forcibly takes his cell phone, and barricades himself in the bathroom where he calls his mother and pleads for her to come get him. Although Sykes appeals to him saying, "I want you to stay," Jared responds, "I read the rules and none of them say you can stop me from leaving." Ultimately Jared's mother arrives banging on the door, demanding to be let in as Jared yells, "Mom, they're not letting me go." One of the other boys, Cameron, breaks away from the group and opens the door, setting Jared free. Later, Jared learns Cameron died of suicide. The film, thus, demonstrates the more terrible ways out of the program—repressing one's homosexuality, faking it, or dying of suicide. Jared is the lucky one. On their way out to the car, his mother even yells at Sykes, asking him, "What are your actual qualifications? I never asked," and adding, "Shame on you! Shame on me too. Shame on you!" Ultimately Jared's mother realizes that "this is not hurting to help," and she tells Jared, "I'll handle your father. He can fall into line with me for a change." Jared thus emerges from the program still under the protection of his mother, who appears ready to accept his sexuality.

In *The Miseducation of Cameron Post*, no adults appear to have such a change of heart, but the film similarly emphasizes how the adolescents realize that adults do not always know best. One of Cameron's peers, Mark, who initially seems enthusiastic about being cured, has a breakdown when he learns of his father's decision to keep him in the program longer than he hoped. In a group therapy session, Mark recites the letter his father sent, which reads, "I am denying your request to return home at the end of the semester. You are still very feminine, and this is a weakness I cannot have in my home." That night, Mark mutilates himself by cutting his penis and pouring bleach on it. When the directors report Mark's hospitalization to everyone in the morning, several of the youth become unhinged, and the directors send them all abruptly to their rooms. When the director Rick comes to see Cameron, she asks him, "If you were worried about him, why'd you leave him alone?" Rick pauses and then responds, "I don't have a very good answer for you." She asks if Adam, Mark's roommate who found him in the bathroom, is alright. When Rick says, "I think so—all things considered. It is going to take him some time to process," Cameron looks shocked, shaking her head in disbelief and then replying, "How the fuck do you process watching your roommate try and cut his dick off?" She then comes to an abrupt realization that she articulates aloud, "You people have no idea what you're doing, do you? You're just making it up as you go along." At this, Rick begins to cry, saying, "I don't know how to answer you right now. I'm so sorry. I'm so sorry." It is Cameron who then stands up and puts her hand on Rick's shoulder to comfort him while he weeps in an obvious reversal of roles. At this moment of crisis, the adults are exposed as not being equipped to protect, guide, or even comfort the adolescents.

Whatever dim spell had kept Cameron in line at this point has been broken. A government authority arrives later to interview the teens about the program, and he asks Cameron, "Do you trust those in charge here?" to which Cameron replies bluntly, "Not really." As he presses further, he clarifies that he's there only to "investigate the care that is given by those who run this facility, not to investigate the mission of this facility unless that includes abuse or neglect." Cameron immediately cuts through this hypocrisy, saying, "But what about emotional abuse?" He asks, "Are you saying you're being emotionally abused by the staff here?" And she responds, "How is programming people to hate themselves *not* emotional abuse?" Thus, adult incompetence is shown as going up the chain of command—the state authorities do not know any better than the program directors or their own parents and guardians. This dramatic realization leads the teens to do what had originally seemed unthinkable—Adam, Jane, and Cameron simply walk off together. There is no clear resolution other than their decision to run away has been made—they have come to recognize they are not safer in the program than on their own. Sitting in the back of a pickup truck adorned with a "Clinton" sticker, the teens have opted to take their chances in an unknown world where they must fend for themselves so they can finally embrace who they are.

Fig. 3.2. In Desiree Akhavan's *The Miseducation of Cameron Post*, three teens—Cameron (Chloë Grace Moretz), Jane (Sasha Lane), and Adam (Forrest Goodluck)—escape a conversion therapy program.

THE QUEER WORLD OF *PRINCESS CYD*

Presumably after the end of many of these films (*Love, Simon, Alex Strangelove, Blockers, Boy Erased, The Miseducation of Cameron Post,* etc.), the queer protagonists are ready to embark on romantic and sexual explorations with more self-acceptance. However, those are moments frequently omitted from teen films. Even over twenty-five years after its release, a depiction like *The Incredibly True Adventures of Two Girls in Love* remains one of the most uniquely positive portrayals of two teenage girls falling in love and exploring sex. The film pairs wealthy Black protagonist Evie with Randy, a poor Caucasian girl raised by two lesbians, and the girls' mutual desire and connection is shown to bring them the confidence to carve their own path. Evie even insists to her peers on a revolutionary concept at the time—a refusal to tie her identity to her sexual desires. Rebecca Beirne in "Teen Lesbian Desires and Identities in International Cinema" argues how director Maria Maggenti's film breaks the mold, stating, "By focusing less on the potentially traumatic aspects of a first same-sex relationship, and more on the positive elements, *Incredibly True Adventures* allows the love story to take center stage as the dominant feature of the film, and is in many ways closer to the generic conventions of romantic comedy than previous lesbian-themed features."⁴¹ Although teen films are not required to be "positive," the fact that so many queer teen films emphasize the struggle of coming out versus the aftermath of exploring queer relationships and sex certainly distinguishes them from their heterosexual counterparts. There are only a handful of contemporary exceptions such as *Unpregnant* (2020) and *Booksmart* where a queer story does *not* center on the challenges of coming out but rather on the teen having their first kiss or homosexual encounter.

Of course, like teen films generally, the themes in queer teen films likely have less to do with US youth today than with adults' own preoccupations and perhaps memories of their own adolescences. Several of the directors of these films self-identify as queer, and they talk explicitly about how their own experiences influenced the making of their films.⁴² In one interview, Berlanti, director of *Love, Simon*, talks about collaborating with the screenwriters and discussing the two things he himself needed to hear after he came out, explaining, "One was that I was still loved. The other was that I deserved love."⁴³ Craig Johnson, the director of *Alex Strangelove*, acknowledges the film is his "most autobiographical," noting that the "spark" came from recalling his own "struggl[e] with confusing sexual identity issues."⁴⁴ In many ways, these films might more accurately represent youth decades ago. Meanwhile we are still waiting for those that better epitomize today's youth. As Johnson notes in an NPR interview, many adolescents today are less phased by queerness—they are "coming out of the closet in middle school" as he puts it.⁴⁵

Nevertheless, we seem to be in a holding pattern where queer adolescent intimacy is most typically an affirming kiss at the story's conclusion—a fact that accentuates how queerness remains transgressive in both Hollywood and independent teen films. When more explicit same-sex encounters are shown, they are often fraught. In *Boy Erased*, the only homosexual encounter is rape, and in *The Miseducation of Cameron Post*, the same-sex experiences are imbued with ambivalence and regret. Certainly, these films have rendered homosexual desires more visible in the genre, but the obvious hesitancy to depict homosexual teens in the throes of passion—without the shame—suggests that queerness continues to be marginalized. Even in the early 2020s, there is still not a body of US films about queer adolescents who simply discover love, romance, and sex—without the need for a pivotal and turbulent coming out moment.

As a result, there remains a dearth of open and communicative explicit queer sexual encounters in the genre. Instead, queer teens are shown contending with a minefield of challenging consent negotiations—unpleasant heterosexual encounters and shameful same-sex experiences. In these moments, sexually questioning youth, who might be conflicted about their own desires, experience sexual encounters muddled by whether consent is what one says/does or what one thinks/feels. Perhaps unintentionally, this pattern exposes an unspoken flaw in our affirmative consent discourse—consent might be the marker between a permissible/impermissible sexual interaction, but we do not always acknowledge ways the "subjective" and "performative" can be at odds. One might say no and feel yes, and one might also say yes and feel no. Seeing that lesbian, gay, and bisexual individuals experience sexual assault at significantly higher rates than their heterosexual counterparts, the stakes are high. The CDC's 2017 National Youth Risk Behavior Survey, based on over fourteen thousand questionnaires in 144 public and private schools, found that lesbian, gay, and bisexual students were 2.6 times more likely to experience dating sexual violence and 4.4 times more likely to have been forced into intercourse.[46] Perhaps what these films indicate is how queer or questioning youth need a consent framework that takes into consideration more than merely their verbal assent.

Noticeably too, when queerness does appear in contemporary teen films, it is nearly always depicted as same-sex desire. Bisexuality, pansexuality, and asexuality remain rare representations—a reminder that we are still waiting for queer teen films to come all the way out of the closet. One of the few exceptions is *Princess Cyd*, a film about a teen girl who spends the summer with her aunt, Miranda. There, Cyd discovers her attraction to partners of varying genders—and the film unproblematically portrays her diverse sexual experiences. As Whitney Monaghan notes in an analysis of the film, *Princess Cyd* resists the depiction of a "conflict (internal or external) as she figures out her sexuality, as one would expect from a queer coming of age film."[47] Rather, the film simply shows Cyd's exploration of romantic and sexual relationships during a formative summer. At the start of the film, Cyd appears to have a boyfriend back home. Then, during the summer, Cyd develops attractions to Katie, who works at the neighborhood coffee shop, and to Miranda's friend's son Josh. This framework completely alters the traditional queer teen film setup where a homosexual teen tests out heterosexual sex, finds it repulsive, and thus concludes that they must be gay. Instead, here, Cyd pursues a mutually passionate sexual interaction with Josh. Afterward, not at all having "ruled out" heterosexuality, Cyd pursues a relationship with Katie. Considering how sexual exploration remains a recurring theme in the teen film genre, one would not expect such a depiction to be so rare in the early twenty-first century, but indeed it is—*Princess Cyd* is one of the only contemporary queer teen films to show a teen's discovery of a complex sexuality without shameful undertones. And Cyd's sexual interactions in the film appear unambiguously consensual.

Such sexual variability is also overtly supported by the adults in the film. When Cyd asks about Josh, her aunt replies that he's "going to attract all the ladies or guys, whatever." Later Cyd confides to her aunt that she wants to have sex with Katie, whom she met in a coffee shop and asks, "Is that weird?" to which her aunt responds, "Of course not." Miranda's adult friends, too, provide a positive reflection of Cyd's sexuality. When Cyd learns that one of the women in a lesbian relationship was previously in a heterosexual marriage, Cyd asks bluntly, "So, you liked it and you didn't?" The friend, amused, responds, "Are you asking me if I like dick? Dick is not terrible—it's the opposite of terrible." They all laugh, and she asks Cyd, "So what are you into?" Hesitant at first, Cyd answers, "I like everything." Here, Cyd's desires are discussed and affirmed openly. Unlike most teen films, *Princess Cyd* also resists recycled narrative patterns regarding bullying or shaming for being queer. At one point in the film, a cameraperson from across the street mistakes Katie as a guy, saying they need a "boy and a girl slow dancing" in the background. Cyd initially seeks to correct the error as she starts to say, "Actually . . . ," but Katie stops her. Instead, they have fun playing along with the request. Later, when Cyd tells Miranda about it, Miranda suggests, "Well maybe she is a he," and Cyd realizes, "Yeah maybe so." Even when Katie and Cyd are approached at one point by a young boy who asks, "Hey, are y'all girlfriends?" Cyd simply shrugs and answers, "Maybe so." The boy then runs off to his friend and says, "They are," as Cyd and Katie laugh. Ultimately, these moments portray innocuous interactions that emphasize the ambiguities of gender and curiosity around queer desire without the bullying and trauma so common in the genre. Here is a more aspirational world—one in which adolescents can explore seemingly contradictory desires.

Princess Cyd does not offer a Pollyannaish world, however. One night, Katie arrives home to find their brother's friend Tab drinking alone in their apartment. Katie rejects his invitation to "hang out," but later he comes in Katie's room and refuses to leave—the look in his eyes makes clear what he's after. When Cyd checks her phone and finds a single text from Katie that says, "Help," she calls for Miranda. We never learn exactly what happened, but when the two arrive at Katie's apartment, Tab is passed out in his boxer shorts with a bloodied nose, and Katie's arm is bruised. Cyd stares at him while Katie packs her things. When Tab opens his eyes and sees Cyd, he says, "What the fuck," as Cyd slowly moves her hand to his throat as if to choke him. Miranda calls Cyd's name repeatedly and pulls her away. This scene certainly represents how queer youth can be targeted—Tab's previous "teasing" of Katie culminates in something much more ominous. Still, Katie is shown to be protected not only through self-defense (we gather Katie has punched him) but also through the support of Cyd and Miranda. Furthermore, the fact that we never see any assault flips the script in a unique way—*Princess Cyd* only provides visual representation for consensual intimate scenes.

Equally groundbreaking is the film's depiction of Cyd's aunt Miranda as asexual. Throughout the summer, Cyd takes an interest in matchmaking when she discovers that one of Miranda's friends has a crush on her. Toward the end of the film, when Miranda has a second piece of cake after the party, Cyd suggests, "Maybe if you had sex once in a while, you wouldn't want to eat as much." But Cyd's assertion is not the epiphany she thought Miranda needed—rather than Miranda's learning that all she needed to be happy was sex, Miranda launches into a speech about the "joy" that reading, discussing literature, and praying bring her. She says, "I can't relate to you the total fulfillment that I get from these things—it's impossible." At the same time, she clearly supports Cyd in her own journey adding, "I understand—you're finding your own joy. You're engaging your own stuff. That's great, that's how it should be, and it's a beautiful thing. But hear me—it is not a handicap to have one thing but not another, to be one way and not another. We are different shapes and ways and our happiness is unique. There are no rules of balance." When Cyd apologizes, Miranda tells her, "Don't be sorry. But I've got a quarter of a century on you, Cyd. Let's just enjoy ourselves. Let's just, like, respect each other's selves." Miranda's declaration that she receives "total fulfillment" from these nonsexual things and that "it is not a handicap" to be like her insists on the validity of her celibacy while simultaneously supporting Cyd's own path to "joy." Miranda's asexuality is shown as her own informed choice and conscious preference. *Princess Cyd*, in other words, offers viewers a world in which a spectrum of sexual desire—from nothing to "everything"—is normal and should be respected. In this way, perhaps *Princess Cyd* offers us a glimmer into a more open future for the genre—moving beyond the coming out trope for homosexual teens and instead presenting more varied depictions of adolescents exploring sex, playing with gender, and finding love stories across a range of sexualities.

NOTES

1. Ryan, "Why Did It Take So Long."
2. Ryan, "Why Did It Take So Long."
3. Rich, *New Queer Cinema*, 9.
4. Schoonover and Galt, *Queer Cinema*, 12.
5. Noreiga, "Something's Missing Here," 21.
6. Benshoff and Griffin, *Queer Images*, 9–11.
7. Schoonover and Galt, *Queer Cinema*, 8.
8. Fischer, "Queer and Feminist Approaches to Transgender Media Studies," 95.

9. Ann, Himberg, and Young, "Queer Approaches to Film," 118.
10. GLAAD, "Glossary of Terms: LGBTQ."
11. See Radi, "On Trans* Epistemology," and Fischer, "Queer and Feminist Approaches to Transgender Media Studies."
12. Benshoff and Griffin, *Queer Images*, 14.
13. Benshoff and Griffin, *Queer Images*, 14.
14. Schoonover and Galt, *Queer Cinema*.
15. Schoonover and Galt, *Queer Cinema*, 90.
16. Schoonover and Galt, *Queer Cinema*, 35.
17. Russo, *Celluloid Closet*, 219.
18. Rich, *New Queer Cinema*, 6.
19. Ringwald, "What about 'The Breakfast Club'?"
20. Russo, *Celluloid Closet*, 252.
21. Russo, *Celluloid Closet*, 88.
22. Conklin, *Campus Life in the Movies*, 112.
23. Ng, "Contesting the Queer Subfield of Cultural Production," 10.
24. Ryan, "Why Did It Take So Long."
25. Hughes, "Boy Wizards," 159.
26. Drushel, "Of Letters and Lists," 1.
27. GLAAD, "Observations & Recommendations." 2021.
28. GLAAD, "Observations & Recommendations." 2019.
29. In an interview, lead actress Ryan Destiny states that her character "was also confused as well with her being a lesbian or not being a lesbian." See Morales, "Exclusive."
30. Geminiyoungster, "Can We Talk."
31. LetterBoxd, "Reviews on a Girl Like Grace (2015)."
32. Another film to consider in this thread would be *First Girl I Loved* (2016), in which boy Clifton pursues intercourse with the clearly reluctant Anne after she has realized her attraction to a girl.
33. See also my 2021 essay "Exposing Flaws of Affirmative Consent through Contemporary American Teen Films."
34. "The APA Ruling."
35. UCLA School of Law, "Conversion Therapy."
36. Movement Advancement Project, "Equality Maps."
37. Conley, *Boy Erased*, 116.
38. Centers for Disease Control and Prevention, "National Intimate Partner and Sexual Violence Survey."
39. Conley, *Boy Erased*, 117.
40. Considine, *Cinema of Adolescence*, 10.
41. Beirne, "Teen Lesbian Desires," 267.
42. The directors of *Love, Simon*, *The Miseducation of Cameron Post*, *Alex Strangelove*, and others have self-identified as queer or homosexual in media coverage pertaining to their films.
43. Hereford, "In Depth Q&A."
44. Saito, "Interview."
45. Johnson, "Craig Johnson."
46. Centers for Disease Control and Prevention, "Infographic about LGB Teen Dating Violence Data."
47. Monaghan, "Not Just a Phase," 108.

FOUR

"I WAS NOT LOLITA"

Child Sexual Abuse and Children's Agency in *The Diary of a Teenage Girl* and *The Tale*

I was shy. I was skinny. I was short. I was underdeveloped. When I played Spin the Bottle, I was the girl everyone didn't want to kiss. I was not Lolita. So I drank in the attention he gave me.

—Jennifer Fox[1]

Does everyone think about fucking as much as I do?

—Minnie in *The Diary of a Teenage Girl* (2015)

Discussing her semiautobiographical film, *The Tale* (2018), writer/director Jennifer Fox explained how for over thirty years, she insisted her first sexual encounter at age thirteen with her coach, an adult man, was consensual. But while working on her docuseries *Flying: Confessions of a Free Woman* (2006–8), Fox interviewed women around the world and encountered a pattern: "every second woman wherever I was—beyond race, class, and color—had a childhood sexual abuse or rape story."[2] This revelation caused her to reexamine her "first relationship" as "sexual abuse," adding that she began to realize her "story wasn't personal and special at all, it was universal."[3] At the same time, Fox also repeatedly has asserted that she does not like the label "victim" because it implies the erasure of agency, stating in another interview, "I think the word victim scares me more than the event itself."[4] As a result, Fox sought a precarious balance in adapting her story for the fictional film *The Tale*—one that recognizes her perpetrators' exploitation of minors while validating the agency of herself as a child survivor. Fox's *The Tale* alongside writer/director Marielle Heller's *The Diary of a Teenage Girl* (2015) epitomizes a shifting depiction of child sexual abuse (CSA) stories in the twenty-first century. While not placing blame with the girls, these films present cisgender white girl CSA survivors who make clear choices and drive the interpretation of their stories, suggesting they are not simply victims to be pitied but resilient individuals with complex beliefs about their abuse.

In discussing her experiences, Fox asserts she was "not Lolita," delineating her child self apart from what has become culturally known as a Lolita—a girl "sexual child"[5] or "our favorite metaphor for a child vixen, a knowing coquette with an out-of-control libido, a baby nymphomaniac."[6] Lolita's name is similarly conjured in articles about *The Diary of a Teenage Girl* and Lone Scherfig's *An Education* (2009). Both these films, like *The Tale*, also have autobiographical roots. The screenplay for *An Education* by Nick Hornby derives from a 2003 autobiographical essay by Lynn Barber about her first sexual relationship with an adult man in the 1960s, and *The Diary of a Teenage Girl* is adapted from Phoebe Gloeckner's semiautobiographical 2002 graphic novel about her first sexual relationship as a teen with her mother's adult boyfriend in the 1970s. In articles and reviews of these films, Lolita supposedly exemplifies the antithesis of the girl protagonists. One *Script Magazine* writer posits that in *An Education*, "David seems very much in control as opposed to his Lolita being the one in control,"[7] and a Vulture writer talks to lead actress Casey Mulligan about "not playing a Lolita" in the film. Similarly in reviews of *The Diary of a Teenage Girl*, critics comment that unlike *Lolita* "the adolescent protagonist isn't the projection of lecherous fantasies,"[8] nor does the film "cleav[e] to a tired Lolita narrative."[9] In each of these cases, Lolita's name is conjured to be disavowed.

However, the concept of a "Lolita" suggests the perpetuation of a misunderstanding of Vladimir Nabokov's 1955 novel *Lolita*. Contemporary feminist readings of the novel commonly emphasize how the novel is not actually a tale of a flirtatious girl's seduction of her stepfather but rather a story of a predatory adult man who kidnaps, abuses, and rapes his stepdaughter. Within consent culture, Lolita is no Lolita either. However, in transforming Lolita into a victim, aspects of her agency are often erased, as if that were the only way to maintain her innocence. What both *The Tale* and *The Diary of a Teenage Girl* present, however, is more complex; the films highlight the exploitation of the girl protagonists by adults without denying the girls authority over the choices they make amid their abuse. Such a formulation warrants a new way of thinking about Lolita and the girls like her—as neither simply "precocious" girls nor victims of abuse but rather a much more nuanced figure. And in fact, this seeming incongruity more closely mirrors a key premise embedded in

Lolita: a prepubescent girl can be sexually curious or even desirous *as* she is exploited and abused.

THE CSA MOVEMENT, SEXUAL AGENCY, AND CONSENT CULTURE

Although there are numerous definitions of CSA, it is commonly referred to as any "sexual activity with a minor."[10] The US Center for Disease Control and Prevention (CDC) defines CSA as "the involvement of a child (person less than 18 years old) in sexual activity that violates the laws or social taboos of society."[11] CSA incorporates not only intercourse but also other types of abuse such as sexual contact, exposure, prostitution, trafficking, and child pornography. There also can be overlap between CSA and what is defined as statutory rape, or "sexual intercourse with a person who has not yet reached the age of consent (determined by state law), whether or not the sexual act is against that person's will."[12] Although federally anyone under the age of eighteen is considered a minor or child, individual US states can still set their own age of consent. Over the last several decades, there has been increasing uniformity of the age of consent across the United States, and it currently ranges from ages sixteen to eighteen in all states—with some "close in age" exceptions.[13] Today, CSA is understood as a widespread problem that affects millions of children. One in four girls and one in thirteen boys experience CSA, and studies often cite how it is an adverse childhood experience (ACE) that impacts "how a person thinks, acts, and feels over a lifetime, resulting in short- and long-term physical and mental/emotional health consequences."[14] The majority of current research around CSA focuses on national and international policies, prevention, impacts, and treatment for survivors.

Girls in particular have been deemed at risk for CSA. In the 2007 "Report of the American Psychology Association (APA) Task Force on the Sexualization of Girls," the authors argue that for girls, CSA is "an extreme form of sexualization, one that always involves both sexual objectification and the inappropriate imposition of sexuality."[15] The report outlines how "sexual abuse victimization" can lead to "risky," "precocious," or "inappropriate" sexual behavior among girls. Although the authors clearly seek to recognize how "girls are fully capable of agency and resistance," they simultaneously acknowledge that "the surrounding cultural milieu ... and, for some girls, their experiences of childhood sexual abuse victimization" cause them to "participate in and contribute to their own sexualization."[16] Since the publication of the report, numerous adolescent sexuality scholars—including several of the report's authors—have sought to refine ways of locating and identifying the sexual agency of girls. For example, Sharon Lamb and Zoë D. Peterson presented their conflicting and overlapping views on girls' sexual empowerment in a joint essay. While Lamb argues that girls' choices are highly constrained by a "sexuality that's highly marketed to girls," Peterson articulates a concern about "prioritizing an 'expert' view of empowerment over girls' own subjective sense of empowerment."[17] What they agree on is how "girls frequently experience ambivalence and uncertainty about their sexual wants and desires" and the assertion that, "To deny or pathologize that ambivalence is harmful to girls."[18] Another report author Deborah Tolman too asks, "At a time when sexual agency itself has been objectified.... how can we understand adolescent women's claims of sexual empowerment?"[19] Tolman recommends that we avoid "diagnosing" girls or assuming their "words are true narrations or false ones," but rather recognize "what they say constitutes ways of making sense and telling a coherent story in an already over-determined discursive theatre."[20] In other words, most contemporary girls' sexuality researchers acknowledge the uncomfortable ambiguities of agency and multifaceted negotiations of consent in girls' sexual interactions.

If consent and sexual agency are elusive for girls, they are even more so for those who experience CSA—approximately a quarter of all US women/girls. To understand how girls might develop their sexuality alongside their abuse, Judith Butler's theory of subjectivity, as outlined in *The Psychic Life of Power: Theories in Subjection* provides a useful framework. According to Butler, the subject is both "the condition for and instrument of agency" while "at the same time the effect of subordination, understood as the deprivation of agency."[21] This contradiction implies that agency emerges within subordination, as Butler states, "The subject might yet be thought as deriving its agency from precisely the power it opposes, as awkward and embarrassing as such a formulation might be, especially for those who believe that complicity and ambivalence could be rooted out once and for all."[22] Thus, survivors of CSA might develop their sexual agency despite and within their abuse, as their sexuality matures amid an introductory experience with their abusers. Ultimately, CSA survivors must make sense of their sexual selves and stories, in part, through their abuse.

Agency, as Laina Y. Bay-Cheng puts it, is a "given: universally and continuously exercised by all sentient beings."[23] A more descriptive definition of sexual agency by Marianne Cense incorporates four components—embodied agency, bonded agency, narrative agency, and moral agency. *Embodied agency* is what we typically imagine as sexual agency—the development of sexual subjectivity and enactment of sexual practices. However, Cense offers more nuance for the term *agency* by incorporating these three other components: *bonded agency* as the "strategies, actions and negotiations involved in maintaining relationships and navigating broader social expectations"; *narrative agency* as "the accounts young people give of themselves and others about their choices and their lives"; and *moral agency* as "the reflection upon and positioning oneself within moral frameworks."[24] Ultimately, Cense acknowledges how, "The concept of choice itself is problematic"—an admission often echoed in other research conceptualizing agency.[25] Still this more varied framework allows us to view agency not only as sexual actions or choices within constrained environments, but also as ways youth seek out and maintain support systems and interpret and reshape the stories of their experiences.

It was not until the 1970s/1980s that CSA came to be recognized as a widespread issue worthy of public attention and policy in the United States. Before then, accounts of CSA were routinely dismissed as normative or flatly denied as false. In Kinsey's own groundbreaking sex research in the 1940s and 1950s, he suggested that the only reason a child might be "disturbed at having [their] genitalia touched, or disturbed at seeing the genitalia of other persons" is "public hysteria."[26] Still, he recognized that women in his study who had "preadolescent" sexual encounters with adults experienced a range of responses— "interested, curious, pleased, embarrassed, frightened, terrified, or disturbed with feelings of guilt."[27] In the 1960s and 1970s, the sexual liberation movement, which sought to relieve society of sexual taboos, emphasized the acceptability of intragenerational sex. However, with this quest came further denial of the existence of CSA—if children were sexual beings and sex could be devoid of its cultural and emotional significance, then intragenerational sex could not be seen as an abusive act perpetrated by adults.

Of course, not all were uniformly on board with these beliefs, and a significant backlash by both feminists and right-wing conservatives followed in the 1970s and 1980s. By 1981, when Judith Lewis Herman published the results of a multiyear study in the book *Father-Daughter Incest*, incest had "been rediscovered as a major social problem."[28] In 1984, Jeffrey Moussaieff Masson published *The Assault on Truth: Freud's Suppression of the Seduction Theory* arguing that Freud had buried his initial discovery of CSA a century earlier because of criticism from the medical community. Although Masson has been accused of oversimplifying both Freud's work and his reasons for forsaking his own theory, *The Assault on Truth* impacted the public discourse around CSA and what would become known as "recovered memory" (the uncovering, often in therapy, of repressed memories of abuse) alongside accusations of "false memory" (the fabrication of imagined traumatic events also often through therapy). Masson's book brought mainstream attention to the fact that in the 1890s, Freud had stumbled on the ubiquity of CSA in working with neurotic patients. Publishing his findings in several papers and presenting a lecture in Vienna titled "The Aetiology of Hysteria" in 1896, Freud described how his patients had been traumatized by CSA. But a little more than a year later, he renounced his own postulation in a personal letter to his friend Wilhelm Fliess.

Why Freud changed his mind has been the subject of much critical debate—his views might have been unpopular or disbelieved, and they might have threatened his patient relationships and source of income. Many argue that the exposure of widespread CSA had the potential to undermine, even destroy, the cultural authority of father figures. Others contend that he simply realized that aspects of his research could not be supported, particularly when he discovered not all survivors of CSA had been traumatized. Whatever the reason, in a letter on September 21, 1897, Freud denied the possibility of these "widespread perversions against children" particularly by their fathers.[29] Freud ultimately found a new theory to explain his findings of CSA. Over the next several years, Freud converted his patient testimonies of abusive episodes into psychoanalytic theories of "seduction-phantasies," or unfulfilled sexual desires of children for their parents. What he initially categorized as "traumatic memories of sexual assault," he later changed to "fantasies of seduction."[30] For example, in one of his most (in)famous cases, *Dora: An Analysis of a Case of Hysteria* (1905), Freud believes that Dora's reports of sexual advances by their family friend Herr K represent Dora's own repressed longings. Although he never openly disavowed his findings of sexual interactions between children and adults, he rerouted them into his theories of the Oedipus complex, psychosexual development, dreams, and the human psyche. Freud's abandoned discovery became labeled "seduction theory," an unfortunate moniker that has stuck despite how it fails to encompass the CSA revealed through his initial hypothesis.

Nearly a century after Freud first shared and changed his theory of sexual abuse, the US media had begun to acknowledge how common CSA was. The widespread attention on CSA during this period has been labeled a long-overdue reckoning by some and a moral panic by others. In 1974, the United States enacted the Child Abuse Prevention and Treatment Act (CAPTA), federal legislation to prevent, investigate, and prosecute child abuse across the country. The CAPTA, which has been renewed and revised numerous times since, focuses not only on childhood sexual abuse but also all types of child abuse and neglect. The focus on CSA during the 1970s and 1980s directly led to legislation, education, and advocacy intended to protect children from adult harm alongside an unprecedented cultural concern over child abductors, molesters, and pedophiles. Possibly due to mandatory reporting laws, an explosion of reported cases of child abuse and neglect occurred between 1976 and 1986—from 669,000 to over 2 million—and it is unclear how many of the 60 percent that remained "unfounded" were false accusations or simply could not be proven.[31] In any case, since the 1980s, Freud's revised theory that children desired adults has become seen as increasingly preposterous—the current understanding is that only adults can desire and exploit children, not the other way around.

In the past few decades, the unveiling of adult men who have leveraged their power to abuse women and children has given further credence to not only the ubiquity of abuse but also the prevalence of cover-ups. In 2002, *The Boston Globe* published its "Spotlight Investigation: Abuse in the Catholic Church," which exposed the sexual abuse of children by priests over many years and the corresponding concealment by the church's hierarchy up through cardinals (one level below the pope). And when Jeffrey Epstein was indicted on sex trafficking charges in 2019, media reports highlighted that despite an FBI investigation upon his initial 2005 alleged sex trafficking of young girls, Epstein was able to arrange a light sentence in 2007 via a favorable plea bargain with Miami's federal prosecutor Alexander Acosta.

Still, the public outcry over CSA at times has appeared misdirected. In *Erotic Innocence: The Culture of Child Molesting*, James R. Kincaid argues how within public discourse, "The eroticizing of children is blamed on somebody else, as if it were an accidental and freakish thing we could wipe out by being sufficiently sanctimonious."[32] Rather, Kincaid argues, our society has consistently eroticized youth, stating, "We see children as, among other things, sweet, innocent, vacant, smooth-skinned, spontaneous, and mischievous. We construct the desirable as, among other things, sweet, innocent, vacant, smooth-skinned, spontaneous, and mischievous." This overlap suggests that the problem is not merely "out there" but embedded within our culture. Kincaid notes, "To the extent that we learn to see 'the child' and 'the erotic' as coincident, we are in trouble. So are the children."[33] Numerous legal scholars too have argued that legislative focus on a child molester/pedophile stranger diverts attention from actual perpetrators of CSA—adults familiar to and trusted by the child.[34]

An insistence on childhood innocence is important in the context of abuse; however, it risks erasing the concept of childhood sexuality itself.[35] As Jacqueline Rose states, "The child victim is desexualized—necessarily—for there does not seem to be a readily available language in which one can talk of childhood sexuality and insist on the reality of child sexual abuse at the same time."[36] If to be a child, or one under the age of consent, means to be free from sexual motives and agency, then *any* sexuality expressed in childhood is presumed perverse and the result of the corruption of adults. In the book *The Fear of Child Sexuality: Young People, Sex, and Agency*, Steven Angelides argues that the "discourse of child sexual abuse ... expanded at the expense of a discourse on child sexuality."[37] Angelides echoes critiques raised by others like Kincaid and Eve Kosofsky Sedgwick, arguing that despite "admirable efforts to protect and empower children from the harmful consequences of abuse," the accompanying moratorium on openly discussing child sexuality has ironically "disempowered" children.[38] Cultural anxieties over protecting children have led to extensive US child pornography laws that have curtailed depictions of adolescent sexuality and erased those of younger children's sexuality. Not surprisingly, such fears also have significantly constrained representations of CSA—until recently.

REFRAMING *LOLITA* AS A CHILD SEXUAL ABUSE STORY

The shift in mainstream perception of CSA elicited feminist rereadings of *Lolita* in the 1980s. Much like Freud's concealment of child abuse, the novel *Lolita* was initially misinterpreted as a love story instead of a story of abuse. As a result, for decades, a widespread misreading of the book persisted—one in which some readers seemed to believe Humbert's declaration, "It was she who seduced me." Consequently, a Lolita became equated with "a precociously seductive girl," a dictionary definition that remains today even as Merriam-Webster acknowledges it has "strayed from its original referent."[39] In offering "a brief history of the nymphet's tribulations," Luke Sayers even suggests that "reviewers who defended *Lolita* the book often did so at the expense of Lolita the girl."[40] If Lolita was a sexual agent "or guilty," Sayers suggests, then "one could not accuse the book of titillating its readers with rape."[41] One had to read precocity into Lolita to avoid seeing the novel as obscene.

Lolita hit a nerve when it was released in the 1950s for many reasons. However, in retrospect, it seems what might have been most transgressive about *Lolita* was not the older man's sexual desire for a young girl or the book's sexual content but rather the depiction of the father figure as a pedophile who threatens both the girl and the family structure. Although discussing the 1962 film version not the novel, Kristen Hatch best summarizes how *Lolita* cut to the core of "fears about the decline of the patriarchal family." Hatch notes that "whereas once the father was understood to guide a girl's sexual development, he is now perceived as vulnerable to her sexualized image; no longer able to protect the bourgeois family from the corrupting influences of the world at large; he is now prone to them."⁴² In another reading of the novel, Jen Shelton too suggests that "the existence of father-daughter incest reveals something unsettling about a culture based on paternal authority," and Shelton quotes the 1981 book *Father-Daughter Incest*, where Herman writes that father-daughter incest "represents an exaggeration of patriarchal norms, not a departure from them."⁴³ Such exploitation of girls by their fathers and father figures undermines the idea that "father knows best" and threatens to reveal the dark side of paternal authority.

Of course, the controversy over the publication of *Lolita* in the 1950s did not explicitly touch on such concerns. When Nabokov finished *Lolita* in 1953, no US publisher would "touch it," and one editor went as far as suggesting "anyone who published it risked being fined or jailed."⁴⁴ So Nabokov looked to Europe, and in 1955, the "pornographic publishing house" Olympia Press published the book in France.⁴⁵ A few years later, in 1958, G. P. Putnam's Sons released the book in the United States. Despite some US reviewers who accused *Lolita* of being "highbrow pornography," most argued it was "not obscene."⁴⁶ Ultimately, *Lolita* would come to be known as "one of the greatest novels of the twentieth century."⁴⁷ It would inspire two film adaptations, one in 1962 by Stanley Kubrick and another in 1997 by Adrian Lyne, as well as countless iterations and references in film, TV, media, and popular culture.

By the 1980s, feminist scholars launched a reinvestigation of the novel to acknowledge the layers of abuse by Humbert in his relationship with Lolita. These critiques not only point out that Lolita was a child without the ability to consent and nowhere else to go but also emphasize how nonconsent emerges clearly through Lolita's accusations in the novel, such as "the word is incest"⁴⁸ or "the hotel where you raped me";⁴⁹ her names for Humbert, including "brute"; and her demeanor, such as when Humbert describes Lolita as "the small ghost of somebody I had just killed."⁵⁰ In pondering why the definition of Lolita is not "a molested adolescent girl" instead of a "seductive" one, scholars have pointed to a "misogynistic" society and "patriarchal culture" that silences and invalidates the experiences and perspectives of women and girls.⁵¹ As this revisionist reading took hold, Lolita the character could no longer be conjured without imagining Lolita the girl. Furthering this association, in 2018, Sarah Weinman published *The Real Lolita: The Kidnapping of Sally Horner and the Novel That Scandalized the World* arguing that the abduction of eleven-year-old Sally Horner by Frank LaSalle in 1948 was the "real-life case" that inspired Nabokov's novel.

Within consent culture, certainly, Humbert's abuse, not Lolita's seductiveness, has become seen as the driving force behind the story, and Lolita is now understood as a victim of CSA. Any consent on Lolita's part is invalid since incest and statutory rape are illegal and immoral, and the adult is always the perpetrator in such cases. However, this reconfiguration, too, comes at the expense of Lolita, the character and the girl. She transforms from sexual perpetrator to sexual victim, and in the exchange, it becomes no longer ethical to imagine any of her sexual curiosity and desire.[52]

ADULT-ADOLESCENT RELATIONSHIPS IN FILM

In the 1940s through the 1960s, Hollywood routinely cast young actresses like Lauren Bacall and Audrey Hepburn in romances with much older men, and as late as the 1980s, high school girls still were depicted in relationships with men decades older in films like *Manhattan* (1979) and *Blame It on Rio* (1984). The 1990s exhibited more confusion over whether girls were dangerous sexual predators who could destroy the lives of older men—*Poison Ivy* (1992), *The Crush* (1993), *Poison Ivy II* (1996), and *Election* (1999)—or innocent victims endangered by older men, as in *Cape Fear* (1991), *Fear* (1996), and *Strangeland* (1998). Although films about CSA and incest became more common in the 1990s, ambivalence still manifested in the coverage of Amy Fisher, the "Long Island Lolita" who as a teenager had a sexual relationship with the married thirty-eight-year-old Joey Buttafuoco. When Fisher shot his wife, Mary Jo Buttafuoco, in 1992, the story made nationwide headlines and continued to do so as details emerged, including Fisher's sex work, which began after her relationship with Joey. Fisher's story inspired three TV movies in 1992 and 1993 (*Amy Fisher: My Story*, *The Amy Fisher Story*, and *Casualties of Love: The Long Island Lolita Story*)—one from Fisher's point of view, one from a journalist's, and another from the Buttafuocos'. While Fisher's version painted her as a victim led astray by the adult Joey, the Buttafuocos' portrayed her as a predator who wreaked havoc on their family. In several of the narratives and media coverage, alleged abuse by Fisher's father and a workman at the house also provided an explanation for either her further victimization or her supposed deviance—depending on the standpoint. A decade later, a teen like Fisher would have garnered both more public sympathy via consent culture and legal protection through the Victims of Trafficking and Violence Protection Act of 2000 (TVPA), but in the early 1990s, Fisher's status as a victim was up for interpretation and public debate.

The awakening to the exploitation of girls is exemplified in a film that literally changed the script—*American Beauty* (1999) about middle-aged Lester's obsession with his teenaged daughter's classmate Angela. Instead of Angela's losing her virginity to Lester as planned in the original screenplay, the film depicts Lester's retreat the moment he has the girl consenting and undressed. Lester stares at Angela's naked breasts, and she confesses, "This is my first time." Her admission snaps Lester abruptly out of his reverie—he cannot continue to see her as a sexual conquest after this statement. He covers her with a blanket, changing his demeanor from an older man who wants to possess the girl to the father figure who seeks to protect her. While *American Beauty* depicts numerous fantasy scenes where Lester (and arguably the film itself) objectifies the girl, ultimately it rejects the idea that an adult man can ethically consummate a relationship with a teen girl, no matter how willing.

It's worth noting that a similar concern has not always extended to teen boys and older women. The same year *American Beauty* was released, *American Pie* (1999) depicted a young man enthusiastically and unproblematically losing his virginity to his friend's mother—a sex comedy plot that had been largely eliminated for girls/adult men at least a decade earlier. In 2004, Jonathan Glazer's *Birth* even depicted the story of an adult woman who falls in love with a ten-year-old boy after he convinces her that he is her reincarnated husband. Although the film, which includes a scene of the two naked in the bathtub, was often described as in "poor taste," it was generally not framed as a CSA story by the media, perhaps because the two have no physical contact. Then in 2011, the independent comedy *Cougars, Inc.* depicted several teen boys having sex with and launching an escort service with older women. More recently, however, there has been pushback on teen boy/adult women relationships. Hannah Fidell's 2013 film *A Teacher*, for example, portrayed the downward spiral of a relationship between a woman teacher and a high school boy. The film was adapted into the 2020 television series *A Teacher*, which features sexual abuse warnings at the start and end of each episode. However, casting works against an interpretation of this story as CSA since the student Eric, who is seventeen and turns eighteen during their relationship, is also played by Nick Robinson at age twenty-five. Furthermore, with the age of consent at least seventeen in most US states and the definition of an adult as eighteen, this story feels forced as a CSA story, or as one reviewer argues, it "seldom . . . feels like a cautionary tale."[53] In retrospect, *The Graduate* (1967) offers a much more compelling depiction of a young man's abuse by an adult woman. Nonetheless, the obvious pivot in *A Teacher* to insist on such a story as abuse represents a considerable cultural change from even a few years earlier in that it signals a belief that older teen boys can be victims of adults.

By the aughts, it became increasingly untenable to depict older men and girls' relationships as light romances or to paint girls unambiguously as seductresses. With the rise of consent culture, it became widely accepted that minors could not consent legally or ethically to sexual relationships with adults. Thus, the die had been cast for these stories with the adult man as predator and the young girl as victim. By 2005, *Hard Candy* embodied the rage at child abusers in a film about a fourteen-year-old girl who catches and tortures a pedophilic adult man. Yet while consent culture has warranted a strict dichotomy between victim and perpetrator, a few independent films have offered a new formulation—one in which girls might be understood as not either survivors or agents, but both. Two such films, *The Diary of a Teenage Girl* and *The Tale*, grant more intricacies to CSA stories, validating girls' choices alongside their exploitation by adults and offering a revised perspective on how girls derive agency through their abuse.

BECOMING THE "HERO"—AGENCY AND RESILIENCY IN *THE TALE*

Over the ten years that Jennifer Fox spent writing *The Tale*, she never deliberated over whether her story should be documentary or fiction. As she put it, there were not enough facts, only memories. Still, she researched her own story like an investigative journalist. She interviewed her coaches, her mom, and the other girls (now adults) in her riding program; she dug out old photographs; and she pored over her own letters, journals, and other writings from when she was a girl. Early on, she knew she would need to reveal the film as an adaptation of her own personal story—she felt her testimony needed to accompany the film for it to be believed. Without that, she feared people would say, "You're making it up. It can't be like that. A little girl can't love the man who abuses her. Memory doesn't work like that." But she knew that it does.

In the beginning of *The Tale*, Jennifer's mother finds a short story written by her daughter at age thirteen that recounts her CSA by her adult coach. Her mother's shock and distress propel the forty-something Jennifer (Laura Dern) to investigate what she had simply called her "first relationship." After talking to her mother, she recalls through a flashback sequence herself as an assured girl who declares, "I always wanted to have a story to tell, but nothing ever happened to me." However, after Jennifer reconnects with an old friend from her riding program, her memory of herself is contested. Her friend recalls, "You were such a tiny little thing—so much smaller than Franny and I. You almost looked like a little boy . . . so afraid, you barely said two words." Jennifer's surprise and confusion at her friend's words prompts her to rush to her mother's house in search of photos from the summer of 1973 when her relationship with Bill started. When she finds the photo of herself at thirteen, she says stunned, "I was so little." Thus, she must re-remember the beginning of that summer—this time, not with the mature and confident Jenny she first imagined but rather the unsure, quiet thirteen-year-old Jenny (played by then eleven-year-old Isabelle Nélisse), who now says in her more wavering child's voice, "I always wanted to have a story to tell, but nothing ever happened to me." Already, we see the discrepancy between what happened and the tale Jennifer has been telling herself for the past three decades.

Jenny is one of five children in her family, which makes her feel "invisible" and means her parents, as she puts it, "barely noticed if I wasn't there." So, it is not surprising later when Jenny eagerly welcomes the personal attention of her future abusers. Jenny's story begins the summer she spends with Mrs. G (aka Jane) to learn horseback riding with a few other girls. There, Mrs. G introduces the girls to her friend Bill as their running coach. On the last night of the program, Jenny's parents are unable to pick her up on time. So, Mrs. G and Bill take Jenny to dinner alone. Bill invites Jenny to be part of a fall running program, saying, "You've got talent and more importantly, you've got guts. Without guts, talent is wasted." When Jenny says sadly, "It's just so hard to leave," Bill comforts her, telling her that she'll be all right and should write to them anytime she wants. Bill then confides in Jenny, "We want us all to be equals, and we respect you too much to lie so we want you to know that Jane and I are lovers." When Jenny says, "I'm happy for you. I'm happy you have each other. I don't want you to be miserable like my parents," Bill says to Mrs. G, "I told you she has a deep soul." This secret serves as a test that proves Jenny's fidelity to the couple against her own parents and other adults. Jenny thinks to herself, "How did they know they could trust me with their secret, that I would never break their confidence? The other girls would've told on them. I would never tell my parents or the other adults. It was like an unspoken oath, and I felt proud of it." After the summer program ends, Jenny keeps her horse at Mrs. G's which enables her to spend weekends there, a time she describes as "pure bliss. It was heaven. I was home." The two adults continue grooming her through flattery, and at one point Bill says, "Your parents can't accept that you're becoming a woman. They can't see you the way we can." One night, when Mrs. G must rush home to make Mr. G's dinner, Bill invites Jenny to stay for dinner and possibly the night. Jenny looks nervous, as Mrs. G says, "It's not up to me. Jenny can make her own mind up."

Because Fox's film is as much about the unreliability of memory as it is about CSA, Jenny's response at this moment remains ambiguous. The film pits the points of view of the thirteen-year-old Jenny against the adult Jennifer. As an adult, Jennifer desperately wants to know if she consented in this moment. She thinks, "What did I say? I don't remember. I must have said something. I only remember them. Why don't I remember myself? Did I say yes?" Her thoughts culminate in a direct conversation with herself as a girl. Adult Jennifer asks, "Why would you do that?" to which young Jenny responds, "Well it's my life. I can make my own decisions." When Jennifer suggests that what Jenny writes in the story later is that she doesn't want to be there, Jenny responds, "That's just a fiction story. . . . Bill is not going to hurt me." When Jennifer pushes back, saying, "What if you're wrong?" Jenny gets angry, saying, "Stop! You've become just like all of them. You just want to tell me what to do. It's my life not yours. Let me live." Jennifer again asks, "What if you're wrong?" and this time the question goes unanswered. As it turns out, this critical "decision" leads to the first instance of CSA. After reading poetry together, Bill tells Jenny, "I want to save you from all those stupid young boys out there. I think you are perfect," and he asks her to take her shirt off. Hesitant at first, Jenny complies, and Bill tells her, "I've been preparing for this moment. I don't think we should tell Mrs. G about us. I don't think she's quite ready." As an audience, we know where this is headed. Jenny, however, might not.

Watching this film in the context of consent culture, there is no way to read the relationship with Bill and Jenny as consensual. Her saying "yes" in this or any other moment appears completely irrelevant—she is a child, and he is an adult, so the only way to view this interaction is as sexual abuse. What happened is not her fault any more than it feels that it could have been her choice. Still, Fox masterfully keeps the child's voice active throughout this pivotal scene and the entire film so that it is simply not possible to see the child's point of view as invalid or irrelevant. In the film's conversations between child Jenny and adult Jennifer, we are forced to contend with the inability of any adult to understand completely the child's experience. Jennifer cannot even understand her own past motives—already she has crossed over and become "one of them" as Jenny puts it. Thus, Fox suggests that to dismiss Jenny's experience as a victimization in which Jenny plays no role, makes no choices, and has no agency is to make the mistake of denying the subjectivity of the girl—one that the girl herself insists on maintaining before and after her abuse.

As they begin a sexual relationship, Bill tells Jenny that they have to keep "stretching" her open slowly and that "no young boy would ever do this for you." In one scene, after determining that she's not ready for intercourse, he guides her head down so she can perform fellatio on him. Later when they do have intercourse, Bill tells her, "Just a little while longer and it will be over, and it will never hurt again." His visible pleasure is countered by her discomfort and pain. Afterward, he tells her, "Now you are a woman, my love," and she smiles. Next, she is in the bathroom vomiting. Fox here depicts CSA more viscerally than most films—and she clarifies in interviews that Nélisse's part in these scenes was shot with a body double or with her alone on a vertical bed.[54] Fox surrounds these disturbing scenes with voices from Jenny's past—Mrs. G's declaring, "Do you know how lucky you were to have a teacher like Bill? I never had anyone like him," or Bill's confession that "no adult can love like that—only children can," or Jenny herself saying, "I find that I trust him so much. I never realize where he's leading me. Once we're that far, I don't know how to say no." As a viewer, we clearly see Bill and Mrs. G's grooming, manipulating, and exploiting Jenny. Consequently, our viewpoint might mirror the adult Jennifer's boyfriend who discovers the nature of her relationship with Bill and bluntly states, "That's rape. That's illegal" and calls her the "victim." But even adult Jennifer does not accept the label victim, telling her boyfriend and vicariously us as the audience, "I am not a victim. I don't need you or anybody to call me a victim because you have no fucking clue about my life." Here, we see that Jenny the child still even maintains an active voice in adult Jennifer.

The Tale accomplishes what most films about CSA do not—Fox never erases or overwrites the child's point of view. Through her investigation into her past abuse, Jennifer recalls how Mrs. G and Bill ultimately had planned a foursome with Jenny and a college student, Iris. Having lied to her parents about going away for the weekend with them for a road race, Jenny wakes up severely ill the morning she is set to leave. Her mother finds her vomiting in the bathroom and tells her daughter they will have to cancel. Jenny thinks, "My body had told me what my mind refused to accept. I'm tired, so tired, tired in ways that I'm afraid. The fear is a fear of a broken dream. I have made a decision." The spell has been broken—and Jenny comes to terms with the fact that these adults are not what she thought them to be. In one imagined conversation with Bill, Jennifer says, "I hoped you would save me from my family," and Bill responds, "Didn't I?" Of course, rather than saving her from her family, Bill exploited her because of it under the pretense of saving her. Jenny's family also does not protect her from Bill and Mrs. G. Although her mother forbids Jenny from going out with a boy her own age, she later rebukes herself for having "failed at the one thing a mother's supposed to do." Even Jenny's grandmother's witnessing Bill and Jenny kiss goes unreported to her parents, and when her mother does suspect Bill at one point, Jenny's father disregards it, criticizing his wife for always seeing "the worst" in people.

The "decision" that Jenny makes after her body's revolt is to end her relationship with Bill and Mrs. G. She secretly calls Bill and tells him, "I don't want to see you anymore." At first, Bill asks, "Is it your parents?" to which Jenny repeats, "I don't want to see you anymore." Bill then cries, pleading, "But Jenny, please I love you. I need you. We can work everything out. Please just... please don't leave me." Jenny declares, "I'm going to hang up now," and she does. She then calls Mrs. G to inform her that she'll be coming to pick up her horse that weekend, to which Mrs. G simply says, "Fine" and hangs up muttering, "stupid girl, stupid, stupid girl." Jenny's decisive action to end the relationship clearly contrasts with the ambiguity in how it began, and it establishes her as her own sole protector. Jenny is not saved by the intervention of adults; she saves herself. Consequently, Jenny sees herself as the primary actor or "hero" of her "story," and in a culminating scene, Jenny walks down a school hallway defiantly looking into the camera as she responds to Jennifer's questions and criticisms:

> **Jennifer**: You lied to me. You told me it was a good thing all these years.
> **Jenny**: It was. You want me to be some pathetic victim. Well, you know what, I'm not. I've got something no one else does. *I'm* the teacher now, not just some invisible kid.
> **Jennifer**: You'll never get married.
> **Jenny**: I don't want to get married. Have you not been listening to me?
> **Jennifer**: You'll never have children.
> **Jenny**: I hate children. I don't want to have children. I'm sure of that. But I know one thing—he loved me. He cried. He cried. Didn't you see? And for years, he's going to send me cards. You see—I'm not the victim of this story. I'm the hero. He fell apart, not me.
> **Jennifer**: You couldn't even think that their lives might continue without you, that there would be others. You froze them in time. But you know, he's still alive, and I'm going to go see him now.
> **Jenny**: No!

As Jenny cries no, the camera pulls back, making her smaller and more powerless. Ultimately, as potent as child Jenny's voice is, this scene reminds us that the story is now adult Jennifer's to reinterpret and tell. Throughout the film we observe adult Jennifer's strained sexual intimacy with her boyfriend and her avoidance of commitment, attributes that could suggest negative impacts of CSA. And Jennifer does ultimately come to see the abusive aspects of her relationship with Bill. Still, Jennifer's self-criticisms about who she is now—an unmarried woman without children—fail to move Jenny who has clearly articulated how she does not want to be anything like her own mother.

Fox's inclusion of Jenny's bold point of view in this scene and throughout the film is indelible. The girl's insistence, "I'm not the victim of this story. I'm the hero," simply cannot be dismissed. In the denouement of the film, adult Jennifer confronts Bill telling him, "I wanted you to know I hated every minute of it," and asking him, "What happened to you that you would do that to me?" After

Bill predictably denies the abuse and his wife calls for security, a series of cuts show how shaken up Jennifer is as she alternates between crying and laughing in the bathroom. After Jennifer retreats to the corner with her head hung low, child Jenny appears and calmly wets a paper towel to hand to adult Jennifer. As Jenny's voiceover of the beginning of her short story comes through ("I'd like to begin this story by telling you something so beautiful. I've met two very special people. . . ."), Jennifer and Jenny sit side by side on the floor of the bathroom. Jennifer looks ahead with furrowed brows, as Jenny looks up at her somewhat expectantly and sympathetically. Undoubtedly, Jennifer now has fully come to terms with the abusive aspects of her first relationship—along with Bill's denial. But child Jenny remains with her, not only to contest her adult vantage point, but also to provide a source of comfort to her adult self. Jennifer might feel torn apart by her abuse, but Jenny is resilient and determined to believe in her agency. Jennifer might feel "damaged," but Jenny insists that she was the "hero."[55]

In adapting her story for the screen, Fox recalls how she "rediscovered" this childhood voice in researching and writing the film. She explains, "In the investigation to write the script, I realized that I actually didn't know who I was at thirteen anymore. I had crossed over and become an adult." Fox decided to include imagined interviews to give her girl self a voice, saying "everywhere I turned" from diaries to letters to poetry, she found her thirteen-year-old self, "knew what she wanted, knew what she thought, was making choices even if they were bad choices, they were her choices. And she definitely had a sense of agency. And the adults around her from her thirteen-year-old point of view were incredibly inept or abusive."[56] In other interviews, Fox insists on the importance of recognizing the child's agency, saying, "By putting the word 'victim' on a child or even an adult, you take away agency. And even though, technically, I had little agency because I was too young, the false . . . belief that you have agency is what keeps us alive and keeps us actually surviving and going beyond trauma. So when you make a child a victim, you destroy the thread that they have to get out of suffering."[57] For Fox, "agency" is essential to controlling one's story as a survivor.

Recalling Marianne Cense's multifaceted description of sexual agency, which encompasses embodied agency, bonded agency, narrative agency, and moral agency, allows us to better understand the stakes for a CSA survivor's controlling their story. Cense says, "One of the narrative challenges for young women lies in negotiating stories of subordination of women, female vulnerability, and dependency as well as stories of responsibility and individual agency."[58] In claiming her hero status, Jenny both mistakes her abuse as empowerment and empowers herself via her abuse. This paradox is not uncommon

Fig. 4.1. Jennifer Fox's *The Tale* gives voice to both grown-up Jennifer (Laura Dern) and child Jenny (Isabelle Nélisse).

for young girls, as Bay-Cheng notes, "Young women's covering or reframing of their victimization might serve adaptive, self-protective functions insofar as they buffer against perpetual feelings of fear and powerlessness."[59] Jenny's story offers her protection as a child and as an adult. Research on CSA survivors supports Fox's sentiments. In "A Review of Child Sexual Abuse: Impact, Risk, and Resilience in the Context of Culture," the authors find that "cognitive coping strategies associated with resilience to CSA include self-enhancing cognitive reappraisals, disclosure and discussion of the abuse, positive reframing, and refusing to dwell on the abuse."[60] In other words, the type of reframing that Jenny applies to her abuse is not merely a delusion; it is an effective coping strategy. In believing herself the "hero," Jenny affords herself a "locus of control" that the authors note "significantly predict[s] resilience to negative mental health outcomes associated with CSA," and she resists "trauma related beliefs such as self-blame, self-stigmatization, betrayal, powerlessness, and traumatic sexualization" which are "negatively related to resilience."[61] Instead of viewing herself as a powerless victim, Jenny insists on herself as the primary actor who makes clear choices. And in ending the relationship, Jenny further harnesses her own agency, self-preservation, and resiliency in response to her abuse.

Fox places the child's perspective literally side by side with the adult's to prove that one is not more valid than the other. Fox states that at the end she wants viewers to "understand that both stories are true and both stories exist simultaneously," adding, "We don't usually let our child's voice exist as adults; we have to squash the voice of our girl self or our boy self in order to assert our adulthood. In fact, it's dangerous to do that for our own development, because we're basically erasing who we were."[62] Jenny's voice thus becomes integral to our understanding of this story of CSA. Recognizing Jenny's relationship with Bill as abusive does not mean denying how the child viewed herself as an actor within the relationship. When her mother asks her at one point, "Did you like it?" Jennifer responds, "Mom. I was a kid. Why are you asking me that?" Her mother explains, "I just don't understand—why did you keep going back?" Jennifer replies, "I got something else. I wanted somebody to think I was special." As disturbing as the depiction of the abuse is in *The Tale*, we also witness how it made Jenny feel "special" or the "hero" as opposed to "invisible." Knowing it was a con played on Jenny and even that there were "others" after her cannot erase how thirteen-year-old Jenny locates her voice, agency, and specialness through the relationship. In this way, *The Tale* is not only about adult Jennifer's revelations and reinterpretation of this relationship, but also about the importance of maintaining the child Jenny's point of view despite its incomprehensibility by adults, even herself.

"IT WAS SHE WHO SEDUCED ME"—SEXUAL AGENCY IN *THE DIARY OF A TEENAGE GIRL*

One of the most troubling aspects of *Lolita* is Humbert's assertion, "I am going to tell you something very strange: it was she who seduced me."[63] Of course, within consent culture, it is not possible for a child to seduce an adult. And even within Nabokov's *Lolita*, such a supposition seems hardly believable. In Humbert's first physical act of child abuse against Lolita, he steals an apple from her to provoke a supposedly playful exchange so that Lolita winds up in his lap. He then uses this opportunity to masturbate with Lolita on his lap, as he describes "every movement she made, every shuffle and ripple" allowed him to get closer to orgasm. When his climax is assured, he states that "Lolita had been safely solipsized," and afterward, he revels, "Blessed be the Lord, she had noticed nothing!"[64] But as other scholars have noticed, Nabokov drops plenty of clues suggesting not only the impossibility of Lolita's consent but also Humbert's lie of her obliviousness.[65] Just before his moment of climax, Humbert recalls that the previous day, he had spied a bruise on Lolita's thigh "which my huge hairy hand massaged and slowly enveloped," causing Lolita to cry, "Oh it's nothing at all" with a "sudden shrill note in her voice."[66] Thus, layered amid Humbert's pleasurable sexual experience with Lolita is his memory of her awareness of his recent breach of boundaries and her nonconsent to being touched.

Similarly, Humbert's predatory motives are embedded in the moments leading up to when Lolita supposedly "seduces" him. When Humbert picks Lolita up at camp, she tells him, "Fact I've been revoltingly unfaithful to you, but it does not matter one bit, because you've stopped caring for me."[67] When he asks her why she thinks that, she replies, "Well, you haven't kissed me yet, have you?" and asks him, "Say, wouldn't Mother be absolutely mad if she found out we were lovers?"[68] Of course, what Lolita does not know during their conversation is that her mother is not sick in the hospital but rather was killed by a car after she ran recklessly into the street after discovering Humbert's journals detailing his obsession with Lolita. At the hotel later, Humbert drugs Lolita. He then furtively tries to use her as before, but the drugs are not strong enough to make her completely unconscious, and he doesn't "dare" to give her more. The next morning, when Humbert and Lolita become "technically lovers," he suggests that her sexual curiosity formed not through his corruption and abuse but through the sexual exploration with one of her girl friends and a boy, Charlie, from her camp. Humbert uses her past sexual experiences to argue, "I am not a criminal sexual psychopath taking indecent liberties with a child. The rapist was Charlie Holmes."[69] But again, Humbert's assertion that, "I was not even her first lover"[70] remains irrelevant in a current ethical and legal framework around CSA. Lolita's consent would be invalid regardless of any of her past experiences, and Humbert has already revealed himself to be an abuser who blatantly uses the child as a tool for his own sexual gratification.

Since reevaluating stories of CSA, it has become increasingly preposterous to uphold any aspect of the assertion that "she seduced me." However, in eradicating blame for the victim/survivor of abuse, what is also often lost is any sense of the child's sexual curiosity, desire, and agency. Moments that imagine how a girl might flirt with her abuser or derive pleasure or attention through her abuse are often ignored in the current scholarship around *Lolita*, just as they are often removed from films about CSA. In both *Precious* (2009) and *Bastard Out of Carolina*, for example, the film adaptations omit key aspects of the girl's sexual experience so notable in the original novels.[71] In the novel *Push* (later adapted to the film *Precious*), Sapphire includes explicit first-person scenes of how Precious cannot control her orgasms as her father rapes her. As a result, she cannot detach her sexual pleasure from the rapes. When she recalls her rapes, she remembers her pleasure, and when she thinks about sex, she imagines rape. The way Precious asserts her agency in this moment is narratively—since she cannot control the physical reality and her own body's seeming complicity, her mind drifts into fantasies of pop culture and fame. While the film maintains the way Precious cuts through the moment of her abuse with fantasy, it completely removes the disturbing ways that Precious ultimately comes to recognize her own sexual desires and responses. Through this omission, director Lee Daniels avoids addressing the shame-filled way a CSA survivor might arrive at sexual subjectivity amid abuse.[72]

A similar omission occurs in the adaptation of the 1992 *Bastard Out of Carolina* novel into the 1996 film directed by Anjelica Huston. In the book, Bone begins to discover her sexual desires as she invents masturbatory fantasies that incorporate her physical and sexual abuse. Bone's rage mixes with her sexual longings and culminates in pleasure that she calls an even more shameful experience than the abuse itself. Yet, again, these aspects from the novel do not make it into the film adaptation. While both films depict the brutality of physical and sexual abuse and the girls' ultimate escape from it, the girls themselves remain safely asexual as if not to contest a belief in their status as CSA victims.

Of course, there could be several reasons for such omissions in *Bastard Out of Carolina* and *Precious* versus the later films *Diary of a Teenage Girl* and *The Tale*. Precious's intersectional identity as poor, overweight, Black, and uneducated might deprive her the same level of narrative agency afforded to white middle-class girls. That said, Bone is white, but also lives in poverty—suggesting it could be class not race that prompted the erasure of sexual subjectivity. The era, too, certainly matters. Bone's story takes place in the 1950s, an era when CSA was dismissed and disbelieved, and Precious's story takes place in the contemporary consent culture era of the early twenty-first century. On the other hand, Jenny's and Minnie's stories take place in the more sexually permissive era of the 1970s—a period before significant child abuse legislation in the United States. Furthermore, both *Precious* and *Bastard Out of Carolina* depict sexual abuse by a father or stepfather as opposed to a coach in *The Tale* or a mother's boyfriend in *The Diary of a Teenage Girl*, a fact that certainly changes the stakes of the victim/perpetrator dichotomy. In any case, films about CSA that remove or deny any sense of desire, pleasure, or agency of the child appear to do so to avoid placing blame on the victim as well as perhaps to avoid an NC-17 rating or accusations of child pornography. When Adrian Lyne attempted a more nuanced adaptation of *Lolita* in the mid-1990s that showed both Humbert's violence and Lolita's agency, the film went unscreened for over a year due to accusations of its being child pornography.[73] Depicting children's sexuality is already transgressive in the United States so visualizing the sexual feelings of a CSA victim becomes even riskier. A tacit belief that sexual subjectivity is antithetical to victimization persists even today. Such a "stance" as Anna Srinivasan argues in *The Right to Sex* has "forced survivors" who have experienced pleasure or exerted agency in abuse "to either deny their experience of agency or to internalize an unaddressed (and, most probably, intense) sense of self-blame."[74] Such a disavowal of the lived experiences of real CSA survivors causes us to "fail to acknowledge how sexual subjectivity does not develop magically and instantly upon adulthood, but rather in and throughout childhood, however violent that childhood might be."[75]

Considering the typical portrayal of CSA victims as asexual, it is not surprising that one of the first questions asked of director Marielle Heller and the original author Gloeckner at the 2015 Sundance Film Festival about their film was, "Don't you think that making a film that glorifies pedophilia is harmful?"[76] *The Diary of a Teenage Girl* goes where most stories about CSA dare not go by emphasizing the girl's sexual curiosity, desire, and pleasure throughout her abuse. Minnie's sexual appetite is palpable in the film, as she wonders at one point, "Does everyone think about fucking as much as I do?" When she begins a sexual relationship at age fifteen with Monroe, her mother's thirty-five-year-old boyfriend, the sex scenes often highlight Minnie's sexual agency with her on top or her initiating physical intimacy. For example, the first time they meet at his apartment, he sits on the bed. Minnie climbs on top, straddling him, and they begin to kiss. As one reviewer comments, in such a contradictory portrayal, "calling him her lover doesn't seem quite right—but neither does predator."[77]

Gloeckner often states how her novel and ultimately the film are not traditionally autobiographical, suggesting in a preface to the revised 2015 edition of the novel that "this is not history or documentary or a confession, and memories will be altered or sacrificed, for factual truth has little significance in the pursuit of emotional truth."[78] Nonetheless, interviewers often seek to link the book and film to her personal experience, particularly to understand her testimony of CSA. In an interview with Heller and NPR journalist Terry Gross, Gloeckner describes how her inspiration for the novel emerged as she rediscovered her own diaries, which "stunned" her, years later. She realized "to hear this child's voice kind of talking to me as an adult, it just—it felt like it was crying out to be heard." When asked about her own experience as a child, Gloeckner, resists any one-sided interpretation. Gloeckner denies she was "misled" into sex, saying, "I was very kind of hypersexual. And it felt very pleasant. And it did feel like love. It did feel like wonderful attention. So in that sense, you know, I look at the story, and I'm trying to express the voice of that girl with no judgment, just to express what she felt." In the same interview, Gloeckner comments on how reviewers frequently attribute the words "agency" and "empowered" to Minnie, which she also labels a misreading, stating, "I can tell you that Minnie was overwhelmed with sex. And I don't think if you had told her, you're empowered and you have agency—it would not have computed." What makes *The Diary of a Teenage Girl* so perplexing and compelling is exactly this incongruous portrait of a girl who enjoys sex while being exploited.

The Diary of a Teenage Girl clearly emphasizes the abusive aspects inherent in the relationship. As Minnie recounts how "it happened," we see her mom head off to bed as Monroe and Minnie are left on the couch together watching TV. When Minnie burps, Monroe looks over and smirks at her. She pushes his shoulder, he pushes her head, and they begin a skirmish that ends with her leaning on Monroe's chest as he puts his arm around her. His hand lands on her breast, as she recalls, "I know it seems weird, but I had this strangely calming feeling that even if he meant to touch my tit, it's probably all right because he's a good guy and he knows how it goes and I don't." Minnie, the child in this scene, was not "safely solipsized," but keenly aware of the sexual implications of his touch. Alone later, Minnie asks her drawing of Monroe, "Oh, Monroe, pitter pat, you touched my tit. How was that?" Monroe's drawing comes to life in an animated/live action sequence where he stutters and says, "T-t-touching your breasts was um, uh. . . . they're really great, Minnie. Fantastic breasts. Perfect." Later, when Charlotte does not feel like going out with Monroe, she offers, "Why don't you take Minnie?" to which he pleads, "No." Reluctantly, he takes Minnie to the bar, where they both get drunk and play with cards. When one drops on the floor, Monroe bends down and starts biting her leg as she squeals with delight. She then bites his hand and ends up sucking on his finger. He sits down quietly, and she says, "You're far away," to which he says, "You just gave me a hard-on." Clearly curious, she comes over and sits next to him, and he says, "You don't believe me?" and takes her hand and puts it down his pants as Minnie thinks, "It didn't feel too hard to me. It was still skin." She then says, "I want you to fuck me." He tells her she's just "shitfaced" and gets up to take her home, but when he sees the serious look on her face, he says, "You really do want me to fuck you, don't you? You really fucking want me to fucking fuck you." This scene purposefully causes us to feel ambivalent about who seduces whom, despite the fact that we know Minnie is only fifteen. Later in the film when Minnie threatens to tell her mother, Monroe answers, "I should tell your mother. You manipulated me." Although a contemporary audience would have little sympathy for Monroe's position, Minnie's sexual curiosity in these scenes mirrors Lolita's challenge to Humbert to kiss her and become

Fig. 4.2. Marielle Heller's *The Diary of a Teenage Girl* depicts the uncomfortable contradictions in a sexual relationship between fifteen-year-old Minnie (Bel Powley) and her mother's boyfriend, Monroe (Alexander Skarsgard).

"lovers." Of course, *The Diary of a Teenage Girl* is not Monroe's story; it's Minnie's. She wields the narrative power here, and as a result, she acknowledges the ambivalence that even she feels about her own story.

Through Minnie's voiceovers, the film forces us as viewers to contend with more than her eagerness to become sexual. Her low self-esteem and self-doubt are also undeniable. Throughout the film, Minnie thinks that she's "fat," and from the first scene of the film, she believes, "I was an ugly child. I suppose I was lucky he was attracted by my youthfulness." After declaring that she wants Monroe to "fuck" her, she internally admits her doubt, thinking, "I didn't know if I wanted him or anyone else to fuck me, but I was afraid to pass up the chance because I may never have another." Her anticipation alongside her neediness is again clear in a scene of her in the bath later as she wonders, "Is this what it feels like for someone to love you? Somebody wants me. Somebody wants to have sex with me." Minnie's desire for attention comes through repeatedly in her voiceovers and diary recordings, such as when she asks herself, "What's the point of living if nobody loves you, nobody sees you, touches you?" In one scene, Minnie stares at herself in the mirror thinking, "I want someone to be so in love that they feel like they would die if I were gone. I want a body pressed up next to me, so I know that I'm really here." Throughout their relationship, Minnie's status as a child emerges through her naïveté. In one scene, after Monroe orgasms, Minnie begs, "No keep going!" He declares, "I have to stop this." She misunderstands his guilt as a lack of attraction saying, "Why would you say that? Do you think I'm fat?" He laughs, and she gets angry saying, "So fucking confusing with your adult codes and bullshit. I'm used to the more honest communication among children—and I'm almost still a child." He responds, "I know that. That's why I say we have to stop." In these moments, Minnie's sexual drive often comes through as a desperate craving for attention, approval, and love. It is also important to remember that while Jenny is played by a minor, Minnie is performed by Bel Powley in her twenties. In other words, the film does not actually depict what it looks like for a fifteen-year-old girl in this scenario. Considering how much Jenny's story—and our impression of it—alters after adult Jennifer finds a photo of herself at age thirteen, we might ask ourselves how we as an audience might feel about *The Diary of a Teenage Girl* if the film were revised with a younger actress in the role.

Still Minnie no doubt develops her own sexual self as a result of her abuse. Heller acknowledges in interviews how her film represents a "much more complicated version of abuse, one in which Minnie often does not feel like a victim." She articulates how her goal was to tell the story "purely from her point of view" so an audience would "feel what she felt." This meant that at moments when Minnie "didn't feel like she was a victim, we shouldn't feel like she was a victim."[79] Although her sexual empowerment always appears tainted by sexualization, it nonetheless feels real to Minnie. She develops a new way of seeing herself as desirable as she says, "Monroe says I exude sexuality. Sometimes I look in the mirror and I can't believe what I see." Not knowing of her daughter's sexual relationship, Charlotte advises Minnie to take more interest in boys, advising her, "You know you're not going to have that body forever. Wear makeup. Get some attention. I know that's not very feminist. You have a kind of power; you just don't know it yet." In this pep talk, Charlotte exposes how women's empowerment is often interpreted as sexualization—not only for girls, but even adult women. Despite the clear imbalance of her relationship with Monroe, Minnie nonetheless unleashes this "power" as she becomes sexually active. When she sees Monroe with her mother on his birthday, she decides to approach one of the boys in her school, Ricky Wasserman. They skinny dip in his pool and then have sex in his pool house. Although this scene starts very much like the scene of lousy sex in *Fast Times at Ridgemont High*, Minnie interjects her own desires for a much different outcome. Initially,

Ricky drives the action. When they get to his house, he dives into his pool naked asking Minnie, "What are you waiting for? Don't be scared." Minnie starts to undress. In the next scene, Ricky speedily and ecstatically humps Minnie, while she seems uncomfortable. But she interrupts him and says, "Let's turn over." Minnie gets on top and then controls the speed, as she says, "See slower." As she moves toward her climax, it is now Ricky who looks uncomfortable and even confused. Later, Ricky tells her, "You're just so intense. Something about having sex with you, Minnie, just kind of scares me. I've just never experienced someone like that." Minnie's intensity, of course, is her insistence on her own sexual gratification, a standpoint that requires an active, not passive role in her sexual encounters.

Certainly, Minnie's sexual empowerment still can be read as her participating in her own sexualization, a phenomenon suggested by the APA report authors. When she and her friend Kimmie are at a bar, they eye two older men across the room who buy them drinks. In jest, Minnie says, "Do you think that they would think that we're prostitutes?" They laugh, and Kimmie says, "That would be amazing. Hookers have all the fucking power. Everybody knows that." Minnie practices her "prostitute walk" over to the men and comes back to report that she informed them, "It's five bucks for us to suck their dicks and fifteen for the fucking fuck of their lives. They're counting their money." The girls laugh. But in the next scene, we see Minnie and Kimmie in the quiet bathroom dispassionately giving the men blow jobs side by side. They hold hands. It turns out that the "power" they had expected from the experience was an illusion. Later, Minnie tells Kimmie, "I don't think we should've done that," adding she feels "weird and creepy about it." Kimmie agrees. They promise each other "never to do anything like that again." Later in the film, the two girls also have a threesome with Monroe. Sitting in a café afterward, Minnie thinks, "What we did makes me sick. It was so pornographic" as she recalls them both kissing Monroe. This sex scene, too, is disconcertingly quiet featuring only sounds of silverware and dishes clanging in the café from the subsequent scene. Such moments suggest how the girls have been conned into mistaking sexualization as empowerment. Still, Minnie and Kimmie are not shown as ruined by these encounters. Seeing themselves as the active agents of these experiences, they believe they also can choose to avoid them in the future. As actress Bel Howley says in talking about her character, "one of the biggest things that we learn when we come out of teenage-hood is, Wow, I can do fucking stupid things and the world won't implode.... I might not even learn from it. I will just move on and things will be fine."[80] Minnie's regrets become part of her testing her own limitations and rejecting what she doesn't want sexually.

Minnie ultimately discovers, like Jenny in *The Tale*, how to extricate herself from the relationship. She might have no choice about growing up in a world where the adults around her are "inept or abusive" as Fox puts it, but she can nonetheless transform how she sees herself and become the primary driver of her life choices. When Monroe and Minnie do acid together, she looks down at herself on the bed and says, "This is incredible. I see everything." She lifts her arms as they turn into wings. "I knew it," she whispers, imagining herself flying over the bed. But Monroe has a bad trip—he insists that Minnie get off the bed or "They're going to see you!" When she gets down, Monroe puts his head in her lap as he pleads, "I need you, Minnie. I need you to take care of me. I love you." When she replies, "What?" he begins to cry repeating, "I love you. You don't love me." And even when she says, "I love you," he doesn't believe her. In a voiceover, she reveals that, "He was vulnerable and weak. It was all I ever wanted, and I had no desire for it." Minnie's drug-induced revelation of her apathy toward Monroe as well as the realization of her freedom and power persist after she sobers up later. In the next scene, Monroe takes a shower while outlining for Minnie how they could date until she turns eighteen and how his business of "vitamin power tabs" should be taking off by then. While he's mid-sentence, she gets up abruptly, runs out of the bathroom, packs her things, and leaves thinking, "I refuse to be some sniveling crybaby. I'm a fucking woman, and this is my life." Much like Jenny's turning point, "I have made a decision," Minnie makes a clear choice to end the relationship.

However, Minnie must save herself a second time after her mother, Charlotte, finds out about the relationship. Charlotte gets drunk and insists Monroe and Minnie get married as a punishment for them both, saying to Monroe, "The point is that you fucked my daughter and so you're going to marry her." Monroe agrees. In making this decision, the adults completely ignore Minnie's own thoughts on the matter. But Minnie has already convinced herself that "this is my life," and she calls Monroe "drunk" and Charlotte "crazy" and walks out. Yet Minnie has nowhere else to go. Like Lolita, Minnie's escape initially puts her in greater jeopardy. She seeks out an acquaintance, Tabatha, and enters a subterranean world of partying and getting high. Here, Minnie's voiceover exposes her emptiness, "I've become nothing. Finally. No home, no school, no money." It turns out Minnie, foggy on drugs, hasn't been home for days. Worse, it turns out Tabatha plans to prostitute Minnie. But when Tabatha leads her to an apartment and speaks in hushed tones to a man, Minnie suddenly emerges from her reverie, rushes out of the building and down the street, and ultimately goes home. Undeniably, the film shows how Minnie's CSA and her lack of family support put her at risk of further sexual violation and exploitation. Nevertheless, the film also clearly positions her as the primary mover of her own story. Despite how she is victimized by an abusive relationship, she locates her sexual agency and emotional resilience through it.

Although Gloeckner clearly resists affixing agency to Minnie, such a label makes more sense when thinking of agency as choices made within a set of personal, social, familial, and cultural constraints. Minnie, like Jenny, finds a narrative where she is the "hero" of her story. At the end, Minnie learns, "I always thought I wanted to be exactly like my mom, but she thinks she needs a man to be happy. I don't." Despite her low self-confidence, she creates a narrative of self-love, saying, "So maybe nobody loves me, maybe nobody will ever love me, but maybe it's not about being loved by somebody else." When she runs into Monroe later, she shakes his hand and looks him in the eye the way her former stepfather taught her and thinks, "I'm better than you, you son-of-a-bitch." Although Minnie's own retelling of the story allows us to see how she is exploited, it simultaneously insists on how she develops both her sexual subjectivity and positive self-image through her abuse.

"FOR ALL THE GIRLS WHEN THEY HAVE GROWN"

In 2005, in a *New York Times* article "50 Years on, *Lolita* Still Has Power to Unnerve," Charles McGrath wrote, "'Lolita' is unlike most controversial books in that its edge has not dulled over time. Where *Ulysses* and *Lady Chatterley's Lover*, say, now seem familiar and inoffensive, almost quaint, Nabokov's masterpiece is, if anything, more disturbing than it used to be." McGrath suggests that the novel "disturbs us more than ever" because although we no longer view their relationship as consensual or Lolita as the "corrupt child," *Lolita* nonetheless "seduces" us to accompany Humbert through his criminal and pedophilic journey.[81] But it's more than that—*Lolita* continues to unnerve because it also timelessly insists on Lolita's sexual curiosity, desire, and choices amid her abuse, aspects that adults do not often acknowledge.

The Tale and *The Diary of a Teenage Girl*, in this way, remind us of the inaccessibility of childhood by adults despite the fact that we as adults tell their stories and watch and analyze them. By the time Gloeckner and Fox write their own stories, they too are adults who find their own childhood voices to be strangely distinct. As Kathryn Bond Stockton says in *The Queer Child*, "The child is precisely who we are not and, in fact, never were. It is the act of adults looking back. It is a ghostly, unreachable fancy."[82] When *The Diary of a Teenage Girl* ends, Minnie declares, "This is for all the girls when they have grown," a line that mirrors the original novel's dedication. Herein lies the irony—this story is for "girls" but only after "they have grown." But when exactly is one grown? As Catherine Driscoll once mused, "I'm still not sure when I stopped being a girl, if I did."[83] Although these stories are based on experiences that happened to children—we also insist that they are not appropriate for children. *The Diary of a Teenage Girl* was rated R, and *The Tale* premiered on HBO with a mature rating. Only "when we have grown" can we see these stories, but that also happens to be when we find the girls' voices more discomfiting and incomprehensible.

Perhaps consent culture's prioritization of women and girl's sexual agency might continue to elicit a reframing of CSA stories that acknowledge the child's voice as these two films indicate. Just as feminists in the 1980s and 1990s reclaimed Lolita's language of abuse, we might now look to recover her language of childhood sexual curiosity. Lolita flirts with Humbert, and he uses that to justify his abuse. Although we find his actions despicable, it can still be true that Lolita enjoys aspects of a relationship by which she is exploited. Understanding Minnie, Jenny, and Lolita as CSA survivors does not mean we must disavow all their agency. And to allow them agency does not mean making them culpable. Films like *The Diary of a Teenage Girl* and *The Tale* suggest ways we might look beyond an oversimplification of consent. In imagining revisionary portrayals of girls' sexuality, both films seek not merely to find some ambiguous middle ground between these two archetypes of victim/perpetrator but rather to show how girls can embody numerous contradictions as they navigate through a minefield of coercive relationships, cultural beliefs, family situations, gender stereotypes, and their own desires as they seek to harness their own sexual subjectivity.

NOTES

1. Kaufman, "Jennifer Fox's Drama."
2. Meek, *Independent Female Filmmakers*, 131.
3. Meek, *Independent Female Filmmakers*, 131.
4. Gross, "'Tale' of Child Sex Abuse."
5. Stockton, *Queer Child*, 119.
6. Durham, *Lolita Effect*, 26.
7. Piluso, "Education."
8. Hornaday, "Review."
9. Buckley, "Birds and the Bees."
10. RAINN, "Child Sexual Abuse."
11. Centers for Disease Control and Prevention, "Preventing Child Sexual Abuse."
12. Cornell University, "Statutory Rape."
13. For example, the age of consent in New Jersey is currently sixteen, but the state has a "close in age" exemption (also known as a "Romeo and Juliet clause") allowing someone ages thirteen to fifteen to consent if their partner is up to four years older than they are.

14. Centers for Disease Control and Prevention, "Preventing Child Sexual Abuse."
15. Zurbriggen et al., "APA Task Force," 27.
16. Zurbriggen et al., "APA Task Force," 18.
17. Lamb and Peterson, "Adolescent Girl's Sexual Empowerment," 704.
18. Lamb and Peterson, "Adolescent Girl's Sexual Empowerment," 710.
19. Tolman, "Female Adolescents," 751.
20. Tolman, "Female Adolescents," 752.
21. Butler, *Psychic Life of Power*, 10.
22. Butler, *Psychic Life of Power*, 17.
23. Bay-Cheng, "Agency Is Everywhere," 469.
24. Cense, "Rethinking Sexual Agency," 255–57.
25. Cense, "Rethinking Sexual Agency," 260.
26. Kinsey et al., *Sexual Behavior*, 121.
27. Kinsey et al., *Sexual Behavior*, 120.
28. Herman, *Father-Daughter Incest*, vii.
29. Blumenthal, "Freud." See also Triplett, "Misnomer of Freud's 'Seduction Theory.'"
30. Triplett, "Misnomer of Freud's 'Seduction Theory'," 654.
31. P. Jenkins, *Moral Panic*, 129.
32. Kincaid, *Erotic Innocence*, 281.
33. Kincaid, *Erotic Innocence*, 14.
34. See the essays in Hessick's compilation, *Refining Child Pornography Law*, for example.
35. Angelides notes that "the question and discourse of child sexuality were rather unfortunate casualties" of the child sexual abuse discourse. See *Fear of Child Sexuality*, 57.
36. J. Rose, *Case of Peter Pan*, xi.
37. Angelides, *Fear of Child Sexuality*, 46.
38. Angelides, *Fear of Child Sexuality*, 46.
39. *Merriam-Webster*, s.v., "Lolita."
40. Sayers, "Brief History of the Nymphet's Tribulations," 6.
41. Sayers, "Brief History of the Nymphet's Tribulations," 7.
42. Hatch, "Fille Fatale," 178.
43. Shelton, "Word Is Incest," 276.
44. Mcgrath, "50 Years On."
45. Sayers, "Brief History of the Nymphet's Tribulations," 6.
46. Book Marks, "Sick, Scandalous, Spectacular."
47. Sayers, "Brief History of the Nymphet's Tribulations."
48. Nabokov, *Annotated Lolita*, 119.
49. Nabokov, *Annotated Lolita*, 202.
50. Shelton, "Word Is Incest," 280; Meek, "Lolita Speaks," 161.
51. Patnoe, "Lolita Misrepresented," 83; Wood, "Lolita Revisited," 70.
52. Meek, "Lolita Speaks."
53. Hale, "Teacher' Review."
54. Cohen, "How Do You Direct."
55. At one point in the film Jennifer says to her mother, "Trust me, it can damage your boundaries," to which her mother says, "At last you admit you were damaged."
56. Meek, *Independent Female Filmmakers*, 135.
57. Gross, "'Tale' of Child Sex Abuse."
58. Cense, "Rethinking Sexual Agency," 257.

59. Bay-Cheng, "Agency Is Everywhere," 466.
60. Sanjeevi et al., "Review of Child Sexual Abuse," 631.
61. Sanjeevi et al., "Review of Child Sexual Abuse," 631.
62. Meek, *Independent Female Filmmakers*, 135.
63. Nabokov, *Annotated Lolita*, 132.
64. Nabokov, *Annotated Lolita*, 61.
65. See Patnoe, "Lolita Misrepresented"; Shelton, "Word Is Incest"; and Meek "Lolita Speaks."
66. Nabokov, *Annotated Lolita*, 60–61.
67. Nabokov, *Annotated Lolita*, 112.
68. Nabokov, *Annotated Lolita*, 113.
69. Nabokov, *Annotated Lolita*, 149.
70. Nabokov, *Annotated Lolita*, 135.
71. Meek, "It Ain't for Children."
72. Meek, "It Ain't for Children."
73. Blades, "Trouble with 'Lolita.'"
74. Srinivasan, *The Right to Sex*.
75. Meek, "It Ain't for Children."
76. McKee, "Diary of a Teenage Girl."
77. Dargis, "Review."
78. Gloeckner, *Diary of a Teenage Girl*, xv.
79. J. Miller, "How 'The Diary of a Teenage Girl.'"
80. J. Miller, "How 'The Diary of a Teenage Girl.'"
81. McGrath, "50 Years On."
82. Stockton, *Queer Child*, 5.
83. Driscoll, *Girls*, 2.

FIVE

THE (IN)VISIBILITY OF TRANS TEENS

3 Generations, *Adam*, and *Boy Meets Girl*

> How do we get the audience to question the usefulness of visibility—in particular when visibility puts populations in harm's way due to systematized oppression via class, race, religion, ability, citizenship, etc. Perhaps visibility isn't the goal after all?
>
> —Sam Feder[1]

The critical acclaim and popularity of Kimberly Peirce's film *Boys Don't Cry* in 1999 brought mainstream attention to trans adolescence. Based on the real-life story of Brandon Teena, a young trans man living in Nebraska, the film evoked an unprecedented empathy for an identity that had been all but invisible in cinema for over a century, and it won several prestigious awards, including Best Actress for Hilary Swank who played Brandon. However, in more recent years, the film has been critiqued by trans activists for how it falls short of an inclusive and progressive agenda. When Peirce showed up for a screening and Q&A at Reed College in 2016, protesters had put up signs that stated, "Fuck Your Transphobia" and "Fuck this cis white bitch," and they interrupted Peirce's Q&A for the first fifteen minutes. Their outrage centered on how the film, which ends with the rape and murder of Brandon, follows a pattern of highlighting only the most tragic and brutal queer and trans stories—and how the film failed to cast a trans actor in the role of Brandon.

As a handful of newer US trans teen films have emerged, social media activists have expressed similar grievances. While Hollywood continues to steer clear of trans teen film protagonists, independent directors who do create trans teen films can find themselves wrestling with public controversies over tactless comments, portrayals, and casting choices, such as in the case of the films *3 Generations* (2015) and *Adam* (2019). Meanwhile, the film *Boy Meets Girl* (2014), despite being a more positively viewed trans teen story, remained under the radar. Consent culture has not only transformed how stories about sex and gender are told but also has changed how audiences react to depictions they do not endorse. These early breakout texts in the genre show how the stakes have remained high as trans teens emerge from invisibility. Trans activists repeatedly find themselves with a challenging paradox—fighting *for* visibility while fighting *against* a certain kind of visibility. Ultimately, both the "canceling" of films like *3 Generations* and *Adam* and the failure to uplift films like *Boy Meets Girl* represent a continuing invisibility of trans youth in the genre. Such invisibility has obscured issues worthy of greater exploration—such as the unspoken cisness of the affirmative consent discourse.

While understanding some scholars prefer to use *trans** as a way of "evoking a multiplicity" of gender identities,[2] in this chapter, the terms *trans* or *transgender* align with GLAAD's definition of an "umbrella term for people whose gender identity differs from the sex they were assigned at birth."[3] Certainly, all umbrella terms carry vagueness and silences that are challenging to overcome. In a 2022 essay in *Feminist Media Studies*, Aiden James Kosciesza calls for gender to be reconsidered as an "intersectional category" across three "dimensions": *gender identity* or "a person's internal sense of their own gender"; *gender expression* or "a person's outward signification and performance of their gender identity"; and *gender experience* or "a person's temporal pattern of conformity or non-conformity with sociocultural gender expectations."[4] In this chapter, I define a contemporary trans teen film as one that portrays a protagonist who does not identify with their sex assigned at birth. At the same time, I invite a fluidity into the history of the genre to recognize past texts that depict not only trans identities but also gender expressions and experiences that defy conventions and resist gender binaries in eras before trans identities had reached legibility.

RENDERING TRANS YOUTH (IN)VISIBLE

In 2012, then US vice president Joseph Biden was overheard describing trans discrimination as the "civil rights issue of our time" while talking with the mother of Miss Trans New England.[5] He has since echoed this statement numerous times, including in a tweet in 2020 before being elected president where he affirmed, "Let's be clear: Transgender equality is the civil rights issue of our time. There is no room for compromise when it comes to basic human rights."[6] Such unequivocal support for trans lives from a prominent US politician seemed unthinkable just a few decades earlier.

Still, the related discourse in the United States has played out amid a political tug-of-war. In 2016, Obama issued an executive order stating that the protections of Title IX against sex discrimination also included trans students, specifically outlining that trans students had the right to use bathrooms and locker rooms consistent with their gender identities. Eleven US states sued his administration, and soon after entering office, Trump rescinded the policy in February 2017. Upon entering office in 2021, President Biden issued the "Executive Order on Preventing and Combating Discrimination on the Basis of Gender Identity or Sexual Orientation" once again reaffirming trans youth's access to sports, restrooms, and locker rooms. A similar back and forth has occurred over employee discrimination—the Obama-era Equal Employment Opportunity Commission ruled in 2012 that the Civil Rights Act of 1964 protects trans employees, while in 2019, Trump's Justice Department filed a brief with the Supreme Court stating that employers could fire trans individuals based on their gender identity. Then in 2020, the Supreme Court of the United States ruled 6–3 that the Civil Rights Act of 1964 *does* protect gay and transgender individuals against employment discrimination. This groundbreaking change rendered moot numerous laws allowing employers to fire individuals based on their sexual orientation and gender identity in over half of US states.[7]

Still, 2022 became a record-breaking year for anti-trans legislation—by the end of March, nearly 240 anti-LGBTQ bills had been filed, the majority targeting trans individuals. And most trans bills target youth—such as their rights to play sports and use bathrooms based on their gender identity.[8] In addition, over a dozen states are considering bills to ban gender-affirming care for youth even with the consent of their parents.[9] In April 2021, Arkansas became the first state to do so.[10] Texas followed in February 2022 when the governor issued an order labeling gender-affirming care for minors "child abuse," causing providers to suspend treatments for youth in the state.[11] Arizona and Alabama followed suit. However, such bans remain in flux as courts sometimes step in to render them temporarily moot. US laws regarding youth trans rights thus vary greatly from state to state—from outright bans on gender-affirming care to laws enabling trans youth to obtain care *without* parental consent, such as in the state of Washington. Meanwhile numerous clinicians note the lack of clear ethical and medical guidelines for children who do not agree with their parents' decisions for their care. For youth, trans rights are not only the civil rights issue of our time; they might also be the consent issue of our time. Of course, the cultural and political battle is far from over as many across the US advocate laws intended to disrupt trans and queer lives, while others fight for greater equality through protests, media, and political and legal battles.

Debates over how to define and categorize trans individuals have also played out in the medical community. In 2019, the World Health Organization (WHO) changed "gender identity disorder" to "gender incongruence," removing the concept from the list of mental and behavioral disorders and placing it instead within a chapter on sexual health. In their guidelines updated in February 2022, the WHO defines gender incongruence as "marked and persistent incongruence between an individual's experienced gender and the assigned sex." In children, the WHO states gender incongruence manifests through over two years of a strong desire to be a different gender, a "strong dislike" of one's own sexual anatomy, and "make-believe or fantasy play, toys, games, or activities and playmates that are typical of the experienced gender rather than the assigned sex." The adolescent/adult definition pertains to an individual after reaching puberty and can include the desire to transition to the experienced gender using hormones and other treatments. Both definitions clarify that "Gender variant behavior and preferences alone are not a basis for assigning the diagnosis."[12] The American Psychiatric Association (APA) has not yet followed suit. In 2022, the APA continues to list "gender dysphoria" in their *Diagnostic and Statistical Manual of Mental Disorders* as characterized by at least six months of "marked incongruence between one's experienced/expressed gender and their assigned gender."[13] However, in February 2021, the APA did release a resolution on "Gender Identity Change Efforts," to state explicitly that "incongruence between sex and gender in and of itself is not a mental disorder" and to clarify that "gender identity change efforts" such as "corrective" or "conversion" therapies cause "harm."[14]

Such classifications impact how trans youth are defined, which can lead to further biases against them. In 2018, Lisa Littman published a peer-reviewed essay coining the term "rapid-onset gender dysphoria" to describe youth whose change in gender expression appears suddenly, according to their parents. Littman outlined several controversial hypotheses, for example, that "gender dysphoria" could be brought on by social influences or "maladaptive" coping strategies. While asserting that it's "unlikely that friends and the internet can make people transgender," Littman nonetheless argued, it is "plausible" that dissatisfaction with one's gender "can be initiated, magnified, spread, and maintained via the mechanisms of social and peer contagion"[15] and that gender incongruence "may represent a form of intentional self-harm."[16] Such a pathologizing theory of social contagion harkens back to numerous other youth panics, including fears over "catching" homosexuality. Not surprisingly, trans advocates disputed both the study's conclusions and methodology, arguing how Littman sought parents from trans-skeptic websites and never interviewed youth.

Critics also argued that what might seem "sudden" to disbelieving parents could be the result of years of their children's closeted gender questioning. Ultimately, the controversy provoked the journal *PLOS One* to conduct a rereview of the essay—a rare acknowledgment of a failing in the peer-review process—and it published a correction and formal comment.[17] Littman's revision emphasizes that the study involved only parental observations and that the "diagnoses" of "gender dysphoria" were not made by clinicians, admitting the subjects would have been "very unlikely... to have met criteria for childhood gender dysphoria if they had seen a clinician for an evaluation."[18] In other words, the subjects of the study likely were not trans and perhaps not even nonbinary—causing the conclusions to be especially off base. It's no wonder that Jack Halberstam has noted, "Transgender bodies seem to be both illogical and illegible to any number of 'experts' who may try to read them."[19] Littman's research epitomizes how trans youth can be rendered invisible, irrelevant, and voiceless even within studies that supposedly focus on them. Despite Littman's concept of "rapid-onset gender dysphoria" being debunked, the term continues to be cited as proof of a rampant "disorder" in numerous transphobic articles and books, such as *Irreversible Damage: The Transgender Craze Seducing Our Daughters* from 2020.

Despite pushback, trans youth are on the rise in the United States. According to 2019 data, nearly 2 percent of US youth surveyed identified as trans, which was more than double the prior estimate two years earlier.[20] The presence of gender clinics has grown exponentially in the United States and so has the number of minors referred to them.[21] These increases have provoked more awareness, dialogue, and debate within academic, parenting, medical, and educational communities. On the one hand, advocates argue that the rise results from greater cultural acceptance of trans lives while stressing that youth should have access to gender-affirming treatments that are scientifically proven to improve mental health outcomes. On the other, skeptics cite risks and irreversible physical effects of hormones and surgical interventions while highlighting stories of "detransitioners" who have reverted to their assigned sex at birth.[22] Even in queer, feminist, and academic communities, trans lives have been attacked by trans-exclusionary radical feminists (TERFs). As these debates play out in the public arena, the category of trans youth is invoked either to elicit empathy for gender variance or a sense of panic over a supposed runaway trend.

THE "RADICAL INCONGRUITIES" OF TRANS VISIBILITY

More positive visibility for trans lives is often touted as an important step toward wider social acceptance. A 2021 Gallup poll found that 31 percent of people say they know someone trans while a 2013 Pew poll showed that 87 percent of people state they know someone gay or lesbian. As a result, GLAAD authors argue that a "stereotypical or defamatory image" of a trans individual can be particularly harmful because "the viewer may assume that all transgender people are actually like that; they have no real-life experience with which to compare it."[23] These facts create a combined urgency—more visibility is needed for trans stories, while the stakes for "fair and accurate stories" remains high.[24] Seeing that trans youth still report "significantly increased rates of depression, suicidality, and victimization compared to their cisgender peers," these representations also might affect trans youth in unique ways.[25]

Twenty-first-century films and television shows have undoubtedly brought more visibility to trans individuals and identities—including youth. In 2014, trans actress Laverne Cox was featured on the cover of *Time* for the story, "The Transgender Tipping Point: America's Next Civil Rights Frontier." The popular Amazon Studios series *Transparent* about a trans woman (played by cis actor Jeffrey Tambor) premiered in 2014, and the reality series *I Am Jazz* about the trans girl Jazz Jennings premiered on The Learning Channel (TLC) in 2015. Both series reached wide audiences and ran for numerous seasons, although *Transparent* ultimately resulted in scandal when Tambor left the show amid sexual harassment accusations. The increasing publicity and inclusion of celebrity trans lives and fictional trans characters led 2015 to be labeled "the year of transgender visibility."[26] Since then, episodic programs such as *Sabrina*, *One Day at a Time*, and *Euphoria* have continued featuring more affirming portrayals of trans youth, and teen films have begun to depict a handful of trans characters.

However, trans studies scholars note how increased visibility has occurred alongside a substantial public backlash. In the introduction to *Trap Door: Trans Cultural Production and the Politics of Visibility*, the authors suggest we must "grapple and reckon with radical incongruities" such as when the "transgender tipping point" is accompanied by increased physical violence against trans individuals and unprecedented anti-trans legislation.[27] In noting such concurrent trends, Sam Feder, director of the documentary *Disclosure* (which advocates more positive media visibility of trans lives) even ponders in a 2016 interview, "Perhaps visibility isn't the goal after all?" Of course, as Feder notes, it would be wrong to suggest that trans visibility *caused* this backlash "because this implies that the backlash wasn't already there."

How best to render trans lives more visible ethically is a recurring theme among trans scholars. In the book *Invisible Lives*, Viviane K. Namaste argues that both in sociological research and gender theory, trans people have been "reduced to the merely figural: rhetorical tropes and discursive levers invoked to talk about social relations of gender, nation, or class that preempt the very possibility of transsexual bodies, identities, and lives."[28] Over the past two decades, as trans studies has undoubtedly gained more visibility in academia, it too has been met with opposition. Some resistances are subtle, such as a tendency to contain trans studies under umbrellas like queer studies, while others are overtly hostile, such as certain radical feminist scholars who outright reject the inclusion of trans studies and trans individuals.

While visibility is often presumed to be "a good thing" or the mark of "success,"[29] it is also a "trap"—offered up as the "the primary path through which trans people might have access to livable lives" while also giving "little support or protection to many, if not most, trans and gender non-conforming people."[30] As Alexandre Baril argues, while "activists are right to fight for greater public visibility" on behalf of a community that has long been "silenced," visibility is nonetheless "not always desirable or possible for all trans people."[31] Baril uses the example of the public's fascination with exposing trans individuals' genitals—not for affirmation, but as spectacle. This pattern, Baril says, leads to a "hypervisibility" that "limits testimonials to a single, dominant script."[32] The promise of visibility can then turn against trans individuals by making them "confessing" others merely for public entertainment and consumption. Similarly, in media depictions, as Feder states, filmmakers have tended to recycle tropes that "reduce transness to medical transition and give cis people the impression they're entitled to information about a transgender person's body or birth given name, or that they can ask for photos of the trans person at different stages of their life." Increasing visibility of trans lives for the purpose of spectacle, many argue, does not realize the desire for more visibility in a constructive way.

As a result of a long history of problematic depictions of transness in the media, several activists and writers have attempted to outline specific criteria for a trans version of the "Bechdel Test" used to evaluate affirming representations of women in cinema. In addition to emphasizing that trans characters should be played by trans individuals, these lists focus on the contrivances of the plot (not about their "transition or surgery, or their struggle with their identity"); the characters' traits ("safe, stable, and secure," "thriving, healthy, and happy," and "in love, loveable, and dating"); and the characters' occupations (not "a sex worker, dealer, or thief"). Undoubtedly, such benchmarks have been put forth as a way of encouraging "more original, authentic, and positive representations" of trans individuals.[33]

However, uncritically adopting a new homogeneity for trans depictions carries its own risks. In the essay "On the Necessity of Bad Trans Objects,"

Cáel M. Keegan suggests that as trans visibility has increased, a division has emerged between what tends to be labeled "good" and "bad" "transgender media objects." Keegan argues that media texts deemed "good" tend to espouse "normative" ideals, including "standards of positivity and respectability," and feature trans characters who are mostly "thin, able-bodied, conventionally attractive, and gender normative."[34] In effect, these depictions "do not problematize the standards for becoming recognizable as a gendered subject."[35] Thus, even as these "good" texts render trans lives more visible, they do so in ways that do not disrupt sex/gender binaries. Just as there are harms from stereotyped depictions of trans characters, there are also issues inherent in supposedly "good" trans texts which, as Keegan summarizes, "effectively assimilate transness, minimizing the threat that transgender embodiment poses to the dominant models of gender and sex."[36] Keegen argues that such standards can erase or ignore "bad" trans texts of the past and present that offer productive intricacies despite their drawbacks. Keegan looks at past "bad" depictions like *Tootsie*, *It's Pat*, and *The Assignment* to show that although they "stereotype or fetishize trans embodiment," each also offers constructive ways of thinking through the complexities of sex and gender.[37] Instead of ignoring or erasing such texts, Keegan encourages critically engaging with them to untangle what exactly their badness might reveal. We might be surprised to find "political resources" as Keegan suggests—such as how "bad" trans texts can threaten "the very stability of sexual difference itself."[38] Keegan's call to action again cuts to the radical incongruities of trans visibility—reminding us how we might find something "good" within a study of "bad" trans texts and vice versa.

Investigating two such "bad" contemporary texts and one "good" one in the teen film genre enables us to consider what they render visible about trans youth, consent, and dissent. In doing so, I seek to avoid "academic objectification"—or the tendency to use trans individuals as objects of study without engaging their voices actively. The mantra "nothing about us without us" that Stryker pulled from the disability movement has been repeated frequently. It is not enough to offer "knowledge of," in other words; as scholars we must provide "knowledge with," or "knowledge that emerges from a dialog that includes trans people who bring an additional kind of experiential or embodied knowledge along with their formal, expert knowledges."[39] With this call to action in mind, I attempt to give prioritization in this chapter to the voices of trans activists, fans, youth, and scholars. I am not trans and neither are many of the film directors of recent US trans teen films. Furthermore, characters in films are, by default, figural representations, and teen films are notoriously inaccurate depictions of adolescents' lives. All of this means that such a study could be doomed to reside purely in the symbolic. Still, I believe that it is time to highlight trans adolescence within the field of youth media studies, and this urgency necessitates scholars like myself to draw more attention to work by and about trans lives. As we respond to appeals for increased inclusion regarding gender, race, and class, we can also reimagine our work to be more open to studies of trans texts. To attempt to offer "knowledge with," I emphasize extratextuality, including fan reactions, social media posts, and trans cast and crew interviews. In addition, I seek to link the teen films here to real ways of being and connecting in the world. If youth are always already subjugated, then trans youth are even more so—and in my study, it becomes evident how many in the community have not appreciated the way their own stories are told, a fact that has become more blatantly obvious during consent culture.

A BRIEF HISTORY OF GENDER VARIANCE IN TEEN FILMS

It is only within the last few years that *any* trans teen characters have appeared in earnest in the genre—and they have been slow to emerge, despite the enormous success and popularity of *Boys Don't Cry* in 1999. Like in the history of queer films, more overt and affirming depictions of trans youth appeared in European films first, such as the French-Belgian film *Ma Vie en Rose* (*My Life in Pink*) in 1997. In the United States, adult trans characters continued to be depicted for shock value well into the late twentieth century in both comedies like *Ace Ventura: Pet Detective* (1994) and dramas like *The Crying Game* (1992), and sympathetic portrayals of openly trans youth simply did not exist before *Boys Don't Cry*. In other words, there is no explicit history of trans teen films in the genre, and scholars continue to question even what it means to call a film "trans."[40] However, this is not to say there aren't abundant examples throughout US cinema history of the varied gender expression of youth. Thus, in seeking a history for trans teen films, it might be useful to identify the flickers and clues within gender-bending characters of the past. Much in the way queerness has been read into films decades before it was openly depicted, glimpses of youth's resistance to gender binaries might be interpreted as offering a trans subtext. As Laura Horak, in the book *Girls Will Be Boys: Cross-Dressed Women, Lesbians, and American Cinema*, notes, scholars have tended to read "cross-dressed women as mirrors of their own concerns" as either "feminists," "lesbians," or "queer and modern."[41] Horak adds that trans studies scholars too "have considered cross-dressed individuals as examples of historical gender variance, though they usually stop short of claiming them as trans," adding "the open meanings" of "cross-dressed" individuals "are a key part of their appeal."[42] In line with Keegan, I consider cross-dressing in my discussion of youth in US cinema history as a means of locating the destabilization of gender before trans identities became depicted more legibly. As Eliza Steinbock argues in "Towards a Trans Cinema," it is "imperative to begin by charting the possibilities for recovering films and cinematic concepts that speak of trans before it reached today's horizon of intelligibility."[43] Although we might not consider cross-dressing characters as trans, I look to them to find early suggestions of gender "nonconformity" in teen films.

Horak locates cross-dressing in US cinema's earliest days, noting that when Marion Davies was credited as "the first girl on the screen. . . . in pantaloons" in *Little Old New York* in 1923, the media had somehow failed to remember "the more than three hundred [US] films with cross-dressed women" released earlier.[44] John E. Conklin, in the book *Campus Life in the Movies: A Critical Survey from the Silent Era to the Present*, locates a similar trend in youth films throughout US cinema history with cross-dressing having been routinely employed for its "entertainment value" in scenarios with youth sneaking into dorms or critiquing gender.[45] However, even when such gender swapping was presented earnestly, it presented a temporary transgression toward a particular end. In *Sylvia Scarlett* (1935), Katharine Hepburn's character, Sylvia, masquerades as a boy while on the run from the law—and while the film does not suggest Sylvia is trans, the film has often been coopted as an early example of gender bending that seems to go beyond mere disguise. In *National Velvet* (1944), Elizabeth Taylor played her first film role at age twelve as Velvet Brown, who disguises as an adult man jockey to ride her horse in the Grand National Race. Again, the film makes no indication of Velvet as trans; rather, the gender swapping is Velvet's act of defiance against rules forbidding girl and women riders.

One of the most affirming past depictions of gender "nonconformity" in the teen film genre appeared in a most unlikely place—a 1980s John Hughes film. In *Some Kind of Wonderful* (1987), the character Watts (played by actress Mary Stuart Masterson) dons short hair, wears boxer shorts, works at an autobody shop, and harbors a secret crush on best friend Keith. In one scene, a classmate who likes Watts confides, "A lot of guys I know think that you're . . . confused. But I know it's just an act. You know how I know?" Watts responds sarcastically, "Enlighten me," to which Ray answers, "Because you radiate the sexual vibe." Watts then declares, "Ray, this is 1987. Did you know that a girl can be whatever she wants to be?" While Watts is teased for masculine gender expression by the highly femininized popular teens at the school, there's no doubt that the film and audience's identification resides with Watts. As such, *Some Kind of Wonderful* might be one of the first empathetic depictions of a teen film protagonist who sincerely transgresses gender expectations. Unlike the characters who came before (and numerous since), Watts's gender expression is neither a disguise nor a costume. Although Watts is not openly trans and neither is the actress who played Watts, the portrayal nonetheless demonstrates an awareness and acceptance of the fluidity of gender expression as an early sign of what was to come.

In the late twentieth-century into the twenty-first century, gender bending for teens has often continued to be depicted as an act that characters could simply adopt and discard through cross-dressing (*Just One of the Guys, Just One of the Girls, She's the Man, Little Sister*),[46] body switching (*It's a Boy Girl Thing, The Swap*), and drag (*The Curiosity of Chance*). Even now, adolescent protagonists who embody gender expressions or identities different than their assigned sex at birth continue to be rare in teen films, and when they do appear, it is often in ways that leave audiences ambivalent or even outraged. For example, in the teen film *Dope* (2015), one of protagonist Malcolm's best friends is Diggy, who appears to identify as one of the guys. But in one scene, the three friends meet resistance in getting into a nightclub when the bouncer wants to let in more girls. So Diggy flashes the bouncer, who then says, "Oh, shit! That is a girl—like some Teena Brandon *Boys Don't Cry* shit!" Played for "humor," both the reference to Brandon Teena and Diggy's exposure as anatomically female come across as highly insensitive. One blogger, Jasmine Alvarez, states being initially excited about the film but leaving disappointed with the actual portrayal, stating, "How could the writers put in such a distasteful joke? Were they not aware of how tragic the Brandon Teena story is?" Alvarez argues that the scene "totally negates the positive impact Diggy's character could have had."[47] Here, Alvarez labels Diggy a "queer girl" not trans or nonbinary, which may in fact be the intent of the film—making it apparent that although, again, a trans subtext might be read here, it certainly would not be obvious to all audiences across all eras. A similar ambiguity might be identified through the protagonist of the film *Freak Show* (2017). Billy Bloom decides to compete for Homecoming Queen, and Billy's elaborate and often feminine outfits at school suggests a gender variance separate from sexuality. However, although both *Dope* and *Freak Show* portray a fluidity of gender expression and expose the performativity of gender, they are not necessarily trans stories.[48] Rather, characters like Watts, Diggy, and Billy offer rare hints at gender variance for teens in the genre.

Overtly trans characters have only recently begun to be integrated into protagonist roles in films like *3 Generations* and *Boy Meets Girl* and an occasional supporting role. For example, in Amy Poehler's 2021 film *Moxie*, a supporting trans character, CJ (played by trans actor Josie Totah), is a participant in the youth feminist movement Moxie. In one scene, they each describe what is "messed up" about their school, and CJ describes how others "refuse to call me by my new name." Although a minor moment in a movie about a cisgender heterosexual teen, this nod to a trans teen played by a trans teen actress indicates an acknowledgment in the mainstream that could foreshadow future depictions. Considering that popular US films started with the "gay best friend" trope, it is not surprising to see teen films begin tentatively by incorporating trans youth in this way. A coming increase in trans representations seems inevitable. While Warner Bros abruptly decided to shelve *Batgirl* featuring DC Extended Universe's first live-action trans character, 2022 also marked the release of Billy Porter's independent feature *Anything's Possible* (2022), produced with a $10 million budget, perhaps the largest yet for a trans teen film. Acquired and released on Amazon Prime in July 2022, the film depicts a trans girl of color (played by trans actress Eva Reign) as she explores a romance with a boy in her high school. Although the film did not have a theatrical release, its sizable budget and acquisition by a major VOD platform indicates an expanding mainstream interest in trans teen stories.

"BAD TRANS OBJECTS" AND "CANCEL CULTURE" IN TRANS TEEN FILMS IN THE TWENTY-FIRST CENTURY

With so few US trans teen films to investigate, it is surprising that two recent films marketed as pro-trans, *3 Generations* and *Adam*, received such intense backlash that it disrupted their theatrical releases. In short, both were deemed "bad" by their target audiences. As a result, individuals coalesced through social media to disrupt, downvote, and "cancel" the films. Examining how people expressed their dissent—the antithesis to consent—toward these films highlights an integral connection between consent culture and what has come to be known as "cancel culture." While the term *cancel culture* has often been conjured by the political right to critique activists' calls for personal responsibility, the dictionary definition is simply "the practice or tendency of engaging in mass canceling as a way of expressing disapproval and exerting social pressure,"[49] and according to a 2020 Pew Research Center study, 49 percent of adults in the United States familiar with the term associate it with "actions people take to hold others accountable."[50] Cancel culture is indelibly linked to consent culture not only because of the way #MeToo advocacy launched a rooting out of powerful serial abusers, canceling their contracts, shows, and careers, but also due to the fact that through cancel culture, audiences, fans, political constituents, and others wield considerable power to express how they feel violated by a particular representation.

A year before the protest over *Boys Don't Cry* at Reed College, director Gaby Dellal was "savaged"[51] by critics in 2015 for, among other things, casting cisgender actress Elle Fanning (who formerly played Princess Aurora in Disney's *Maleficent*) as Ray, a trans boy in *3 Generations* (originally titled *About Ray*). The film chronicles Ray's quest to obtain the legal consent of his mother (Naomi Watts) and his estranged father to begin testosterone treatment. Initially, the film, which also stars Susan Sarandon as Ray's intolerant lesbian grandmother Dodo, seemed destined for success with early positive support from the industry, including a piece in Women and Hollywood, which reported that although Fanning's role in the film might attract some controversy, "it's hard not to be excited for a multigenerational project focused on sexually diverse women and transgender people with female writers and filmmakers in key roles behind the scenes."[52] The film was acquired by the Weinstein Company (TWC) for an impressive $6 million at Cannes Film Festival, and it received a standing ovation at its Toronto International Film Festival screening.[53] Critics frequently mentioned the film as an Oscar contender.

The tides turned quickly in August 2015 when Dellal's interview with Refinery29 exposed a surprising lack of sensitivity in talking about the film and character. In the interview, Dellal used feminine pronouns to discuss Ray—especially ironic considering that in the film itself, Ray's mother constantly corrects herself and others to use "he" not "she" in referencing Ray.[54] Immediately, activists and writers criticized Dellal, who had exposed "how little she gets it, and why she probably shouldn't have told this story in the first place" and how she had decided to "shoehorn in being trans to make [the] story more interesting."[55] On Twitter, naysayers panned Dellal's casting choice with comments like "why is elle fanning (cis woman) portraying a (trans)boy"; "I want to be excited about #3Generations, but are you telling me there were no pre-T trans actors who could have played Ray?";[56] and "Why isn't a real trans person cast? Things haven't changed since Boys Don't Cry w/H. Swank."[57] TWC pulled the film days before its expected release, and it sat in limbo for a year and a half until being slated for release in theaters (a contractual obligation of the acquisition) in 2017.[58] By then the controversy had died down but so had enthusiasm for the film. According to IMDb, the film only grossed $680,000 worldwide ($156,000 in the United States) at the box office—a brutally poor showing for a $6 million acquisition. It received no Oscar nomination nor any other significant industry award nominations.

All movies are subject to their extratextuality, but films with trans characters are perhaps even more so since it is not merely the suspension of disbelief that is disrupted when a cis person plays a trans character or a director talks about a boy protagonist as a girl but also the audience's understanding of the film and filmmaker as pro-trans that becomes undermined. In interviews, Dellal clearly hoped to position the film as a positive and sensitive portrayal that sought to "normalize.... not sensationalize" trans experiences, adding, "I really hope this film has a social impact and is far-reaching."[59] Yet Dellal's description of Ray as "a girl who is presenting in a very ineffectual way as a boy" and her explanation that "to actually use a trans boy was not an option because this isn't what my story is about,"[60] cannot be untangled from the text of the film itself—particularly for audiences seeking authentic and affirming portrayals of trans lives.

The fact that nearly all trans teen movies are written and directed by cisgender individuals has been problematic, although stories have not always fared better under a trans director. The 2019 film *Adam*, based on the novel by lesbian writer Ariel Schrag and directed by trans filmmaker Rhys Ernst, premiered at Sundance and initially garnered numerous glowing reviews in *Hollywood Reporter*,[61] *Out* magazine,[62] and others. The film was lauded for its depiction of early 2000s trans and queer New York City culture and its casting of numerous queer and trans actors. Yet the film itself presents an unusual premise—Adam, a heterosexual cis adolescent, is mistaken as a trans adult man by Gillian, a lesbian woman he has a crush on. Although at times he wavers, wanting to tell Gillian the truth, Adam pursues their relationship under these pretenses. The two begin dating, and Adam fills in the details of his pretended trans identity by researching online. Although the film does not go as far as the novel—Adam never has intercourse with Gillian using his penis without her knowledge—he does have intercourse with her repeatedly using a strap-on.

Undoubtedly, queer and trans reviewers initially wanted to like this film despite its premise—in *Out*, a critic admits, "On paper, the whole idea could honestly be considered transphobic and gross.... But why this film works as well [as] it does is because transgender filmmaker Rhys Ernst is at its helm."[63] The wider public of potential fans, however, was not as forgiving. Although the 2014 book had received its own "backlash of transphobic claims,"[64] such criticism remained relatively low key until May 13, 2018, when a Tumblr user created a post titled "Do Not Support Adam." The blogger argued for avoiding the upcoming film due to numerous aspects of the plot, including Adam's guise as trans and sex with Gillian, "which is fucking rape" that the book does "worse" than "justify."[65] The blogger also critiqued the ending of the book (omitted from the film) in which Gillian has a straight cis boyfriend,[66] a plot conclusion they argued supported corrective rape, the false belief that homosexuality can be altered through heterosexual rape. Within just a few weeks, the post had over fifty thousand comments, and a #BoycottAdam trend had found its way through Twitter. Many posters screenshotted and shared the author's main takeaway:

> "So. We have
> An underage cishet boy lying about being an adult trans man in order to trick a lesbian into dating him!
> A scene in which he actually rapes her!
> The lesbian in question becomes attracted to cis men making Adam, essentially, conversion therapy!
> Do NOT support Adam (2018)"

Individuals on Twitter called out the film for its transphobia and lesbophobia—expressing how the film posed a "threat"[67] and could cause "extreme harm"[68] to the LGBTQ+ community. In many cases, individuals referenced the impact that art has on real lives, such as "Trans art that hates trans people & others is hate."[69] This outpouring of public outrage fueled a forceful yearlong campaign to disrupt the release of the film.

Ernst, who had anticipated controversy for the film, responded soon after with a June 5, 2018 Medium post which begins with, "I'm a queer transgender man and film director who has dedicated my life to telling trans stories, to expanding the boundaries of what a trans story can be, while seeking to improve the condition of trans people's lives through storytelling."[70] Ernst explains that he too had some "concerns" about Schrag's book, so when he received the script, he was initially "apprehensive" and "ready to be offended." However, after reading it, he found himself "stunned and pleasantly surprised." In particular, he was taken by the way the "screenplay flipped the 'trans deception' narrative trope on its head. It was poking fun at, but also challenging, cis people's obsession with transness." Ernst argued that "Adam is trapped in a lie, but he is ultimately culpable," suggesting that in his own retelling of the story, "what Adam does is wrong, it affects people, and that is the point." Ernst stated that although he understands that "our community is rightfully distrustful of material" that might add to an already "negative legacy," he argued that "creating trans art often requires difficult conversations, and I strive to show up, be present and responsible to this dialogue." Ernst repeatedly articulated that because he is a member of the trans community, his film too is a "trans story."[71] Still, Ernst's post did little to sway audiences—calls to boycott the film mounted from its premiere at Sundance in January 2019 to its screening at Outfest in July 2019 to its scheduled release soon after. Individuals downvoted the film until it plunged to 1.7/10 on IMDb, and they created hundreds of posts demanding a boycott of the film as well as several petitions calling for canceling its release.[72] The distributor, however, proceeded with the film's theatrical release. Having been acquired by Wolfe Releasing in May 2019 for an undisclosed amount, the film went into theaters as scheduled on August 14, 2019. But the damage had undoubtedly been done—it would be hard to imagine a film with as much publicity getting so little positive traction on social media. Years later, its Twitter account has only a few dozen followers and Instagram only a few hundred.[73] And despite award nominations and wins at Sundance, Outfest, and the GLAAD Media Awards, the film currently has a 4.0 rating on IMDB.[74]

Based on the reaction from bloggers and social media posters, it is evident that many in the queer and trans communities did not agree with the way trans lives were represented via *Adam* and *3 Generations*. They voiced their refusal to see the films and encouraged others to do the same, protesting what they believed to be harmful portrayals of an already vulnerable population. The visibility that these films offered, they believed, was neither acceptable nor desirable. As a result, trans individuals and allies sought and largely succeeded at rendering these films less visible for their depictions, plot contrivances, and casting choices. In a sense, they expressed their dissent or lack of affirmation/consent to each film—loudly and clearly—and as a result, they likely limited each film's theatrical potential. Both films were, indeed, seen as "bad" and, on some level, canceled.

In an industry guided by both public reception and return on investment, the resistance to both *3 Generations* and *Adam* carries consequences beyond these individual films. Trans critic Jude Dry, who disagreed with the backlash, articulates, "*Adam* has some big producers behind it, and they took a gamble on Ernst. That's a huge fucking deal. There aren't a lot of trans filmmakers making movies of this size, and it's not even that big. It's a pretty small-budget movie, and it's probably not even going to make that much money. What do these people even think they're boycotting?"[75] This argument points to the fact that to not see and to not support a film is more than an act of protest for that particular film—it carries an economic impact that might alter future productions. Because there are so few, each trans film that fails to find a wide audience inevitably increases the risk of further reduced visibility for trans individuals—not just for that film, but via the industry as a whole.

RENDERING VISIBLE THE (IN)VISIBLE REPRESENTATIONS OF TRANS YOUTH

Is anything lost by a refusal to engage with "bad" films like *Adam* and *3 Generations*? Do such films have something to offer us if not as consumers, then as trans allies and film scholars? If we look more closely at these breakout texts themselves, do we find moments of value—or of deeper concern? Might we locate in them, as Keegan suggests, productive possibilities that "good" trans media objects typically fail to explore? Ultimately, all three films (3 Generations, Adam, and Boy Meets Girl) have remained much less visible than they could have been—3 Generations and Adam due to a backlash that sought to erase them and Boy Meets Girl due to its lack of a substantial fan base to propel it to wider visibility. However, these films represent some of the earliest forays into the still developing US trans teen genre. As cultural artifacts, they can help us understand how the US independent film industry both reflects trans teen lives and reshapes them into stories for mainstream audiences. Furthermore, assessing the nuances and details of these depictions might help inform writers, filmmakers, producers, and critics to think more actively about the meaning made by the stories we tell.

In fact, each of these films renders trans adolescence visible in important ways. In 3 Generations, Ray, assigned female at birth, desperately wants to begin T (testosterone) and restart his life at a new school as a boy. However, he cannot proceed without a signed parental consent form from his hesitant mother and his estranged father. As such, the film depicts the nonconsent of Ray's very existence—he does not consent to his body's being categorized as female nor does he have the legal right to transition without parental consent due to his age. In this way, he is subjugated on multiple levels—it's no wonder he describes his "whole existence" as "shit." When Ray reminds his mother to sign the form, her response is routinely, "We agreed to take this slow." Considering that we learn in the film that Ray, now age sixteen, has felt like a boy since age four and has been out to his family for five or six years, Ray's desire to transition is not at all framed as a hasty decision but rather one borne out of over a decade of life experience in his changing body. By depicting the ambivalence of his mother and initial reluctance of his father, the film evokes compassion for a trans youth who must contend with adults who constantly run interference to his wishes in both their words and actions. Significantly, the film underscores that Ray knows best what he wants and needs. Ray's parents do eventually consent to sign the papers, and Ray begins hormone treatments. His sense of relief at the end is evident—and overall, the film draws in audiences to identify with both his lack of agency and his journey of overcoming the obstacles of his parents, grandparents, and peers so that he can be himself. Considering how the debates on trans youth continue to be played out in US politics, such an empathetic depiction could offer visibility to a youth's point of view in impactful ways.

Of course, 3 Generations also has problematic elements upon closer look. Ray desperately wants to pass, and the film repeatedly stresses that Ray hopes to be on testosterone for several months before beginning at a new school. Ray longs for a "conventional experience" as his mother puts it, or as he says himself in the film, "I just want to be normal in a regular school" and "I'm not starting a new school in this body—I'm just not." This emphasis on passing is not further investigated in the film—it is seen simply as a worthwhile and "authentic" goal. Again, it is nearly impossible to separate the extratextuality of the film here, as we might recall Dellal's describing Ray's failure to "pass" when talking about the character as "a girl who is presenting in a very ineffectual way as a boy." In fact, passing has been often problematized by trans advocates as an ideal that can do more harm than good. If ideal femininity or masculinity can be elusive standards for cis individuals, they are even more challenging for trans individuals. Much of the film—through Ray's character—imagines gender as a strict binary. For example, the film starts with Ray's voiceover describing how when he was younger, he wanted to be a "cowboy" not a "princess." Later when Ray sits with some masculine friends, he enjoys their "locker room talk" about a girl at school, until one of them says "I'm blessed" for being a "big dude." Ray appears eager to fit into heteronormative culture—even including the objectification of women and girls—until it omits him. Since the film ends just as Ray begins his treatment, we do not have access to how he or his story might allow for more complexities and ambiguities in the future. As a result, the film depicts testosterone as a panacea—an overly simplistic portrayal of a trans teen.

Boy Meets Girl offers a more nuanced approach to sexuality and gender identities. Despite a cisgender director, *Boy Meets Girl* epitomizes many of the criteria for a "good" depiction of a trans individual. Ricky (played by trans actress Michelle Hendley in a debut performance) is beautiful, talented, and self-confident—and the film focuses on her goal to be a fashion designer and her journey through romances. Although *Boy Meets Girl* had a limited theatrical release, it had a successful festival run and was acquired by Wolfe Video in 2015. As writer/director Eric Schaeffer is not trans himself, he relied on a combination of research and interviews to make the film more authentic, and Hendley notes in several interviews how Schaeffer encouraged her to change dialogue to reflect her own experiences. The film has since received overwhelmingly positive reviews both from critics and fans, and it launched Hendley's acting career.

In the film, the trans girl protagonist, Ricky, who previously has been attracted only to men, decides to embark on a relationship with the cis woman Francesca, after a mutual attraction brings them together. Sexual fluidity connects the threads of the plot—Ricky's best cis guy friend Robby harbors a crush on her; Francesca is engaged to be married to a cis man, David, despite her attraction to Ricky; and, as is later revealed, David previously had sex with Ricky.

Fig. 5.1. Eric Schaeffer's *Boy Meets Girl*, starring trans actress Michelle Hendley, depicts the nuances of sexualities and gender identities.

In other words, Ricky attracts them all at various points—David, Francesca, and Robby. As well as the relationships, the dialogue in the film points to how Schaeffer sought to break down labels, which he suggests often "alienate us."[76] After Francesca and Ricky are intimate together, Francesca wonders, "I'm curious. I mean does this make me gay?" Ricky says, "I don't think so." "Bi-curious?" Francesca asks. Ricky responds, "I don't know." Francesca declares, "Well, it has to make me *something*," to which Ricky responds, "Human?" and they both laugh and kiss. Later, Robby attempts to contest such ambiguity insisting to Ricky that heterosexual sex is only "penis in vagina," as he declares himself perfectly straight. Ricky suspects otherwise and begins to question him about his "queer" practices asking, "And during this good clean normal god-fearing American 'boy meets girl' heterosexual sex, do you ever like when a girl sticks her finger up your butt?" Robby doesn't deny her suggestion, but nevertheless initially insists on his flawed logic.

Ultimately, *Boy Meets Girl* depicts the futility of labels—even for oneself. In the denouement, Robby realizes his love and attraction to Ricky, frantically searches her out, finds her swimming in the lake, and confesses his love to her. When he tells her, "You are so beautiful, Ricky," she walks out of the lake—and both Robby and us as viewers see her naked. The film's depiction of Hendley's non-op trans body undoubtedly runs risks since, as Baril argues, in our "sensationalist" media culture "trans bodies are an ideal target to satisfy public curiosity."[77] It is worth noting how Hendley mentions in interviews how the nudity was integral to the story and "non-negotiable" for the role.[78] She states how it was "important" to her that the scene not be for "shock value," merely showing, "Oh, look at that lady with the dick."[79] Instead, Hendley argues for the affirming visibility of this scene, stating, "I think there's a lot of mystery associated with trans people. And I think that mystery can often lead to fear, which leads to people being judged. Why not just demystify the whole thing? Why not show people that, hey, even naked I'm just a person."[80] In the film, when Ricky steps out of the water, she asks Robby, "Do you still think I'm beautiful?" He responds by kissing her passionately. His affirmation to her body is further validated when Ricky says, "It's OK if you want to ignore it," to which Robby responds, "I don't want to ignore anything about you ever." This scene thus renders trans adolescence and romance visible in an affirming and mutual way, and it does so without the typical shock or tragic undertones. *Boy Meets Girl* thus reimagines the scenario of a cisgender heterosexual guy who falls in love with a trans girl.

Boy Meets Girl also presents trans embodiment with its many ambiguities. Ricky does "pass" effectively as a girl, but the film specifically addresses Ricky's own feelings about her gender fluid body. When she first informs Francesca that she's trans, Ricky explains, "I wish I'd been born a genetic girl. I do plan on getting the full surgery someday. It's just so expensive. But, for now, I might as well just dance with the one that brung me, right? And it's not really about hating my body, so I've learned to live with it." Hendley attests to validity of this sentiment—in fact at her request, Schaeffer's original line that she "loved" her body was changed to "I've learned to live with it" to better reflect her own view of trans embodiment.[81] Although Ricky's ambivalence is clear, her openness in the film about her gender identity and body presents a refreshing example of someone living beyond the binary. When Francesca asks if she keeps it a secret, Ricky responds, "I am completely comfortable with who I am and I like to make sure everyone else in my life is too." In this way, the film models a world in which acceptance is possible both by oneself and others.

While *Boy Meets Girl* relies on some tired tropes, it also depicts how youth assert themselves in a gender normative world. For example, in one flashback scene, young Ricky scares off a pedophilic predator on Halloween by lifting up her dress—a contrivance that relies on the clichéd shock of her unexpected genital revelation. But at other points, the film depicts more nuance in how youth defend trans lives. In another flashback scene, Robby defends his friendship with Ricky amid the teasing of his masculine high school friends—who quickly grow quiet when they see her and clearly find her attractive. The film also shows Ricky's asserting and defending herself. When Francesca's mom shows up at the coffee shop to persuade Ricky to break it off with her daughter, telling her, "Transgender just sounds so ugly. You'd be better off just telling everybody you have a birth defect," Ricky comes back with, "Thanks, Helen. Sage words, indeed. Is that what you tell people is your excuse?" Similarly, when David verbally and physically attacks Ricky after learning of her relationship with his fiancée, he pins Ricky on the ground, and she says, "You like being on top David? From what I recall, you like being on bottom much more." The recollection of their intimacy together snaps him out of his rage. Although David's character conforms to the cliché of a self-hating queer character's lashing out, the more open resolution for David and Francesca upends the traditional trajectory. In their final scene together, Francesca tells David that she still loves him, but she doesn't like how he can "hate." He confesses that he slept with Ricky his sophomore year, adding, "So, no I don't hate her. And if you don't hate me for doing it, it might go a long way for me not hating myself for doing it either." Francesca, although shocked, answers immediately, "Of course, I don't hate you." The plot comes together perhaps a bit too neatly here when they decide to postpone the wedding and "get to know each other again." Still, the film resists pathologizing or demonizing any of the characters so that the couples (Robby and Ricky; Francesca and David) can have their happy endings in a true rom-com style albeit with much more acceptance for a spectrum of sexualities and gender identities.

So too does 3 *Generations* present a combination of tired patterns but also a more unexpected depiction of discrimination that warrants more attention. At one point, Ray is attacked and beaten up by another student who demands, "Show me your tits, girl" and yells, "Where you running to faggot?" as Ray escapes with a black eye. Later, Ray's crush, Lola, exhibits some sympathy calling him "brave," but his excitement gets derailed when she follows it with, "pretty lame beating up on a girl, right?" Such scenes reiterate scenarios that have been depicted in queer films for decades and, as such, feel like stock scenes meant to convey transphobia. However, 3 *Generations*, through the character of Ray's grandmother Dodo, portrays a lesbian character's bias against trans individuals—a form of discrimination not commonly depicted in films. Early in the film, Dodo and her girlfriend have a conversation with Ray's mother, Maggie, while Ray is in earshot. Dodo asks, "Why can't she just be a lesbian?" to which Ray's mother responds, "Because she's not a lesbian, Mom. She's a boy." In discussing the medical interventions, Dodo says, "It feels like mutilation to me" and then equates trans treatments with female genital mutilation. By portraying a lesbian grandmother who does not initially support trans lives and gender-affirming care, 3 *Generations* demonstrates that acceptance is not only something hard to come by in the wider world but also within families. Significantly, it also demonstrates how a queer person might not always be an ally to trans rights—a fact made evident in anti-trans writings by certain radical feminists. In an interview, Sarandon mentions her own shock at hearing one of her gay friends saying, "It's so self-indulgent this trend that's going on. Can't they just be lesbians?"[82] Sarandon expresses that her "job" in the film is to show a character who evolves into understanding the "difference between gender identity and sexual preference."[83] By the end, Dodo has come around. She meets Ray after school and says, "Look, sometimes I'm wrong—not often, but sometimes. And I thought you were too young to know what you wanted, but you *do* know. And I was just afraid. And now I realize that who you are and who I love is staying the same, and everything that's changing is just details." Through Dodo, the film exposes queer individuals who are intolerant of trans lives while providing an idealistic outcome of how they might arrive at a new way of thinking.

These two films, 3 *Generations* and *Boy Meets Girl*, represent some of the only recent teen films with a trans teen protagonist. As a result of the lack of visibility for each of these films, albeit for different reasons, audiences did not have the benefit of empathizing with trans youth through the issues these films raised—parental consent, queer biases, and the unsustainability of sex/gender binaries. Still, each of the films are now available on VOD platforms, and they might continue to garner viewers as trans youth emerge from invisibility.

THE PRODUCTIVE WORK OF THE VERY "BAD TRANS OBJECT": *ADAM*

Adam might be considered the worst trans text. In fact, the protagonist Adam is not even trans but instead disguising as trans. As a result, even to call it a trans text requires a conceptual leap—one must accept Ernst's assertion that the film is a "flipped" trans narrative. The film follows cisgender high school student Adam, who spends the summer in New York City with his queer older sister Casey and her roommates June and Ethan (played by trans actor Leo Sheng). With no other friends, job, or family in the city, Adam winds up tagging along with Casey and her community of queer and trans friends to parties, restaurants, and bars. As outlined earlier, social media users "canceled" *Adam* based on a premise considered transphobic and lesbophobic as well as the sexual interactions deemed nonconsensual between Gillian and Adam. However, inspired by Keegan, I look here to the "bad" text of *Adam* for what its badness reveals. Keegan suggests examining such texts "can help expose how the exemplary trans media of the current moment might actually reflect new restrictions on the transgender imaginary."[84] In other words, it might be necessary to do more than simply look away—but rather to examine more closely what exactly is so egregious and so transgressive in a film like *Adam*.

In numerous interviews about *Adam*, Ernst, the film's producers, and several actors argue that the public's refusal to see and engage with the film itself represented a self-destructive shutdown of issues important to the queer and trans communities. In interviews, Ernst often targets "cancel culture," which he argues "has become toxic and harmful to all kinds of people in marginalized communities." He states, "I think it's an important cultural moment in this conversation, to question this response. Boycotting movies before they are out by marginalized artists, is that the kind of world we want to live in?"[85] Ernst specifically criticizes the attacks on two points—people had not yet seen the film, and trans filmmakers should not be limited to "safe work." At a Q&A after the Outfest screening, Ernst declared that we are experiencing a "war on nuance," arguing that despite the "pressure," he resists the idea "that trans filmmakers or queer filmmakers.... shouldn't push boundaries, and we shouldn't make people question things or be uncomfortable."[86] *Adam* most certainly pushed boundaries, and upon a closer look, the film offers a rare representation of consent issues for trans youth.

The crux of discontent over *Adam* appears to be Adam's disguise as trans which leads him to a sexual relationship with Gillian. At first, Adam's misunderstood identity is accidental. Before meeting Gillian, Adam's sister and friends bring him to a "dyke bar." The knowing nod that the bouncer gives him when he offers up his fake ID shows that he has been accepted into this club—and world—under a mistaken belief regarding his gender identity. At the bar, Adam meets an intoxicated woman who declares it's her thirtieth birthday. As they make out in the bathroom, she says, "Fuck me with that dick of yours," and Adam stutters responding he thinks he has a condom. She laughs saying, "Is it dirty? Did you fuck another girl tonight? Naughty" and adds, "You wouldn't come here packing if you didn't want to use it. Don't be shy—I love tranny cock." At that, Adam suddenly realizes the confusion. Flustered, he backs away and begins to make excuses as he rushes out the door to find Casey and June.

The world of *Adam* is inverted—here, being queer is the norm. Although Casey has kept her sexuality secret from her parents (which Adam uses as blackmail when she discovers Adam lied about his age to Gillian), queer and trans characters in the film are embraced for their various gender identities and sexualities. As one of the attendees at Camp Trans at the end of the film declares, "Some women have penises; some men don't. And the rest of the world is just going to have to get the fuck over it." Through this declaration and others like it, *Adam* clearly seeks to affirm and normalize trans and queer bodies and identities. As a cisgender heterosexual youth, Adam is the odd man out in the world of the film—*he* is the one who must learn to understand and adapt. And that he does. In one scene, Casey tells Adam that no girls would be interested in him at the party since they are all gay. So, when Adam spots Gillian at a queer party, he makes his (clumsy) move, sidling up to Gillian and then abruptly tossing a drink all over her chest. When he apologizes, saying he tripped, Gillian's friend accuses bluntly, "You didn't trip. You literally turned around and threw a drink on her." He admits, "I wanted to talk." Gillian and her friend laugh, and despite Gillian's saying, "That's the dumbest thing I've ever heard," she follows it up with, "So what'd you want to talk to me about?" Adam benefits by being mistaken as trans—he behaves badly, but all is forgiven because he is thought to be trans—and he knows it. He immediately demonstrates a willingness to play along. When Gillian asks him who he knows at the party, he points to Boy Casey and some of the other trans men stating, "They're my bros." When Adam walks Gillian home, she says, "I've never dated a trans guy before. Like I've only had girlfriends. And I think I'm open. I mean, I know I'm open to it. I just thought I should tell you." Gillian's honesty is countered by Adam's secrecy as he, a bit flustered, mumbles, "Yeah I never really dated too so." She gives him a quick kiss on the mouth and says, "See you later OK." After she leaves, Adam begins laughing in satisfaction.

Undoubtedly the outrage the film inspires has much to do with the premise of a cisgender heterosexual teen boy's infiltrating this otherwise safe and insular queer world. Even as *Adam* positions the titular cis character as the odd man out in a queer world, the film still prioritizes Adam's point of view. As a result, *Adam* is a film not only about how a cis heterosexual person learns to understand and adapt to queer culture but also how that culture learns to understand and accept *him*. Like the book, the film attempts to justify Adam's actions when he confesses at the end, and Gillian responds that she already knew. But this premise is unconvincing based on the plot, which repeatedly depicts Gillian's obliviousness to Adam's cisness. For example, more than halfway through the film when Gillian and Adam have already had intercourse with a strap-on multiple times, Gillian suggests they watch the lesbian love story *The Incredibly True Adventures of Two Girls in Love*. Adam lets it slip that his mom can't even say the word *lesbian* without it being in a "vampire voice." Gillian is surprised and says, "Really? But she's cool with you." He tries to cover by saying, "Yeah but not my sister. It's fucked up." Gillian tells him, "We never really talk about trans stuff, and you don't have to obviously, but I just didn't want you to think that I was avoiding it," and he responds, "Uh, no, no. It's like not a big part of who I am. Like *really* not a big part." Perhaps Adam's nervousness at this moment could have given Gillian a clue about his nontrans identity, but there is no earlier indication in the film that Gillian suspects he is cis—certainly it seems she begins this scene still believing he is trans.

Critiques of the film often point to how Gillian's consent is not fully aware and, thus, not freely given. In a consent culture that prioritizes "informed" and "specific" consent, the underlying belief is "There's no room for ambiguity or assumptions when it comes to consent,"[87] which is exactly why Adam's actions seem so wrong. However, where does such a framework leave trans individuals? Is one's gender identity irrelevant, a matter of privacy, or a requisite disclosure? By exploring *Adam* as a flipped trans story, it homes in on how the terms of affirmative consent and consent culture might be problematic for trans individuals. In the reversed story, Adam would be a trans protagonist who did not disclose his trans identity before engaging in sexual activity with Gillian. He might still be feigning friendship with his "bros" but instead would not be disputing Gillian's assumption that he is cis. While *Adam* might leave audiences feeling outraged by the concept of a cis person allowing someone to believe he is trans, the fact is that if Adam *were* trans in the story, some of those same individuals might argue for his right to share his identity if, when, and how he wants.[88] Most trans advocates agree with the sentiment that "gender identity is a private matter and people should not be forced to figure it out or communicate it to others to have an intimate life."[89] In a perhaps unpalatable way, *Adam* ultimately exposes this important point—consent culture's emphasis on full disclosure might not be inclusive for those who have gender identities or gender expressions different than their sex assigned at birth.

The film *Adam* delves specifically into this issue in a scene when Adam and his cis friend Brad arrive at the apartment as the roommates are watching TV news about a trans teen girl who has been murdered. The report details how the male suspects felt "tricked" by "him" to which Casey, in tears, responds "her, her" and Ethan looks visibly angry. Brad, new to this world, immediately reveals his ignorance by stating, "So he tricked those guys into thinking he was a girl?" Casey snaps back, "*She* didn't trick anybody." Thus, the argument ensues—and Adam is caught between Brad's insistence that "you shouldn't pretend to be a girl and have sex with guys if you're a dude. You wouldn't understand. It's a straight guy thing. I mean it could really fuck you up," and Casey's argument that "they had sex with her because they wanted to—she did not have to tell them that she was trans." Of course, in the story, the irony is that Adam has not yet told Gillian that he is cis, despite his obvious growing guilt. Ernst's attempt to equate Adam's actions with what he calls "trans deception" becomes more obvious here. When Adam quietly adds, "I mean, I guess she could have told them," Ethan breaks in abruptly, "You know, I don't tell people when I hook up with them." At this moment, Adam cannot immediately process what Ethan has just revealed (before this point, Adam—and perhaps the audience—had assumed Ethan was cis). Adam responds, "Tell them, tell them what?" to which Ethan says, "That I'm trans. I've hooked up with people and not told them." Adam stares in disbelief as Ethan gets up and goes to his bedroom and closes the door.

Which point of view is the audience meant to identify with here? If we support Ethan's actions to not disclose his transness, do we also excuse Adam's concealment of his cisness? Certainly, the parallel is uncomfortable—and perhaps that is the point. *Adam* is a very "bad trans object" indeed. However, this scene, and the film itself, exposes a key flaw of the affirmative consent discourse regarding noncisgender sexual consent—exactly what should be included in a definition of "informed" and "specific" consent? Although the United States does not have federal laws against what has been labeled "gender fraud," several other countries such as the United Kingdom and Israel do. In those cases, trans individuals who do not reveal their gender identity before sexual interactions can be brought up on sexual assault charges—a fact that many criticize for legalizing "trans panic."[90] *Adam* identifies the crux of this consent question— why should one's gender identity even matter? If one consents to a sexual act (e.g., intercourse with a dildo) with a partner, why would that partner's sex assigned at birth matter at all?

Adam resists an unambiguously negative reading if we accept Ernst's determination that the story be understood as a flipped narrative of "trans deception." Advocates have long argued that trans individuals do not need to disclose their trans identities—and that, in fact, being trans is not "deception" at all. The fact of Adam's cisness as something both he and Gillian must accept at the end presents an obvious irony—and perhaps even a tasteless one. After Adam admits to being cis, Gillian says, "I wanted you to keep pretending so I could keep pretending too. Like I needed you to be a trans guy for me to be able to like you.... which is pretty fucked up and transphobic when you think about it." But what Gillian does is not only transphobic—it's also heterophobic and cisphobic. In the film, Gillian is a self-identified lesbian cis woman who initially only wants to be with a trans man believing his sex assigned at birth is female. But if we flip this narrative, Gillian is a woman who only wants to be with a cis man thinking his sex assigned at birth was male. When Gillian concludes at the end of the film that she must expand her definition of her own sexuality to accommodate her desires, it suggests that she was wrong to have been focused on Adam's cisness/transness at all. Although this portrayal comes across as offensive in *Adam*, in its flipped iteration, it makes more sense, which calls into question the inconsistencies embedded in the affirmative consent discourse regarding sex/gender/sexuality.

In discussing the "bad trans object," Keegan argues that sometimes the "bad trans object threatens the very stability of sexual difference itself"—and it is for that reason that others seek to "ignore" or "erase" it. *Adam* most certainly presents this assertion in a most discomfiting way. When Gillian, at the end of the film at Camp Trans, admits her sexuality, shouting, "I'm bisexual," into the air, Adam follows suit yelling, "I'm a straight cis male." Here, gender and sexuality are slippery concepts from which Adam as a cis heterosexual teen boy too benefits. In this way, *Adam* presents the strange contradictions and possibilities in a world beyond sex/gender divisions.

"NOTHING ABOUT US WITHOUT US"— CONSENTING TO STORIES

Consent culture has transformed not only how films about sex and gender are told but also audiences' expectations and reactions to those films. In short, fans want to feel they have consented to the stories told about them. When they don't, it feels like a violation and affront, and audiences are quick to shut them down. For trans teen stories, the stakes continue to be particularly high since there are still only a handful of breakout texts.

In 2016, Jack Halberstam wrote a blog post in response to the protests against *Boys Don't Cry* and Peirce. Halberstam articulates that the protesters raise "interesting critiques and queries . . . worthy of conversation" but ultimately argues that it is not "a worthy activist goal to try to suppress the film, to cast it as transphobic." Halberstam states how *Boys Don't Cry* needs to be contextualized historically—having been produced at a point in time when trans actors were uncommon and empathetic representations of a trans protagonist were nonexistent. Written soon after Trump was elected president, Halberstam's piece argues the political landscape necessitates that we pick our "enemies" carefully, adding, "Spending time and energy protesting the work of an extremely important queer filmmaker is not only wasteful, it is morally bankrupt and misses the true danger of our historical moment."[91] Halberstam's critiques mirror many of those expressed by Ernst and others who argue that anger toward trans and queer filmmakers and their work is misdirected.

Of course, to suggest that students should not be outraged by screening *Boys Don't Cry* also might be out of step with a generation that insists on the power of both narrative and dissent. Underlying the Reed College protest is a desire to move on to a new phase of trans stories—away from ones that focus primarily on trauma and violence and those that make a spectacle of trans suffering. The students might not have expressed their views kindly or even wisely. But they did know how to be heard as demonstrated by the national news coverage their actions attracted. The more recent social media movements against 3 *Generations* and *Adam* carried out this opposition virtually, similarly expressing enough is enough. At the same time, Ernst is not wrong to note that by casting aside films without watching them means we miss the opportunity to engage with the complex issues they might raise. If films like *Adam* and *3 Generations* hit sore points, it might still be worth exploring more fully what those are and what we might glean so we don't create a new generation of trans stories that simply swap one homogeneity for another. By rendering invisible problematic depictions, we might also unintentionally keep the issues they illuminate out of sight.

Seeing that trans representations in cinema have been marked by over a century of narratives alternating spectacle with complete invisibility, it's no wonder that trans activists remain eager for a better variety of stories about the lives of trans youth—not only about coming out or gender transitioning, but also about falling in love, exploring sexuality, and struggling with the typical ups and downs of adolescence. In many ways, over twenty years after *Boys Don't Cry*, we are still waiting for the trans teen genre to emerge fully. Certainly, breakout texts represent "small cracks in the glass ceiling of cultural consciousness" that make "room for future breaks."[92] But in fact, teen films remain largely guided by the gender and sexuality binaries that have ruled romantic and sexual representations of adolescents for over a century. As trans activists remain alert to depictions that reflect them in ways they do not agree with, perhaps future writers and directors might seek to tell more stories that incorporate the individuals they wish to represent. It might still be years away, but trans teen stories will likely enter the mainstream just as queer films have. Small independent films—even not-so-commercially successful ones—have often been integral to paving the way for Hollywood depictions. Audiences impacted by such depictions are fully aware of that, which is exactly why they seek to influence how these stories are told. Likely, they will.

NOTES

1. Feder and Juhasz, "Does Visibility Equal Progress?"
2. Radi, "On Trans* Epistemology," 45.
3. GLAAD, "Transgender."
4. Kosciesza, "Intersectional Gender Measurement," 3.

5. Bendery, "Joe Biden."
6. Biden, "Let's Be Clear."
7. Liptak, "Civil Rights Law Protects Gay and Transgender Workers."
8. Lavietes and Ramos, "Nearly 240 Anti-LGBTQ Bills."
9. UCLA School of Law, "Prohibiting Gender-Affirming Medical Care for Youth."
10. In April 2021, the Arkansas General Assembly passed the "Save Adolescents from Experimentation (SAFE) Act," which states that a "physician or other healthcare professional shall not provide gender transition procedures to any individual under eighteen (18) years of age." Also see Cox, "As Arkansas Bans Treatments for Transgender Youth."
11. Dey, "Texas Health Providers Are Suspending."
12. *ICD-11 for Mortality and Morbidity Statistics*, "Gender Incongruence."
13. American Psychiatric Association, "What Is Gender Dysphoria?" The term "gender dysphoria" was adopted by the APA when they replaced "gender identity disorder" in 2013 in the DSM-5.
14. American Psychiatric Association. "APA Resolution on Gender Identity Change Efforts."
15. Littman, "Parent Reports," 33.
16. Littman, "Parent Reports," 34.
17. Brainard and You state that "retractions appeared to be relatively rare, involving only about two of every 10,000 papers."
18. Littman, "Correction," 5.
19. Halberstam, *In a Queer Time and Place*, 54.
20. The Trevor Project, "Research Brief: Data on Transgender Youth."
21. In an *Economist* article titled "An English Ruling on Transgender Teens Could Have Global Repercussions," the author states that while there was only one gender clinic in the United States 2007, there were fifty in 2020. In addition, numerous studies suggest increasing rates of children identifying as trans—also see Tanner, "More U.S. Teens Identify as Transgender."
22. In a study of over 17,000 participants, Turban et al. found that 82.5 percent of detransitioners "reported at least one external driving factor" in their decision to detransition such as "pressure from family and societal stigma."
23. "GLAAD, "Transgender People."
24. GLAAD, "Transgender People."
25. The Trevor Project, "Research Brief: Data on Transgender Youth."
26. Holiday, Bond, and Rasmussen, "Coming Attractions," 1157.
27. Gossett, Stanley, and Burton, *Trap Door*, xvi.
28. Namaste, *Invisible Lives*, 52.
29. Feder and Juhasz, "Does Visibility Equal Progress?"
30. Gossett, Stanley, and Burton, *Trap Door*, xv.
31. Baril, "Confessing Society," 7.
32. Baril, "Confessing Society," 11.
33. In addition to the "May Test" by Kiley May cited here, GLAAD has published the "Vito Russo Test" and writer Cassie Brighter suggested the "Brighter Test" in a 2019 Medium post.
34. Keegan, "On the Necessity of Bad Trans Objects," 26 and 28.
35. Keegan, "On the Necessity of Bad Trans Objects," 28.
36. Keegan, "On the Necessity of Bad Trans Objects," 27.
37. Keegan, "On the Necessity of Bad Trans Objects," 29.
38. Keegan, "On the Necessity of Bad Trans Objects," 29.

39. Radi, "On Trans* Epistemology," 48.
40. See Leung, "Film," and Steinbock, "Towards Trans Cinema."
41. Horak, *Girls Will Be Boys*, 2.
42. Horak, *Girls Will Be Boys*, 2. See also Helen Hok-sze Leung, "Film."
43. Steinbock, "Towards Trans Cinema," 395.
44. Horak, *Girls Will Be Boys*, 125.
45. Conklin, *Campus Life in the Movies*, 111.
46. Referenced here is the 1992 film *Little Sister* directed by Jimmy Zeilinger.
47. Alvarez, "Myth of Diggy."
48. In "The New Queer Spectator," Michele Aaron points out that a key difference between Brandon in *Boys Don't Cry* and the numerous gender-bending characters that came before is that "Brandon is not so much trying to pass as someone else as trying to be 'him' self" (190).
49. *Merriam-Webster*, s.v., "cancel culture."
50. Vogels et al., "Americans and 'Cancel Culture.'"
51. Jackson, "Gaby Dellal."
52. Women and Hollywood, "Elle Fanning to Play Transgender Character."
53. Busch, "About Ray."
54. Zuckerman, "Why 'About Ray's' Director Cast Elle Fanning as a Trans Teen."
55. Jusino, "About Ray's Gaby Dellal."
56. McCormick, "Trans Film."
57. Your Faux Mom (@JustBeNicer), "@Peoplemag Why isn't a real trans person cast? Things haven't changed since Boys Don't Cry w/ H. Swank #3generations," Twitter, November 20, 2014, https://twitter.com/JustBeNicer/status/535250114550706176.
58. Siegel, "Weinstein Co."
59. Jackson, "Gaby Dellal."
60. Zuckerman, "Why 'About Ray's' Director Cast Elle Fanning as a Trans Teen."
61. Rooney, "Adam."
62. Solzman, "'Adam' Proves the Importance."
63. Solzman, "'Adam' Proves the Importance."
64. Keeley, "Film Adaptation."
65. Call Me Out Scotty, "Do Not Support Adam (2018)."
66. Keeley, "Film Adaptation."
67. Lomas, "You Are a Threat."
68. CK (@itscourtkendall), "#BoycottAdam bc perpetuating a gross fetishizing account of a cishet rapist fantasizing about raping lesbians/wlw under the guise of being a pre-op trans man is harmful...," Twitter, May 15, 2018, https://twitter.com/itscourtkendell/status/996216915751243777.
69. Homan, Lucy (@lucypaw), "You can #boycottadam for being cis-centric and being transphobic. Or for hating on queer and trans politics. Or for its racism. Or for its misogyny." Twitter, August 10, 2019, https://twitter.com/lucypaw/status/1160252829111422976.
70. Ernst, "On 'Adam.'"
71. Ernst, "On 'Adam.'"
72. Keating, "People Are Calling."
73. Numbers are as of July 28, 2021. See the @adamthefilm Instagram profile at https://www.instagram.com/adamthefilm/ and Twitter profile at https://twitter.com/AdamTheFilm.

74. Internet Movie Database, "Adam." IMDb lists the box office for *Adam* as $364,921 worldwide. However, since Wolfe Releasing does not always make their US box office numbers public, these numbers might be inaccurate.
75. Osenlund, "Cancel Culture."
76. G. Kramer, "Frameline Interview."
77. Baril, "Confessing Society," 9.
78. Musto, "Michelle Hendley."
79. Wickman, "How One Young Trans Woman."
80. Kurchak, "Boy Meets Girl's Michelle Hendley."
81. Giacobbe, "24-Year-Old Trans Actress."
82. Whitney, "Not Just a Phase."
83. Whitney, "Not Just a Phase."
84. Keegan, "On the Necessity of Bad Trans Objects," 29.
85. Bravo, "'Adam' Presents Controversial View."
86. Reynolds, "'Adam' Director Rhys Ernst Addresses."
87. Healthline, "Your Guide to Sexual Consent."
88. The author of the book *Adam* states in an interview, "But people are really angry specifically about appropriating an oppressed identity. I just think that's fascinating to think about because what is so terrible about appropriating an oppressed identity? And what's terrible is that people are oppressed. But ultimately his deception is just a deception. He's also lying about his age, but no one seems to care about that. Why is one deception worse than another? I just think it's interesting to think about that." See Seggel, "Ariel Schrag."
89. Ashley, "Genderfucking Non-Disclosure," 339.
90. Ashley, "Genderfucking Non-Disclosure."
91. Halberstam, "Hiding the Tears."
92. Cavalcante, "Breaking into Transgender Life," 541.

CONCLUSION

Adolescent Sexuality and the Adult Imagination

IN THE PAST TWO DECADES, as consent culture has become increasingly normalized in US society, teen films have followed suit by depicting sexual consent explicitly in dialogue and plots. At the same time, teen films offer important clues about how an affirmative consent framework might still fall short for youth—and likely adults. If teen films are any indication, consent culture has not once and for all eliminated unpleasant, regrettable, or even unwanted sexual interactions nor have they clarified every ambiguous sexual experience. In fact, teen films reveal how emphasizing "performative" over "subjective" consent and prioritizing disclosure might undermine complex aspects of consent particularly for questioning, queer, and trans teens. Several of these films also belie adults' insistence that youth lack agency and cannot make competent choices or articulate their own coherent narratives.

In other words, even in consent culture, the ideal of consent has remained somewhat confounding as evidenced by teen films. Although consensual sexual interactions remain a worthwhile goal, to oversimplify sexual consent might be to reiterate gender roles, deprive youth of deserved agency, marginalize certain identities and sexualities, and erroneously imply consent in practice is straightforward. While the affirmative consent discourse has been shown, through these films, to offer a clearer framework, it is not seen as eliminating all the perplexing aspects of sexual negotiations and interactions. And while many continue to insist in public discourses on strict boundaries between a "minor" and an "adult" or "consent" and "nonconsent," this body of films pushes us to acknowledge the inevitable blurriness of such delineations.

Teen films are not the same as adolescents' lives, and they likely do not accurately or thoroughly represent adolescent sexuality. Although David

M. Considine was discussing movies from over a half century ago when arguing that the US "film industry has been spectacularly unsuccessful in realistically depicting adolescence,"[1] the same might be said of the genre today. In fact, teen films portray only the aspects of adolescents' lives that adults choose to depict visually. Ultimately, more is concealed than shown—necessarily so due to US laws regarding child pornography. By definition, teen films represent the ethos of what Linda Williams calls "on/scene" as opposed to "ob-scene (literally, off scene)."

So, what adolescent sexuality realities have we, as adults, chosen not to see? What remains too "obscene" to show? What is still "off scene"? In this conclusion, I look to clues related to teen sexting, the sexual images created by and for adolescents themselves.[2] While teen films represent the publicly available visual stories that adults create about youth, teen sexting is the result of adolescents' using their own cameras to produce and share their sexual selves privately. Teen films might render visible certain fictional aspects of adolescent sexuality, but youth sexting comprises the real images that adults are not permitted to see—and in this way, youth sexting is the invisible and "real" counterpart to the contrived world of sexuality in teen films. Remarkably, in only a few years, youth themselves forced a change in the overall perception of teen sexting from a state of "panic" to an acceptance of it as normative adolescent behavior. Such a dramatic reversal points to the influence youth exert on transforming adults' beliefs of normative adolescent sexual behavior. Even as adults surveil, make laws, publish news stories, make films, and set educational standards about youth sexuality, adolescents themselves wield considerable power to change adult discourses, perhaps more than we (or they) might realize. In the past decade, the evolving sexting discourse has upended seemingly intractable beliefs about adolescent sexuality, even challenging one of the most formidable notions in the United States—what constitutes child pornography. Ultimately, this transformation of public opinion is a reminder that the future of teen films rests in the hands of today's youth.

IMAGINING ADOLESCENT SEXUALITY

In the 2014 article "Why Kids Sext" in *The Atlantic*, Hanna Rosin recounted the trajectory of a teen sexting "scandal" in Louisa County, Virginia. It began when a mother learned about her "goody-goody" fifteen-year-old daughter's naked picture on an Instagram page and reported it, launching an investigation by Major Donald Lowe in March 2014. As authorities questioned high school students, confiscated their cell phones, and took names of their peers with similar images, soon dozens of teens across six counties were implicated regarding hundreds of "sexually explicit"[3] photos that might be classified as child pornography. Local media initially called the situation a "massive teen sexting ring" and a story "every parent needs to hear."[4] But as teens led authorities to other teens who led them to other teens, the underlying premise of the investigation—that sexting was a rare and deviant adolescent behavior—became called into question. In a matter of days, Lowe had collected dozens of cell phones, found over one thousand videos and pictures of girls as young as age fourteen, and saw no end in sight. He told his deputies, "We got to draw the line somewhere or we're going to end up talking to every teenager in the damned county!"[5] Instead, Lowe worked with Instagram to shut down the accounts and began to educate youth and their families about sexting, saying, "I'm glad people are talking about it.... That's what needs to be done." Ultimately, no one was charged.[6] What had begun as a wide-ranging criminal investigation wound up reconfigured as an adolescent sexual behavior that authorities believed would be best managed discursively.

Sexting is defined as "the sharing of sexually explicit images, videos, or messages" via electronic means.[7] While US teen films with explicit or naked sex scenes routinely cast adults in teen roles, when real teens sext, there is no body double. Due to US child pornography laws, any person who creates sexual images of someone under age eighteen automatically creates child pornography—even if the creator is a minor. Similarly, anyone who possesses or shares such images can also be brought up on child pornography charges. State age of consent laws are moot since possession of child pornography is a federal crime. Crafted with the intent of protecting children from sexual exploitation and abuse by adults, such laws initially had no loophole for minors who photographed or recorded themselves. And the strictness of the laws ensures they encompass an enormous range of images and videos—any naked image of a minor or even any clothed image of a minor in a "suggestive" pose potentially could be classified as child pornography. US law enforcement agencies had spent half a century policing and punishing how children are depicted visually by rooting out such images, only to face the unforeseen circumstance that minors had taken matters into their own hands and produced sexual images to share among themselves. US laws had only imagined one nefarious purpose for such imagery—and children's desires had nothing to do with it.

Adults—including researchers like myself—cannot view the photos and videos they study. For that reason, in the introduction to the book *Sexting Panic*, Amy Adele Hasinoff acknowledges there remains "considerable speculation" about "the specifics" of these images.[8] In other words, the youth sexting controversies over the past decade plus have had to play out discursively. Although there might be certain parents, educators, police, and, of course, many adolescents themselves who have seen these images, most adults can only imagine them based on vague textual descriptions such as "racy" or "inappropriate pictures"; "sexually explicit photos, videos, and texts"; "nude selfies"; "nude photos"; "nude or seminude cellphone pictures"; "nude photographs of students under the age of 18"; "images of a 'questionable nature'"; and "X-rated pictures, which are almost always nudity and not sex acts."[9] Despite the fact that girls and boys report sexting in equivalent numbers, articles often highlight photos of girls such as "semi-nude photos of female students"; "351 images, most of which were of girls"; "sexually explicit photos of more than 30 girls"; "pictures of girls' breasts"; or a "topless photo of a classmate."[10] When they mention boys, writers generally describe a photo of a penis.[11] In most cases, these textual accounts omit much—there is often little to no indication on poses, camera angles, proximity, or sometimes even body parts included. How better to demonstrate how youth sexuality must be "imagined" by adults than these scant descriptions that rely on us to fill in the ellipses?

In a few isolated cases, journalists provide more specifics, generally in the words of one of the parents or teens being interviewed. One *New York Times* piece interviews young people, and a teen describes, "In eighth grade, four girls were having a sleepover and they took off their clothes, covered themselves with whipped cream and sent pictures to boys of themselves licking it off."[12] But this type of detailed description is rare. In a 2009 ACLU case, two photos by girls brought up on charges are described specifically to highlight how nonsexual they are—one of two girls "from the waist up wearing white bras" and one of a girl "standing outside a shower with a bath towel wrapped around her body beneath her breasts." The ACLU press release states that "Neither of the two photos depicts sexual activity or reveals anything below the waist."[13] So too must Rosin rely on secondhand reports of the photos, which are described as mostly pictures of girls "scantily clad in a bra and panties, maybe in a suggestive pose" with a few exceptions of more explicit images like "high-school girls masturbating, and then one picture showing a girl having sex with three boys at once."[14] While most articles mention photos, there are a few about videos, such as one where several teen boys "filmed themselves engaging in sex acts with at least six teenage girls"[15] and another of a teen boy "allegedly filming a sex act that took place with a female in October."[16] What these reports suggest is an incredibly wide range of visual depictions—from a photo of a young girl in a bra to a video of multiple teens having sex—that all have been discussed under the name of "sexting."

YOUTH SEXUALITY AND THE PORNOGRAPHIC

Clearly at issue within the discourse of sexting has been how the images or videos conform to the pornographic. The mother in Rosin's article who critiques the photos for being "porny" wonders, *Where did they pick this up?*" She describes, "There were all these girls with their butts cocked, making pouty lips, pushing their boobs up, doing porny shots" while the photo of her own daughter in contrast presented her "just standing there, with her arms down by her sides." The emphasis here is on the woman's "innocent" daughter who does not fit in with the rest of the girls—Rosin describes the woman's daughter as having "long, silky hair and doe eyes and a sweet face that seemed destined for a Girl Scouts pamphlet" and clearly not fit for "an Instagram account where girls were called out as hos or thots." Rosin's own introduction to the story also picks up the idea of the pornographic with the line, "It looked like a porn site—shot after shot of naked girls—only these were real teens, not grown women in pigtails." What appears to be most shocking is the fact of real girls not only being sexualized but also sexualizing themselves. The fervor over the naked images of prepubescent Brooke Shields in the 1970s might have become a distant memory. But suddenly in the twenty-first century, adults had to contend with an even more disquieting premise—children's taking and sharing naked images of themselves.

Even when the pornographic is not mentioned directly, adults often allude to it when describing the images. In a 2014 video news story about one girl whose selfie in her underwear had been shared, the mother expresses feeling, "shock, disbelief, and at first anger."[17] Without seeing the photo, the only way to conceive of an image that provokes such a reaction is to imagine it as pornographic. Stories like these contain no pushback, but one might wonder what could possibly be so shocking about an image of girl in her underwear when youth can wear bikinis on the beach and pose however they choose. When Lowe said the "majority" of the images discovered in their investigation were "sexually explicit," the statement automatically suggests the pornographic since any sexually explicit images of a minor equals child pornography. But what exactly does it mean to call something "sexually explicit"? In Rosin's article, those same photos are also described as mostly clothed girls with a "suggestive pose"—possibly illegal, but not necessarily interpreted as obscene if we saw them. In fact, Lowe even goes back on the claim that the photos were sexually explicit.[18] It appears the recurring theme of what is most "shocking" is the simple revelation that children have sexual feelings and might express them visually. Of course, it is quite possible—even likely—that these photos and videos do draw from or reflect porn culture, but whose fault is that? If, as James R. Kincaid has suggested, our society eroticizes youth while denying doing any such thing, then the exposure of adolescent sexting brings with it the uncomfortable reality that minors are in fact developing their sexual agency amid a culture that can only imagine their sexuality as perverse.

Ultimately, it is hard to untangle if such images are obscene in themselves or we imagine them to be so because of a ready cultural association between youth, sexuality, and the obscene. Obscenity itself is yet another slippery concept. Often defined legally based on criteria from the 1973 US Supreme Court case Miller v. California, a work is deemed obscene if it 1) "as a whole" evokes a "prurient interest"; 2) depicts sexual behavior in a "patently offensive way"; and 3) lacks "serious literary, artistic, political, or scientific value."[19] Obscene works are not protected by the First Amendment according to this case, and in fact, child pornography need not even be deemed obscene to be illegal. Teen films necessarily must not be child pornography. But what is often overlooked is just how much we have erased from depictions of youth on screen through these laws—not only the exploitation of children but also depictions of normative sexual curiosity and discovery among minors.

Parents, educators, and police often voice concern in many of these articles about how photos of children can land in the "wrong" hands. An oft quoted but difficult to confirm statistic attributed to the FBI is that "at any given time, 50,000 predators are on the Internet actively seeking out children." This supposed lurking and ever-present menace fuels the argument to stamp out and control youth sexting—despite the fact that the statistic itself appears unsubstantiated.[20] Because youth sexting does not typically involve an adult offender, reports on sexting must imagine a presumed pedophile "out there" waiting to grab these photos as the inevitable danger we must protect children against. Attorney Amy Adler in the essay "The Perverse Law of Child Pornography," in the *Columbia Law Review* recognizes an embedded irony here, stating, "Child pornography law explicitly requires us to take on the gaze of the pedophile in order to root out pictures of children that harbor secret pedophilic appeal."[21] Adler argues, "Child pornography law has changed the way we look at children. I mean this literally. The law requires us to study pictures of children to uncover their potential sexual meanings, and in doing so, it explicitly exhorts us to take on the perspective of the pedophile."[22] Ironically, the eagerness to prevent the sexualization of children leads to an adult gaze that sexualizes them in tandem with a robust discussion on how to prevent children from being sexualized. In other words, if we have little faith in youth to keep within normative sexual behavior, clearly, we have much less for adults.

REVISING THE NORMS OF ADOLESCENT
SEXUALITY—AND ITS VISUALIZATION

By automatically classifying all sexual imagery of minors as child pornography in the United States, there has been no way to visualize youth sexuality with actual youth as anything other than pornographic. However, the sexting discourse evoked a conundrum—how could a child be a perpetrator and victim of the same crime? Although authorities' initial instinct was to find and punish youth who had created or shared sexually explicit images and videos of themselves, nearly immediately that became an unwieldy and even absurd goal. If the intent of child pornography laws was to protect children from sexual exploitation by adults, then youth sexting cases should not meet the criteria—in most situations, the minor had not been sexually abused by an adult through the creation of the photos or videos, nor were adults in possession of the images until parents, schools, or the police intervened. Many seemed to agree that the laws had been made to *protect* children, not *punish* them. As a result, despite the hullabaloo in the media, from the onset, municipalities and states were not actually eager to prosecute youth for the production and dissemination of their own sexual images. In one study of thousands of police cases on youth-produced sexual images from 2008 to 2009, researchers discovered "most youth were not arrested" and "sex offender registration was rare."[23] During the 2010s, over two dozen US states even developed new laws and diversion programs to prevent minors from harsh punishments associated with child pornography crimes. Similar to "close in age" exemption laws, which started to be passed by states in 2007 to allow exceptions to statutory rape laws (for example a seventeen-year-old having sex with a fifteen-year-old), the legal exemption or classification for youth-produced sexual images demonstrates a rare recognition that minors are not, in fact, asexual. It acknowledges that in certain situations, youth even can consent. Although technically in many US states, minors still can be prosecuted and receive lifetime sex offender status,[24] it is evident that youth sexting has been largely decriminalized in the United States. As the authors of a *Journal of American Medical Association* (*JAMA*) study declare in 2018, "sexting between minors is generally not prosecuted in the United States."[25]

Not only did the vast number of minors sending and receiving sexts make it challenging to prosecute as a crime, but it also suggested that youth sexting might be more "normal" than initially imagined. As a teen in one focus group put it, "How would you catch somebody when everyone does it?"[26] Although youth typically do not admit to producing their own sexual images in media interviews (unless they already have been caught), they suggest something along the lines of "everybody does it," implying sexting is a ubiquitous and normative practice.[27] Similar to masturbation, adolescent sexting might be seen as a common practice not readily admitted publicly. It seems that many youth see these images from an early age—in a 2016 *Today* show focus group, seven out of eight of the youth raised their hands when asked if they had seen a naked picture of someone at their school, and several of them said they had first seen one in middle school.[28] Research, too, has confirmed youth sexting as a common adolescent behavior. In a 2018 meta study of thirty-nine differing studies about minors' sexting practices, researchers discovered that 14.8 percent of minors has sent a sext, while 27.4 percent has received them. In looking at nonconsensual sexts, they found that, on average, 12 percent had forwarded a sext without consent and 8.4 percent had received a sext forwarded without consent. Considering how youth might "consent" despite ambivalence or even after being coerced, such numbers might be underestimated. And while it is often implied that the frequency of girls' sexting is higher, the gender breakdown overall across studies has been fairly even, with 47.2 percent of young men, on average, sexting. In looking at the studies over time, the researchers found that more recent studies had higher rates of youth sexting, suggesting that the practice could be becoming increasingly common.[29]

Ironically, while adolescent sexting increases, research shows that youth are having less sexual intercourse than in the past. According to the CDC's Youth Risk Behavior Survey (YRBS), 38.4 percent of ninth through twelfth graders who identified as heterosexual reported ever having sexual intercourse in 2019—down from 54.1 in 1991.[30] Sexting could be a cause or a result (or perhaps both) of such a trend. Of course, this focus on intercourse omits a range of adolescent sexual behaviors and sexualities. In a 2018 study of over seven thousand US adolescents and young adults ages 15–24, researchers found that more than half had engaged in oral sex, for example.[31] And in the YRBS report, 44.9 of self-identified lesbian, gay, and bisexual youth reported having had "sexual contact."[32] The CDC also acknowledges that the YRBS and other studies have not incorporated questions about transgender and questioning/queer youth—doing so could illuminate other patterns.[33] In other words, it might not be that adolescents are having less "sex" at all—it could simply be that the type of sex they're having does not fit into the definition researchers have traditionally constructed.

Like teen films, the discourse on youth sexting—what it highlights and what it omits—exposes adults' concerns. Despite queer and trans adolescents' experiencing sexual assault at higher rates than cisgender heterosexual youth, little apprehension about how this demographic might be exploited or pressured into sexting emerges in news stories. Instead, articles focus primarily on heterosexual, cisgender, Caucasian girls—a fact that reveals the public's demographic of concern. Of course, girls can be victimized through sexting and coerced in innumerable subtle or not-so-subtle ways that conform to dominant sexual scripts—just as they can during physical sexual encounters. But youth themselves actively dispute the belief that it is only boys who send unsolicited sexts. In the *Today* show focus group, one teen says, "Guys will just send them," but several jump in to articulate, "Girls will too."[34] In other words, a fear illuminated by the youth sexting discourse—girls' images being obtained and shared without their consent—is likely only one potential consent problem sexting raises. Just as teen films reveal our cultural bias of prioritizing consent for cisgender heterosexual girls, so too does the sexting discourse.

As we have moved toward an era of decriminalizing adolescent sexting, many adults (parents, educators, lawmakers, journalists, researchers, and others) continue to discuss and regulate such images and videos without ever having seen them. Even as the emphasis has shifted toward guidelines for "safe sexting," the characterization of such images has remained incredibly vague. As one writer advised, "A rule of thumb is if they can't send a photo to their grandmother, then it's not a picture they should take or send."[35] Almost no one comments on the irony of policing a type of image we have not seen; the presumption seems to be "you'd know it if you saw it." At the same time, youth themselves often do not seem to share adults' anxieties over the visual depiction of their sexuality. In one interview, teen girls articulate, "People don't think it's that big of a deal anymore" and "We see virtual images all day long, so if someone sends you an image, it loses the identity of the person. It's just a picture."[36] Other teens assert their own agency even more clearly. Rosin notes how "a handful of senior girls became indignant during the course of the interview" as they attested, "This is my life and my body and I can do whatever I want with it" and "I don't see any problem with it. I'm proud of my body." In fact, in that particular case, some of the girls even "had taken pictures especially for the Instagram accounts and had actively tried to get them posted." In a 2019 short online documentary, one teen even refers to sexting as "first base," saying, "when people say, 'we started dating,' that's almost like saying first base, like you guys send pictures back and forth. Oh yeah, like, we did that. Then everything in person happens."[37] To assert that youth-produced sexual images are "first base" or not "a big deal" and even something to be "proud" of marks a dramatic reversal in how sexual images of minors have been understood by adults for the past several decades. Such a significant shift in a short amount of time, largely brought on by the simple fact of adolescent behavior impervious to change, reveals the power adolescents wield. Youth not only craft their own visual sexual stories but they also can bend the discourse and even the research and the laws toward their inclinations.

CONSENT CULTURE, ADOLESCENT SEXTING, AND THE FUTURE OF TEEN FILMS

Every era harbors its anxieties even as it lets go of some of the old ones, as we saw in chapter 1. While the youth sexting discourse began by presuming the impossibility of minors' consent, the US adult public since has largely embraced consent as an ethical framework for advising youth how to ensure such images are sent and received consensually and privately.[38] Although these changes might mean more acceptance in the United States for visual evidence of youth sexuality—this imagery nonetheless remains "off scene" or hidden to adults. So while youth share sexual images of themselves with each other, adults still only can imagine youth sexuality by recalling their past selves through a "gauzy lens"[39] or by visualizing it through the opaque depictions in teen films. In other words, for most adults who have not seen youth-produced sexual images, such images are perhaps no more "real" than teen films.

Much is rendered intentionally invisible through both adolescent sexting and teen films. At the same time, both illuminate ongoing misconceptions amid consent culture about our current delineations of consent/nonconsent and minor/adult. They highlight how sexual agency and victimization cannot so easily be contained or defined. Consent is not the wrong framework. But if we fail to acknowledge the numerous complexities and inconsistencies embedded in an affirmative consent discourse that underscores "yes means yes," then we might also fail to navigate these contradictions effectively. Teen films, like adolescent sexting, can provide a unique opportunity to expose issues that warrant more intentional thought: the need to build a more inclusive consent framework that considers queer, questioning, and trans youth; the fact that performative and subjective consent might not always align; the importance of not perpetuating compulsory gender roles *or* their flipped iterations via our discussions on consent; and the urgency to ensure that adolescents and children can access and enact their agency without causing them harm.

It could be significant that today's youth will grow into adults who have normalized youth-produced sexual images. More changes about how we visualize youth sexuality will likely follow. How might we rethink youth rights to free speech, sexual privacy, and bodily autonomy? Might adults start to imagine youth as not just sexualized but also sexual? Will consent culture ultimately liberate childhood sexuality from a cultural lens that denies minors' claims to sexual agency? How will adolescents' ability to talk back to studios, platforms, producers, and filmmakers via social media continue to alter how stories about youth get told? How will adolescents' access to media-making tools and distribution networks continue to offer possibilities for them to create and market their own stories? When the first generation of youth who grew up with ubiquitous smart phones become parents and filmmakers themselves, will this lead to even more acceptance of youth sexuality and sexting, or will it result in a backlash to prevent their own children from doing as they themselves have done? Such changes carry enormous implications for both real adolescents and the future of depictions of youth sexuality across media—including teen films. The results of a discursive turn toward imagining adolescent sexual desire and agency might not be evident immediately, but it is a pivot that could reverberate in depictions of youth for decades to come. Teen films might be adults' stories about youth, but adolescents themselves clearly continue to shape the overarching narrative.

NOTES

1. Considine, *Cinema of Adolescence*, 9.
2. Brennan and Phippen prefer the phrase "youth-involved sexual images" to "youth sexting" to "move the focus away from the victim." However, I use *youth/adolescent/teen sexting* here since that is how it was largely refered to in the discourses I elaborate here.
3. Goldstein, "Underage Virginia."
4. Rupcich, "Deputies Bust Massive Teen Sexting Ring."
5. Rosin, "Why Kids Sext."
6. PBS, "Felony for a Selfie?"
7. Englander and McCoy, "Sexting," 328.
8. Hasinoff, *Sexting Panic*, 6.
9. Sources include: "racy" (Jouvenal, "Sexting"); "inappropriate pictures" ("Students Accused of Sending Explicit Photos," *The Sun*, November 28, 2013); "sexually explicit photos, videos, and texts" (Mendoza); "nude selfies," "nude photos," and "nude photographs of students under the age of 18" (Mitchell, "Sexting Scandal"); "nude or seminude cellphone pictures" and "X-rated pictures, which are almost always nudity and not sex acts" (Boccella, "On Youth Sexting"); and "images of a 'questionable nature'" (S. Rose, "No. 1 Story of 2015").
10. Sources include: "351 images, most of which were of girls" (Paul, "No Charges"); "sexually explicit photos of more than 30 girls" (McCrystal, "Sexting Investigation"); "pictures of girls' breasts" ("What They're Saying about Sexting," *New York Times*, March 26, 2011, https://www.nytimes.com/2011/03/27/us/27sextingqanda.html); a "topless photo of a classmate" (Jouvenal, "Sexting").
11. Friedersdorf, "Anti-Sexting Crusade."
12. "What They're Saying."

13. American Civil Liberties Union, "ACLU Sues Wyoming County D.A." See also Hasinoff, *Sexting Panic*.
14. Rosin, "Why Kids Sext."
15. Jouvenal, "Sexting."
16. Mendoza, "Sexting Scandals."
17. WCCO–CBS Minnesota, "Teen Shares Sexting Story."
18. The 2014 article "No charges forthcoming in Louisa sexting scandal" states, "At the start of the investigation, Lowe said the majority of images were sexually explicit, but he now says they were not."
19. See Legal Information Institute Miller v. California and "Obscenity."
20. The statistic is referred to in numerous reports such as "Project Safe Childhood" and "Inside Dateline: To Catch a Predator III." In the US congressional report "Sexual Exploitation of Children over the Internet" from 2007, it is attributed to the FBI, but it is unclear how old this statistic is or if it remains accurate despite its continued use.
21. Adler, "Perverse Law of Child Pornography," 213.
22. Adler, "Perverse Law of Child Pornography," 256.
23. Finkelhor and Mitchell, "How Often Are Teens Arrested for Sexting?"
24. Strasburger et al., "Teenagers."
25. Englander and McCoy, "Sexting," 317.
26. "What They're Saying."
27. Thomas, "What Should I Do?," 194.
28. Today NBC, "Teens Tell All."
29. Madigan et al, "Prevalence," 330.
30. Centers for Disease Control and Prevention, "Youth Risk Behavior Survey (YRBS)."
31. Holway and Hernandez, "Oral Sex and Condom Use."
32. Centers for Disease Control and Prevention. "Sexual Behavior (Sexual Minority Youth)."
33. On their webpage "LGBT Youth," the CDC acknowledges "Historically, YRBS and other studies have gathered data on lesbian, gay, and bisexual youth but have not included questions about transgender and questioning/queer youth. As that changes and data becomes available, this content will be updated to include information regarding transgender and questioning/queer youth."
34. Today NBC, "Teens Tell All."
35. Pahr, "Is Teen Sexting Cause for Concern."
36. "What They're Saying."
37. OK, Inc., *Sexting: A Documentary*.
38. Hasionff, in the book *Sexting Panic*, for example, argued for an "explicit consent standard for the production, distribution, or possession of private media and information."
39. In *The Queer Child*, Kathryn Bond Stockton writes, "From the standpoint of adults, innocence is alien, since it is 'lost' to the very adults who assign it to children. Adults retrospect it through the gauzy lens of what they attribute to the child" (30).

FILMOGRAPHY

1890s	The Dolorita Passion Dance	1934	Imitation of Life
1908	The James Boys in Missouri	1934	The Road to Ruin
1909	To Save Her Soul	1935	Sylvia Scarlett
1912	The Painted Lady	1936	These Three
1915	The Birth of a Nation	1938	Bringing Up Baby
1916	Her Defiance	1938	Girls on Probation
1916	The Realization of a Negro's Ambition	1940	Stolen Paradise
		1942	Always in My Heart
1919	Broken Blossoms	1943	The Constant Nymph
1919	The Homesteader	1944	National Velvet
1920	The Brute	1944	Youth Runs Wild
1921	The Burden of Race	1945	Mom and Dad
1923	Little Old New York	1946	To Each His Own
1925	The Red Kimono	1947	Are You Popular?
1927	The House behind the Cedars	1947	Junction 88
1928	Our Dancing Daughters	1948	Bob and Sally
1928	The Road to Ruin	1949	Not Wanted
1929	Our Modern Maidens	1953	The Moon Is Blue
1929	The Pagan	1955	Rebel without a Cause
1929	Untamed	1956	Baby Doll
1929	The Wild Party	1956	Tea and Sympathy
1930	All Quiet on the Western Front	1957	Band of Angels
		1957	Motorcycle Gang
1930	The Right to Love	1957	Sorority Girl
1931	Are These Our Children	1957	Tammy and the Bachelor

1958	Joy Ride	1981	Goin' All the Way!
1958	Unwed Mother	1981	Private Lessons
1959	Blue Denim	1982	Fast Times at Ridgemont High
1959	Diary of a High School Bride		
1959	Ghost of Dragstrip Hollow	1983	Losin' It
1959	Gidget	1983	The Outsiders
1959	Shadows	1983	Risky Business
1959	Suddenly, Last Summer	1983	Spring Break
1960	Where the Boys Are	1983	Valley Girl
1961	Splendor in the Grass	1984	Blame It on Rio
1961	Susan Slade	1984	Hot Moves
1962	Lolita	1984	The Joy of Sex
1965	A Patch of Blue	1984	Preppies
1967	The Graduate	1984	Revenge of the Nerds
1967	Guess Who's Coming to Dinner	1984	Sixteen Candles
		1985	The Breakfast Club
1968	Three in the Attic	1985	Just One of the Guys
1969	The First Time	1985	Once Bitten
1969	Last Summer	1985	Smooth Talk
1971	Harold and Maude	1985	Teen Wolf
1971	The Last Picture Show	1985	Weird Science
1971	Summer of '42	1986	Peggy Sue Got Married
1973	Nymph	1986	Stand by Me
1975	Cooley High	1987	The Big Bet
1976	The Little Girl Who Lived Down the Lane	1987	Dirty Dancing
		1987	Some Kind of Wonderful
1976	Norman, Is That You?	1988	Mystic Pizza
1976	Taxi Driver	1988	School Daze
1978	Animal House	1989	Loverboy
1978	Du er ikke alene (You Are Not Alone)	1989	Say Anything
		1990	House Party
1978	Grease	1991	Boyz n the Hood
1978	Pretty Baby	1991	Cape Fear
1979	H.O.T.S.	1991	House Party 2
1979	Manhattan	1991	Virgin High
1980	The Blue Lagoon	1992	Amy Fisher: My Story
1980	Fame	1992	Just Another Girl on the I.R.T.
1980	Little Darlings	1992	Little Sister

FILMOGRAPHY

1992	Poison Ivy
1993	The Amy Fisher Story
1993	Casualties of Love: The Long Island Lolita Story
1993	The Crush
1993	Just One of the Girls (aka Anything for Love)
1993	The Sandlot
1993	Totally F***ed Up
1994	House Party 3
1995	The Basketball Diaries
1995	Clueless
1995	The Incredibly True Adventures of Two Girls in Love
1995	Kids
1995	Welcome to the Dollhouse
1996	Bastard Out of Carolina
1996	Fear
1996	Foxfire
1996	Girls Town
1996	Manny & Lo
1996	Poison Ivy II
1997	All Over Me
1997	Lolita
1997	Ma Vie en Rose (My Life in Pink)
1998	Edge of Seventeen
1998	Slums of Beverly Hills
1998	Strangeland
1999	American Beauty
1999	American Pie
1999	Boys Don't Cry
1999	But I'm a Cheerleader
1999	Coming Soon
1999	Cruel Intentions
1999	Election
1999	Never Been Kissed
1999	She's All That
1999	The Virgin Suicides
2000	Love and Basketball
2000	The Truth about Jane
2001	Bully
2001	House Party 4: Down to the Last Minute
2001	Riding in Cars with Boys
2001	Save the Last Dance
2003	Thirteen
2004	Birth
2004	The Girl Next Door
2004	Mean Girls
2004	Saving Face
2005	Hard Candy
2006	The Curiosity of Chance
2006	It's a Boy Girl Thing
2006	She's the Man
2007	Juno
2007	Superbad
2008	Poison Ivy: Secret Society
2008	Sex Drive
2008	Twilight
2009	An Education
2009	Precious
2009	Wrecked
2010	Easy A
2010	The Kids Are All Right
2011	Cougars, Inc.
2011	Pariah
2012	Moonrise Kingdom
2012	The Perks of Being a Wallflower
2013	Geography Club
2013	House Party: Tonight's the Night
2013	The To Do List
2014	Boy Meets Girl
2015	The Diary of a Teenage Girl

2015	Dope	2018	To All the Boys I've Loved Before
2015	Fifty Shades of Grey		
2015	A Girl Like Grace	2018	We the Animals
2015	Henry Gamble's Birthday Party	2019	Adam
		2019	Booksmart
2015	3 Generations	2019	Good Boys
2016	As You Are	2019	Premature
2016	Edge of Seventeen	2019	Trapped: The Alex Cooper Story
2016	First Girl I Loved		
2016	Moonlight	2019	Yes, God, Yes
2016	The Swap	2020	American Pie: Girls' Rules
2017	Beach Rats	2020	Banging Lanie
2017	Freak Show	2020	The Half of It
2017	Lady Bird	2020	Never Rarely Sometimes Always
2017	Princess Cyd	2020	Prom
2017	Speech & Debate	2020	To All the Boys I've Loved Before: PS I Still Love You
2018	Alex Strangelove		
2018	Blockers	2020	Unpregnant
2018	Boy Erased	2021	Moxie
2018	The Kissing Booth	2021	Plan B
2018	Love, Simon	2021	To All the Boys: Always and Forever
2018	The Miseducation of Cameron Post		
		2022	Anything's Possible
2018	Sierra Burgess Is a Loser	2022	Sex Appeal
2018	The Tale	2022	Three Months

BIBLIOGRAPHY

Aaron, Michele. "The New Queer Spectator." In *New Queer Cinema: A Critical Reader*, edited by Michele Aaron, 187–200. New Brunswick, NJ: Rutgers University Press, 2004.

Adalian, Josef. "Inside Netflix's TV-Swallowing, Market-Dominating Binge Factory." *Vulture*, June 11, 2018. https://www.vulture.com/2018/06/how-netflix-swallowed-tv-industry.html.

Adler, Amy. "The Perverse Law of Child Pornography." *Columbia Law Review* 101, no. 2 (2001): 209. https://doi.org/10.2307/1123799.

Alvarez, Jasmine. "The Myth of Diggy: How *Dope* Got the Queer Experience Wrong." For Harriet | Celebrating the Fullness of Black Womanhood, August 20, 2015. http://www.forharriet.com/2015/08/the-myth-of-diggy-how-dope-got-queer.html.

American Civil Liberties Union. "ACLU Sues Wyoming County D.A. for Threatening Teenage Girls with Child Pornography Charges over Photos of Themselves." ACLU, press release, March 25, 2009. https://www.aclu.org/print/node/13998.

American Psychiatric Association. "APA Resolution on Gender Identity Change Efforts." February 2021. https://www.apa.org/about/policy/resolution-gender-identity-change-efforts.pdf.

American Psychiatric Association. "What Is Gender Dysphoria?" Patients & Families. Accessed July 28, 2021. https://www.psychiatry.org/patients-families/gender-dysphoria/what-is-gender-dysphoria.

Angelides, Steven. *The Fear of Child Sexuality: Young People, Sex, and Agency*. Chicago: University of Chicago Press, 2019.

Ann, Patty, Julia Himberg, and Damon R. Young. "Queer Approaches to Film, Television, and Digital Media." *Cinema Journal* 53, no. 2 (2014): 117–21. https://www.jstor.org/stable/43653571.

"The APA Ruling on Homosexuality." *The New York Times*, December 23, 1973. https://nyti.ms/3zbcifI.

Archard, David. *Sexual Consent*. Boulder, CO: Westview Press, 1998.

Ashley, Florence. "Genderfucking Non-Disclosure: Sexual Fraud, Transgender Bodies, and Messy Identities." *Dalhousie Law Journal* 41, no. 2 (2018): 339–77.

Baril, Alexandre. "Confessing Society, Confessing Cis-Tem: Rethinking Consent through Intimate Images of Trans* People in the Media." *Frontiers: A Journal of Women Studies* 39, no. 2 (2018): 1. https://doi.org/10.5250/fronjwomestud.39.2.0001.

Barnhill, Anne. "Just Pushy Enough." In *Dating—Philosophy for Everyone: Flirting with Big Ideas*, edited by Kristie Miller and Marlene Clark, 90–100. Hoboken, NJ: Wiley, 2011.

Bay-Cheng, Laina Y. "Agency Is Everywhere, but Agency Is Not Enough: A Conceptual Analysis of Young Women's Sexual Agency." *Journal of Sex Research* 56, no. 4–5 (2019): 462–74. https://doi.org/10.1080/00224499.2019.1578330.

Behm-Morawitz, Elizabeth, and Dana E. Mastro. "Mean Girls? The Influence of Gender Portrayals in Teen Movies on Emerging Adults' Gender-Based Attitudes and Beliefs." *Journalism & Mass Communication Quarterly* 85, no. 1 (2008): 131–46. https://doi.org/10.1177/107769900808500109.

Beirne, Rebecca. "Teen Lesbian Desires and Identities in International Cinema: 1931–2007." *Journal of Lesbian Studies* 16, no. 3 (2012): 258–72. https://doi.org/10.1080/10894160.2012.673925.

Benavente, Gabby, and Julian Gill-Peterson. "The Promise of Trans Critique: Susan Stryker's Queer Theory." *GLQ: A Journal of Lesbian and Gay Studies* 25, no. 1 (January 2019): 23–28. https://doi.org/10.1215/10642684-7275222.

Bendery, Jennifer. "Joe Biden: Transgender Discrimination Is 'The Civil Rights Issue of Our Time.'" *HuffPost*, October 31, 2012. https://www.huffpost.com/entry/joe-biden-transgender-rights_n_2047275.

Benshoff, Harry M., and Sean Griffin. *Queer Images a History of Gay and Lesbian Film in America*. Lanham, MD: Rowman & Littlefield Pub., 2006.

Bergelson, Vera. "The Meaning of Sexual Consent." *Ohio State Journal of Criminal Law* 12 (2014): 171–80. https://doi.org/https://papers.ssrn.com/sol3/papers.cfm?abstract_id=3631204.

Biden, Joe (@JoeBiden). "Let's be clear: Transgender equality is the civil rights issue of our time. There is no room for compromise when it comes to basic human rights." Twitter, January 25, 2020. https://twitter.com/joebiden/status/1221135646107955200?lang=en.

Blades, John. "The Trouble with 'Lolita.'" *Chicago Tribune*, August 30, 2018. https://www.chicagotribune.com/news/ct-xpm-1997-04-13-9704120210-story.html.

Blumenthal, Ralph. "Freud: Secret Documents Reveal Years of Strife." *New York Times*, January 24, 1984. https://www.nytimes.com/1984/01/24/science/freud-secret-documents-reveal-years-of-strife.html.

Blumer, Herbert, and Philip Morris Hauser. *Movies, Delinquency, and Crime.* New York: Macmillan Company, 1933.
Boccella, Kathy. "On Youth Sexting, Pa. and Other States Act to Prosecute, Not Persecute." *Philadelphia Inquirer,* October 19, 2012.
Bond, Keosha T., Natalie M. Leblanc, Porche Williams, Cora-Ann Gabriel, and Ndidiamaka N. Amutah-Onukagha. "Race-Based Sexual Stereotypes, Gendered Racism, and Sexual Decision Making among Young Black Cisgender Women." *Health Education & Behavior* 48, no. 3 (2021): 295–305. https://doi.org/10.1177/10901981211010086.
Book Marks. "Sick, Scandalous, Spectacular: The First Reviews of *Lolita*." Literary Hub, August 17, 2020. https://bookmarks.reviews/sick-scandalous-spectacular-the-first-reviews-of-lolita/.
Boyar, Jay. "Frantic 'Weird Science' Never Pauses to Think." OrlandoSentinel.com, October 12, 2018. https://www.orlandosentinel.com/news/os-xpm-1985-08-05-0320080282-story.html.
Brainard, Jeffrey and Jia You. "What a massive database of retracted papers reveals about science publishing's 'death penalty.'" *Science,* October 2, 2018. https://www.science.org/content/article/what-massive-database-retracted-papers-reveals-about-science-publishing-s-death-penalty
Bravo, Tony. "'Adam' Presents Controversial View of TRANS Identity, SPARKS Community Boycott." Datebook. *San Francisco Chronicle,* August 12, 2019. https://datebook.sfchronicle.com/movies-tv/film-adam-presents-controversial-view-of-trans-identity-sparks-community-boycott.
Brennan, Maggie, and Andy Phippen. "'Youth-Involved Sexual Imagery'—A Better Term to Challenge Blame Culture in Youth Sexting Cases?" *Entertainment Law Review* 29, no. 3 (2018). https://pearl.plymouth.ac.uk/handle/10026.1/12703.
Brook, Tom. "*The Birth of a Nation:* The Most Racist Movie Ever Made?" BBC, February 6, 2015. https://www.bbc.com/culture/article/20150206-the-most-racist-movie-ever-made.
Buckley, Cara. "The Birds and the Bees as Seen at 15, in 'The Diary of a Teenage Girl.'" *New York Times,* July 29, 2015. https://www.nytimes.com/2015/08/02/movies/the-birds-and-the-bees-as-seen-at-15-in-the-diary-of-a-teenage-girl.html.
Busch, Anita. "'About Ray' Pushed from This Weekend's Release Schedule by TWC." *Deadline,* September 15, 2015. https://deadline.com/2015/09/about-ray-susan-sarandon-elle-fanning-transgender-film-release-date-change-1201528419/.
Butler, Judith P. *The Psychic Life of Power: Theories in Subjection.* Stanford, CA: Stanford University Press, 2006.
Butters, Gerald R. "Capitalizing on Race: White Producers of All-Black Cinema." In *Early Race Filmmaking in America,* edited by Barbara Tepa Lupack, 105–22. New York: Routledge, 2016.

Callister, Mark, Lesa A. Stern, Sarah M. Coyne, Tom Robinson, and Emily Bennion. "Evaluation of Sexual Content in Teen-Centered Films from 1980 to 2007." *Mass Communication and Society* 14, no. 4 (2011): 454–74. https://doi.org/10.1080/15205436.2010.500446.

Call Me Out Scotty. "Do Not Support Adam (2018)." Archive.org. Tumblr, May 13, 2018. Snapshot from the Internet Archive from May 6, 2019. https://web.archive.org/web/20190506210406/https://peach-course.tumblr.com/post/173869039893/i-recently-heard-the-news-that-adam-by-ariel.

Canby, Vincent. "Film: 'Pretty Baby' by Louis Malle." *New York Times*, April 5, 1978.

Carter, Bill. "'Lolita' Reaches a U.S. Audience." *New York Times*, May 6, 1998. https://www.nytimes.com/1998/05/06/movies/tv-notes-lolita-reaches-a-us-audience.html.

Catholic News Archive. "Pledge of the Legion of Decency." *Catholic Transcript*. Accessed July 28, 2021. https://thecatholicnewsarchive.org/?a=d&d=CTR19340712-01.2.12&e=-------en-20--1--txt-txIN--------.

Cavalcante, Andre. "Breaking into Transgender Life: Transgender Audiences' Experiences with 'First of Its Kind' Visibility in Popular Media." *Communication, Culture & Critique* 10, no. 3 (February 8, 2017): 538–55. https://doi.org/10.1111/cccr.12165.

Cense, Marianne. "Rethinking Sexual Agency: Proposing a Multicomponent Model Based on Young People's Life Stories." *Sex Education* 19, no. 3 (2018): 247–62. https://doi.org/10.1080/14681811.2018.1535968.

Centers for Disease Control and Prevention. "Infographic about LGB Teen Dating Violence Data." Injury Center, Violence Prevention, September 28, 2016. https://www.cdc.gov/violenceprevention/communicationresources/infographics/yrbs-lgb-tdv.html.

Centers for Disease Control and Prevention. "LGBT Youth." June, 21, 2017. https://www.cdc.gov/lgbthealth/youth.htm.

Centers for Disease Control and Prevention. "National Intimate Partner and Sexual Violence Survey: 2015 Data Brief—Updated Release." National Center for Injury Prevention and Control, November 2018. https://www.nsvrc.org/sites/default/files/2021-04/2015data-brief508.pdf.

Centers for Disease Control and Prevention. "Preventing Child Sexual Abuse." Injury Center, Violence Prevention, April 30, 2021. https://www.cdc.gov/violenceprevention/childsexualabuse/fastfact.html.

Centers for Disease Control and Prevention. "Sexual Behavior (Sexual Minority Youth)." https://www.cdc.gov/healthyyouth/data/yrbs/slides/dstr/smy_sexual_behavior.pptx.

Centers for Disease Control and Prevention. "Youth Risk Behavior Survey (YRBS)." Trends in the Prevalence of Sexual Behaviors and HIV Testing

National YRBS: 1991–2019, August 20, 2020. https://www.cdc.gov/healthyyouth/data/yrbs/factsheets/2019_sexual_trend_yrbs.htm.

The Central Virginian, "No charges forthcoming in Louisa sexting scandal." September 11, 2014. https://www.thecentralvirginian.com/news/local/no-charges-forthcoming-in-louisa-sexting-scandal

Chuba, Kirsten. "Seth Rogen, Evan Goldberg on How 'Good Boys' Echoes 'Superbad.'" *Hollywood Reporter*, August 15, 2019. https://www.hollywoodreporter.com/news/seth-rogen-evan-goldberg-how-good-boys-echoes-superbad-1232213.

CK (@itscourtkendall). "#BoycottAdam bc perpetuating a gross fetishizing account of a cishet rapist fantasizing about raping lesbians/wlw under the guise of being a pre-op trans man is harmful . . ." Twitter, May 15, 2018. https://twitter.com/itscourtkendell/status/996216915751243777.

Cohen, Anne. "How Do You Direct a Child in a Movie about Sexual Abuse?" Refinery29, May 24, 2018. https://www.refinery29.com/en-us/2018/05/200084/the-tale-true-story-sexual-abuse-director-jennifer-fox.

Conklin, John E. *Campus Life in the Movies: A Critical Survey from the Silent Era to the Present*. Jefferson, NC: McFarland, 2009.

Conley, Garrard. *Boy Erased: A Memoir of Identity, Faith, and Family*. New York: Riverhead Books, 2018.

Considine, David M. *The Cinema of Adolescence*. Jefferson, NC: McFarland, 1985.

Considine, David M. "Get Real: Representations of Adolescent Sexuality in the Media." In *Adolescent Sexuality: A Historical Handbook and Guide*, edited by Carolyn Cocca, 65–84. Westport, CT: Praeger, 2006.

Constabile, J. Paul. "Censorship." *Globe and the Mail*, April 12, 1978.

Courtney, Susan. *Hollywood Fantasies of Miscegenation: Spectacular Narratives of Gender and Race*. Princeton, NJ: Princeton University Press, 2005.

Cox, Chelsey. "As Arkansas Bans Treatments for Transgender Youth, 15 Other States Consider Similar Bills." *USA Today*, April 8, 2021. https://www.usatoday.com/story/news/politics/2021/04/08/states-consider-bills-medical-treatments-transgender-youth/7129101002/.

Coyne, Sarah M., L. Monique Ward, Savannah L. Kroff, Emilie J. Davis, Hailey G. Holmgren, Alexander C. Jensen, Sarah E. Erickson, and Lee W. Essig. "Contributions of Mainstream Sexual Media Exposure to Sexual Attitudes, Perceived Peer Norms, and Sexual Behavior: A Meta-Analysis." *Journal of Adolescent Health* 64, no. 4 (2019): 430–36. https://doi.org/10.1016/j.jadohealth.2018.11.016.

Dargis, Manohla. "Review: In 'The Diary of a Teenage Girl,' a Hormone Bomb Waiting to Explode." *New York Times*, August 6, 2015. https://www.nytimes.com/2015/08/07/movies/review-in-the-diary-of-a-teenage-girl-a-hormone-bomb-waiting-to-explode.html.

Davis, Ivor. "Pre-pubescent Superstar Brooke May Be Only 13 but She Rates $500,000 a Movie." *Globe and the Mail*, December 11, 1978.

Dennis, Jeffery P. *Queering Teen Culture: All-American Boys and Same-Sex Desire in Film and Television*. New York: Harrington Park Press, 2006.

Dey, Sneha. "Texas Health Providers Are Suspending Gender-Affirming Care for Teens in Response to GOP Efforts." *Texas Tribune*, March 22, 2022. https://www.texastribune.org/2022/03/22/texas-transgender-teenagers-medical-care/.

Doherty, Thomas. *Pre-Code Hollywood: Sex, Immorality and Insurrection in American Cinema, 1930–34*. New York: Columbia University Press, 1999.

Doherty, Thomas. *Teenagers and Teenpics: The Juvenilization of American Movies in the 1950s*. Philadelphia: Temple University Press, 2002.

Dresner, Lisa M. "Love's Labor's Lost? Early 1980s Representations of Girls' Sexual Decision Making in *Fast Times at Ridgemont High* and *Little Darlings*." In *Virgin Territory: Representing Sexual Inexperience in Film*, edited by Tamar Jeffers McDonald, 174–200. Detroit: Wayne State University Press, 2010.

Driscoll, Catherine. *Girls: Feminine Adolescence in Popular Culture and Cultural Theory*. New York: Columbia University Press, 2002.

Driscoll, Catherine. *Teen Film: A Critical Introduction*. Oxford: Berg, 2011.

Drushel, Bruce E. "Of Letters and Lists: How the MPAA Puts Films Recommended for LGBTQ Adolescents Out of Reach." *Journal of Homosexuality* 67, no. 2 (2020): 174–88. https://doi.org/10.1080/00918369.2018.1528072.

Dumaraog, Ana. "Why John Ambrose Was Recast for to All the Boys 2." ScreenRant, February 13, 2020. https://screenrant.com/to-all-boys-2-netflix-john-ambrose-mcclaren-actor-recast-reason/.

Durham, Meenakshi Gigi. *The Lolita Effect: The Media Sexualization of Young Girls and What We Can Do about It*. London: Duckworth, 2009.

Dymock, Alex. "Towards a Consent Culture: An Interview with Kitty Stryker." *Journal of the International Network of Sexual Ethics and Politics* 2, no. 1 (2014): 75–91.

Ebert, Roger. "Pretty Baby." RogerEbert.com, June 1, 1978. https://www.rogerebert.com/reviews/pretty-baby.

Ebert, Roger. "The Young and the Restless." RogerEbert.com, June 19, 2005. https://www.rogerebert.com/reviews/great-movie-rebel-without-a-cause-1955.

The Economist. "American Teens Are Sexting More and Sexing Less." March 26, 2020. https://www.economist.com/united-states/2020/03/26/american-teens-are-sexting-more-and-sexing-less.

The Economist. "An English Ruling on Transgender Teens Could Have Global Repercussions." December 12, 2020. https://www.economist.com/international/2020/12/12/an-english-ruling-on-transgender-teens-could-have-global-repercussions.

Egan, R. Danielle. *Becoming Sexual: A Critical Appraisal of the Sexualization of Girls*. Cambridge: Polity, 2013.

Encyclopedia of Chicago, s.v., "Film Censorship." Accessed July 21, 2021. http://www.encyclopedia.chicagohistory.org/pages/453.html.

Englander, Elizabeth, and Meghan McCoy. "Sexting—Prevalence, Age, Sex, and Outcomes." *JAMA Pediatrics* 172, no. 4 (2018): 317. https://doi.org/10.1001/jamapediatrics.2017.5682.

Erb, Cynthia. "Jodie Foster and Brooke Shields: 'New Ways to Look at the Young.'" In *Hollywood Reborn: Movie Stars of the 1970s*, edited by Jim Morrison, 82–100. New Brunswick, NJ: Rutgers University Press, 2010.

Ernst, Rhys. "On *Adam*" Medium, June 5, 2018. https://medium.com/@rhys.ernst/on-adam-129982a3119b.

@Euphocity. "Fuck Noah Centineo for pretending to be a Latino to get a Latin role." Twitter, September 22, 2020. https://twitter.com/Euphocity/status/1308475436360298498.

Feder, Sam, and Alexandra Juhasz. "Does Visibility Equal Progress? A Conversation on Trans Activist Media." *Jump Cut: A Review of Contemporary Media* 57 (Fall 2016). https://www.ejumpcut.org/archive/jc57.2016/-Feder-JuhaszTransActivism/index.html.

Ferzan, Kimberly Kessler. "Clarifying Consent: Peter Westen's *The Logic of Consent*." *Law and Philosophy* 25, no. 2 (Mar. 2006): 193–217.

Finkelhor, David, and Kimberly J. Mitchell. "How Often Are Teens Arrested for Sexting? Data from a National Sample of Police Cases." *Pediatrics* 129, no. 1 (2011). https://doi.org/10.1542/peds.2011-2242.

Fischer, Mia. "Queer and Feminist Approaches to Transgender Media Studies." In *Feminist Approaches to Media Theory and Research*, edited by Dustin Harp and Ingrid Bachmann, 93–107. New York: Springer International Publishing, 2018.

Forman, Henry J. *Our Movie Made Children*. New York: Macmillan Company, 1933.

Foucault, Michel. *The History of Sexuality*. Vol. 1, *An Introduction*. New York: Vintage Books, 1978.

Foucault, Michel. *Politics, Philosophy, Culture: Interviews and Other Writings, 1977–1984*. Edited by Lawrence D. Kritzman. New York: Routledge, 1990.

Friedersdorf, Conor. "The Moral Panic over Sexting." *The Atlantic*, September 2, 2015. https://www.theatlantic.com/politics/archive/2015/09/for-sexting-teens-the-authorities-are-the-biggest-threat/403318/.

Friedman, Jaclyn, and Jessica Valenti. *Yes Means Yes!: Visions of Female Sexual Power & a World without Rape*. New York: Seal Press, 2019.

Gaines, Jane M. *Fire & Desire: Mixed-Race Movies in the Silent Era*. Chicago: University of Chicago Press, 2001.

Gardner, Chris. "Transgender Artists Applaud Scarlett Johansson's 'Rub & Tug' Exit." *Hollywood Reporter*, July 15, 2018. https://www.hollywoodreporter.com/news/transgender-artists-applaud-scarlett-johanssons-rub-tug-exit-1127165.

Geltzer, Jeremy. *Film Censorship in America: A State-by-State History*. Jefferson, NC: McFarland, 2017.

Geminiyoungster. "Can we talk about the Movie 'A Girl like Grace'? *Spoiler*" Lipstick Alley, September 28, 2020. https://www.lipstickalley.com/threads/can-we-talk-about-the-movie-a-girl-like-grace-spolier.1134295/.

Giacobbe, Alyssa. "24-Year-Old Trans Actress Michelle Hendley on Her Rise from YouTube Fame to Movie Stardom." *Teen Vogue*, August 18, 2015. https://www.teenvogue.com/story/michelle-hendley-transgender-actress-interview.

GLAAD. "Glossary of Terms: LGBTQ." GLAAD Media Reference Guide. Accessed July 28, 2021. https://www.glaad.org/reference/lgbtq.

GLAAD. "Observations & Recommendations." 2019. https://www.glaad.org/sri/2019/additional-recommendations.

GLAAD. "Observations & Recommendations." 2021. https://www.glaad.org/sri/2021/observations-recommendations.

GLAAD. "Transgender." GLAAD Media Reference Guide, March 28, 2021. https://www.glaad.org/reference/transgender.

GLAAD. "Transgender People." GLAAD Media Resource Guide, November 3, 2020. https://www.glaad.org/reference/covering-trans-community.

Gloeckner, Phoebe. *The Diary of a Teenage Girl: An Account in Words and Pictures*. Berkeley, CA: North Atlantic Books, 2015.

Goldstein, Sasha. "Underage Virginia 'Sexting' Ring Ensnares 100 Teens, Uncovers 1,000 Pictures: Police." *New York Daily News*, April 4, 2014. https://www.nydailynews.com/news/national/virginia-sexting-ring-ensnares-100-teens-uncovers-1-000-pictures-police-article-1.1746393.

Gossett, Reina, Eric A. Stanley, and Johanna Burton. *Trap Door: Trans Cultural Production and the Politics of Visibility*. Cambridge, MA: MIT Press, 2019.

Greenhouse, Linda. "'Virtual' Child Pornography Ban Overturned." *New York Times*, April 17, 2002. https://www.nytimes.com/2002/04/17/us/virtual-child-pornography-ban-overturned.html.

Gross, Terry. "A 'Tale' of Child Sex Abuse Was Inspired by Filmmaker's Real-Life Trauma." NPR, August 8, 2018. https://www.npr.org/transcripts/636536848.

Gross, Terry. "'Why Kids Sext' Describes Nude Photos as 'Social Currency' among Teens." NPR. *Fresh Air*, October 15, 2014. https://www.npr.org/transcripts/356393531?storyId=356393531%3FstoryId.

Gruber, Aya. "Anti-Rape Culture." *Kansas Law Review*, 2016. https://doi.org/10.17161/1808.25540.

Halberstam, Jack. "Hiding the Tears in My Eyes—*Boy's Don't Cry*—A Legacy." *Bully Bloggers*, December 7, 2016. https://bullybloggers.wordpress.com/2016/12/07/hiding-the-tears-in-my-eyes-boys-dont-cry-a-legacy-by-jack-halberstam/.

Halberstam, Jack. *In a Queer Time and Place: Transgender Bodies, Subcultural Lives*. New York: New York University Press, 2005.

Hale, Mike. "'A Teacher' Review: After School, Not So Special." *New York Times*, November 9, 2020. https://www.nytimes.com/2020/11/09/arts/television/a-teacher-review.html.

Hall, G. Stanley. *Adolescence: Its Psychology and Its Relations to Physiology, Anthropology, Sociology, Sex, Crime, Religion and Education*. Vol. 2. New York: D. Appleton, 1917.

Halley, Janet. "The Move to Affirmative Consent." *Signs: Journal of Women in Culture and Society* 42, no. 1 (2016): 257–79. https://doi.org/10.1086/686904.

Han, Jenny. "An Asian-American Teen Idol Onscreen, Finally." *New York Times*, August 17, 2018. https://www.nytimes.com/2018/08/17/opinion/sunday/crazy-rich-asians-movie-idol.html.

Hardesty, Melissa, Sarah R. Young, Allison M. McKinnon, Ann Merriwether, Richard E. Mattson, and Sean G. Massey. "Indiscrete: How Typical College Student Sexual Behavior Troubles Affirmative Consent's Demand for Clear Communication." *Sexuality Research and Social Policy*, June 25, 2021. https://doi.org/10.1007/s13178-021-00611-9.

Hasinoff, Amy Adele. "Blaming Sexualization for Sexting." *Girlhood Studies* 7, no. 1 (2014): 102–20. https://doi.org/10.3167/ghs.2014.070108.

Hasinoff, Amy Adele. *Sexting Panic: Rethinking Criminalization, Privacy, and Consent*. Urbana: University of Illinois Press, 2015.

Hatch, Kristen. "Fille Fatale: Regulating Images of Adolescent Girls, 1962–1996." In *Sugar, Spice, and Everything Nice: Cinemas of Girlhood*, edited by Frances K. Gateward and Murray Pomerance, 163–81. Detroit: Wayne State University Press, 2002.

Healthline. "Your Guide to Sexual Consent." Accessed March 21, 2022. https://www.healthline.com/health/guide-to-consent.

Hereford, André. "In Depth Q&A: *Love, Simon* Director Greg Berlanti." *Metro Weekly*, March 15, 2018. https://www.metroweekly.com/2018/03/interview-love-simon-director-greg-berlanti/.

Herman, Judith Lewis. *Father-Daughter Incest*. Cambridge, MA: Harvard University Press, 2000. Originally printed 1981.

Hessick, Carissa Byrne, ed. *Refining Child Pornography Law: Crime, Language, and Social Consequences*. Ann Arbor: University of Michigan Press, 2016.

Hickman, Susan E., and Charlene L. Muehlenhard. "'By the Semi-Mystical Appearance of a Condom': How Young Women and Men Communicate Sexual Consent in Heterosexual Situations." *Journal of Sex Research* 36, no. 3 (August 1999): 258–72. https://doi.org/10.1080/00224499909551996.

Hok-sze Leung, Helen. "Film." *Transgender Studies Quarterly* 1, no. 1–2 (May 2014): 22–23. https://doi.org/10.1215/23289252-2399686.

Holiday, Steven, Bradley J. Bond, and Eric E. Rasmussen. "Coming Attractions: Parental Mediation Responses to Transgender and Cisgender Film Trailer

Content Targeting Adolescents." *Sexuality & Culture* 22, no. 4 (2018): 1154–70. https://doi.org/10.1007/s12119-018-9517-3.

Holway, Giuseppina Valle, and Stephanie M. Hernandez. "Oral Sex and Condom Use in a U.S. National Sample of Adolescents and Young Adults." *Journal of Adolescent Health* 62, no. 4 (April 2018): 402–10. https://doi.org/10.1016/j.jadohealth.2017.08.022.

Homan, Lucy (@lucypaw). "You can #boycottadam for being cis-centric and being transphobic. Or for hating on queer and trans politics. Or for its racism. Or for its misogyny . . ." Twitter, August 10, 2019. https://twitter.com/lucypaw/status/1160252829111422976.

hooks, bell. "The Oppositional Gaze." In *Black Looks: Race and Representation*, 1st ed., 115–31. Boston, MA: South End Press, 1992.

Horak, Jan-Christopher. "Preserving Race Films." In *Early Race Filmmaking in America*, edited by Barbara Tepa Lupack, 197–230. New York: Routledge, 2016.

Horak, Laura. *Girls Will Be Boys: Cross-Dressed Women, Lesbians, and American Cinema*. New Brunswick, NJ: Rutgers University Press, 2016.

Hornaday, Ann. "Review: 'Diary of a Teenage Girl' Is Funny, Forthright and Daringly Frank." *Washington Post*, August 13, 2015. https://www.washingtonpost.com/goingoutguide/movies/review-diary-of-a-teenage-girl-is-funny-forthright-and-daringly-frank/2015/08/13/76a5c66e-4041-11e5-bfe3-ff1d8549bfd2_story.html.

Hughes, Katherine. "Boy Wizards: Magical and Homosocial Power in *Harry Potter and the Goblet of Fire* and *The Covenant*." In *Queer Youth and Media Cultures*, edited by Christopher Pullen, 158–69. New York: Palgrave Macmillan, 2014.

Hullender, Tatiana. "Sydney Park, Anjelika Washington & Josie Totah Interview: Moxie." Screen Rant. February 25, 2021. https://screenrant.com/sydney-park-anjelika-washington-josie-totah-interview-moxie/.

Hurd, Heidi. "The Moral Magic of Consent." *Legal Theory* 2, no. 2 (June 1996): 121–46. https://doi.org/10.1017/S1352325200000434.

ICD-11 for Mortality and Morbidity Statistics. "Gender Incongruence." World Health Organization, March 2022. https://icd.who.int/browse11/l-m/en#/http%3a%2f%2fid.who.int%2ficd%2fentity%2f411470068.

Illinois Supreme Court. Block v. City of Chicago, 239 Ill. 251 (1909). Available from Caselaw Access Project, Harvard Law School Library Innovation Lab. https://cite.case.law/ill/239/251/.

Independent Film Channel. "Indie Sex: Teens." Episode. *Indie Sex* 1, no. 2 (August 3, 2007). Video.

Internet Movie Database. "Adam." IMDb.com, July 28, 2022. https://www.imdb.com/title/tt1715344/.

Internet Movie Database. *The Story of Bob and Sally* movie poster. IMDb.com. Accessed July 28, 2021. https://www.imdb.com/title/tt0040177/mediaviewer/rm885235713/.

Jackson, Noah. "Gaby Dellal on the Controversies Surrounding Her Movie '3 Generations.'" Nylon, May 5, 2017. https://www.nylon.com/articles/gaby-dellal-3-generations-interview.

Jenkins, Henry. "Just a Spoonful of Sugar: Permissive Childrearing and Walt Disney's *Mary Poppins* (Part One)." *Confessions of an Aca-Fan*, March 10, 2021. http://henryjenkins.org/blog/2021/2/21/just-a-spoonful-of-sugar-permissive-childrearing-and-walt-disneys-mary-poppins-part-one.

Jenkins, Philip. *Moral Panic: Changing Concepts of the Child Molester in Modern America*. New Haven, CT: Yale University Press, 2004.

Johnson, Craig. "Craig Johnson on 'Alex Strangelove.'" Interview by Lulu Garcia-Navarro. *Weekend Edition Sunday*, June 10, 2018. https://www.npr.org/2018/06/10/618648655/craig-johnson-on-alex-strangelove.

Jouvenal, Justin. "'Sexting' Case Fuels Debate over Punishment for Teens." *Washington Post*, April 18, 2013.

Jusino, Teresa. "*About Ray's* Gaby Dellal Proves Why She Wasn't the Best Person to Tell This Story." Mary Sue, August 21, 2015. https://www.themarysue.com/about-ray-director-gaby-dellal/.

Kaplan, Ilana. "'American Pie' at 20: That Notorious Pie Scene, from Every Angle." *New York Times*, July 9, 2019. https://www.nytimes.com/2019/07/09/movies/american-pie.html.

Kaufman, Amy. "Jennifer Fox's Drama 'The Tale' Brings #MeToo to Sundance." *Los Angeles Times*, January 25, 2018. https://www.latimes.com/entertainment/movies/la-ca-mn-sundance-the-tale-jennifer-fox-20180125-story.html.

Keating, Shannon. "People Are Calling for This Queer Indie Film to Be Canceled before It Hits Theaters." BuzzFeed News, August 4, 2019. https://www.buzzfeednews.com/article/shannonkeating/rhys-ernst-adam-controversy-transgender-queer.

Keegan, Cáel M. "On the Necessity of Bad Trans Objects." *Film Quarterly* 75, no. 3 (2022): 26–37. https://doi.org/10.1525/fq.2022.75.3.26.

Keeley, Matt. "A Film Adaptation of the Novel 'Adam' Is Facing Backlash over a Character Who Pretends to Be Trans." Hornet, May 15, 2018. https://hornet.com/stories/adam-movie-transphobia-two/.

Kelly, Casey Ryan. *Abstinence Cinema: Virginity and the Rhetoric of Sexual Purity in Contemporary Film*. New Brunswick, NJ: Rutgers University Press, 2016.

Kelly, Charles M., and James N. Norman. "The Fusion Process for Productivity Improvement." *National Productivity Review* 2 (Spring 1983): 164–72.

Kincaid, James R. *Erotic Innocence: The Culture of Child Molesting*. Durham, NC: Duke University Press, 2000.

Kinsey, Alfred C., Wardell B. Pomeroy, Cylde E. Martin, and Paul H. Gebhard. *Sexual Behavior in the Human Female*. Bloomington: Indiana University Press, 1998. Originally published 1953.

Kirby, David A. "Regulating Cinematic Stories about Reproduction: Pregnancy, Childbirth, Abortion and Movie Censorship in the US, 1930–1958." *British Journal for the History of Science* 50, no. 3 (September 19, 2017): 451–72. https://doi.org/10.1017/S0007087417000814.

Klein, Verena, Roland Imhoff, Klaus Michael Reininger, and Peer Briken. "Perceptions of Sexual Script Deviation in Women and Men." *Archives of Sexual Behavior* 48, no. 2 (2018): 631–44. https://doi.org/10.1007/s10508-018-1280-x.

Klemesrud, Judy. "Jodie Foster's Rise from Disney to Depravity." *New York Times*, March 7, 1976. https://timesmachine.nytimes.com/timesmachine/1976/03/07/121597664.html?pageNumber=96.

Koresky, Michael. "Queer & Now & Then: 1956." *Film Comment*, January 16, 2019. https://www.filmcomment.com/blog/queer-now-then-1956/.

Kosciesza, Aiden James. "Intersectional Gender Measurement: Proposing a New Metric for Gender Identity and Gender Experience." *Feminist Media Studies* (2022): 1–16. https://doi.org/10.1080/14680777.2021.2018008.

Kramer, Gary M. "Frameline Interview: Eric Schaeffer on His Trans Rom Com 'Boy Meets Girl.'" IndieWire, June 25, 2014. https://www.indiewire.com/2014/06/frameline-interview-eric-schaeffer-on-his-trans-rom-com-boy-meets-girl-214018/.

Kramer, Rita. "What Every Parent Needs to Know about Movies (and Isn't Told)." *New York Times*, April 4, 1971. https://www.nytimes.com/1971/04/04/archives/what-every-parent-needs-to-know-about-movies-and-isnt-told-movie.html.

Kung, Andrew. "The Desexualization of the Asian American Male." CNN, March 3, 2020. https://www.cnn.com/style/article/andrew-kung-asian-american-men/index.html.

Kurchak, Sarah. *"Boy Meets Girl's* Michelle Hendley: On Transphobia and Inclusivity in Film." Consequence, May 21, 2015. https://consequence.net/2015/05/boy-meets-girl-michelle-hendley/.

Lamb, Sharon, and Zoë D. Peterson. "Adolescent Girl's Sexual Empowerment: Two Feminists Explore the Concept." *Sex Roles* 66, no. 11–12 (2011): 703–12. https://doi.org/10.1007/s11199-011-9995-3.

Lavietes, Matt, and Elliott Ramos. "Nearly 240 Anti-LGBTQ Bills Filed in 2022 So Far, Most of Them Targeting Trans People." NBC News, March 20, 2022. https://www.nbcnews.com/nbc-out/out-politics-and-policy/nearly-240-anti-lgbtq-bills-filed-2022-far-targeting-trans-people-rcna20418.

LD. "What Is 'Sex Critical' and Why Should We Care about It?" *Sex Critical*, July 27, 2012. http://sexcritical.co.uk/2012/07/27/what-is-sex-critical-and-why-should-we-care-about-it/.

Leff, Leonard J., and Jerold Lee Simmons. "Appendix: The Motion Picture Production Code." In *The Dame in the Kimono: Hollywood, Censorship, and the Production Code*, 285–300. Lexington: University Press of Kentucky, 2001.

Legal Information Institute. Miller v. State of California 413 U.S. 15 (1973) 93 S.Ct. 2607, 37 L.Ed.2d 419. Cornell Law School. 1973. https://www.law.cornell.edu/supremecourt/text/413/15.

Legal Information Institute. "Obscenity." Cornell Law School. June 2017. https://www.law.cornell.edu/wex/obscenity.

Legal Information Institute. "Statutory Rape." Cornell Law School. November 2021. https://www.law.cornell.edu/wex/statutory_rape.

Legal Information Institute at Cornell Law School. Ashcroft v. Free Speech Coalition (00-795) 535 U.S. 234 (2002) 198 F.3d 1083, affirmed. Cornell Law School. 2002. https://www.law.cornell.edu/supct/html/00-795.ZS.html.

Leibowitz, Ed. "Kissing Vivian Shing." *New York Times*, May 29, 2005. https://www.nytimes.com/2005/05/29/movies/kissing-vivian-shing.html.

LetterBoxd. "Reviews on *A Girl Like Grace* (2015)." Accessed July 28, 2021. https://letterboxd.com/film/a-girl-like-grace/.

Leung, Helen Hok-sze. "Film." *Transgender Studies Quarterly* 1, no. 1–2 (May 2014): 86–89. https://doi.org/10.1215/23289252-2399686.

Lewis, Jon. *The Road to Romance and Ruin: Teen Films and Youth Culture.* New York: Routledge, 1992.

Liptak, Adam. "Civil Rights Law Protects Gay and Transgender Workers, Supreme Court Rules." *New York Times*, June 15, 2020. https://www.nytimes.com/2020/06/15/us/gay-transgender-workers-supreme-court.html.

Littman, Lisa. "Correction: Parent Reports of Adolescents and Young Adults Perceived to Show Signs of a Rapid Onset of Gender Dysphoria." *PLOS One* 14, no. 3 (2019). https://doi.org/10.1371/journal.pone.0214157.

Littman, Lisa. "Parent Reports of Adolescents and Young Adults Perceived to Show Signs of a Rapid Onset of Gender Dysphoria." *PLOS One* 13, no. 8 (August 16, 2018). https://doi.org/10.1371/journal.pone.0202330.

Lomas, Stephanie (@stephanielomas). "You are a threat to the LGBT+ Community #BoycottAdam." Twitter, July 18, 2019. https://twitter.com/stephanielomas/status/1151942112881119232.

Lukianoff, Greg. *Unlearning Liberty: Campus Censorship and the End of American Debate.* New York: Encounter Books, 2014.

Madigan, Sheri, Anh Ly, Christina L. Rash, Joris Van Ouytsel, and Jeff R. Temple. "Prevalence of Multiple Forms of Sexting Behavior among Youth." *JAMA Pediatrics* 172, no. 4 (April 1, 2018): 327–35. https://doi.org/10.1001/jamapediatrics.2017.5314.

Madman. "Noah Centineo." Ethnicity of Celebs | What Nationality Ancestry Race. September 3, 2017. https://ethnicelebs.com/noah-centineo.

Mary Baldwin University. "Race Films: Getting Started." Martha S. Grafton Library, January 24, 2022. https://libguides.marybaldwin.edu/racefilms.

Massood, Paula J. "African-Americans and Silent Films." *Wiley-Blackwell History of American Film*, November 13, 2011. https://doi.org/10.1002/9780470671153.wbhaf009.

May, Kiley. "There Wasn't a Bechdel Test for Trans Representation, So I Made One." *Vice*, November 26, 2019. https://www.vice.com/en/article/7x5nje/there-wasnt-a-bechdel-test-for-trans-representation-so-i-made-one.

Mayer, Geoff. "A Parallel Universe? Hollywood in the 'Pre-Code Era.'" Screening the Past, March 1, 2000. http://www.screeningthepast.com/issue-9-reviews/a-parallel-universe-hollywood-in-the-pre-code-era/.

McCormick, Joseph. "Trans Film 'Three Generations' Criticised for Casting of Elle Fanning as Trans Boy." PinkNews, April 11, 2017. https://www.pinknews.co.uk/2017/04/11/trans-film-three-generations-criticised-for-casting-of-elle-fanning-as-trans-boy/.

McCrystal, Laura. "Sexting Investigation at Plymouth Whitemarsh." *Philadelphia Inquirer*, November 21, 2015.

McDonald, Tamar Jeffers. *Romantic Comedy: Boy Meets Girl Meets Genre*. New York: Wallflower Press, 2007.

McDonald, Tamar Jeffers. *Virgin Territory: Representing Sexual Inexperience in Film*. Detroit: Wayne State University Press, 2010.

McGrath, Charles. "50 Years on, 'Lolita' Still Has Power to Unnerve." *New York Times*, September 24, 2005. https://www.nytimes.com/2005/09/24/books/50-years-on-lolita-still-has-power-to-unnerve.html.

McKee, Jenn. "'Diary of a Teenage Girl' Author/U of M Prof Talks Controversy and Movie Cameos." mlive, August 15, 2015. https://www.mlive.com/entertainment/ann-arbor/2015/08/diary_of_a_teenage_girl_author.html.

McKenna, John L., Lizabeth Roemer, and Susan M. Orsillo. "Predictors of Sexual Consent Communication among Sexual Minority Cisgender and Nonbinary Young Adults during a Penetrative Sexual Encounter with a New Partner." *Sexuality & Culture* 25, no. 4 (2021): 1490–508. https://doi.org/10.1007/s12119-021-09831-y.

McMurran, Kristen. "'Pretty' Brooke." *People*, May 29, 1978. https://people.com/archive/cover-story-pretty-brooke-vol-9-no-21/.

Meek, Michele. "Exposing Flaws of Affirmative Consent through Contemporary American Teen Films." *Girlhood Studies* 14, no. 1 (Spring 2021): 101–16.

Meek, Michele, ed. *Independent Female Filmmakers: A Chronicle through Interviews, Profiles, and Manifestos*. New York: Routledge, 2019.

Meek, Michele. "'It Ain't for Children': 'Shame-Interest' in *Precious* and *Bastard Out of Carolina*." *Literature/Film Quarterly* 45, no. 4 (2017). https://lfq.salisbury.edu/_issues/45_4/it_aint_for_children.html.

Meek, Michele. "Lolita Speaks: Disrupting Nabokov's 'Aesthetic Bliss.'" *Girlhood Studies* 10, no. 3 (2017): 152–67. https://doi.org/https://doi.org/10.3167/ghs.2017.100312.

Meek, Michele. "Marriage, Adultery, and Desire: A Subversive Subtext in *Baby Doll*." *Tennessee Williams Annual Review* 12 (2011). http://www.tennesseewilliamsstudies.org/journal/work.php?ID=109.

Melnick, R. Shep. "Analyzing the Department of Education's Final Title IX Rules on Sexual Misconduct." Brookings, June 11, 2020. https://www.brookings.edu/research/analyzing-the-department-of-educations-final-title-ix-rules-on-sexual-misconduct/.

Mendoza, Jessica. "Sexting Scandals: How to Protect Kids from Risky Behavior— And Legal Fallout." *Christian Science Monitor*, November 13, 2015.

Merriam-Webster, s.v., "cancel culture." Accessed July 28, 2021. https://www.merriam-webster.com/dictionary/cancel%20culture.

Merriam-Webster, s.v., "Lolita." Accessed July 28, 2021. https://www.merriam-webster.com/dictionary/Lolita.

Milano, Alyssa (@Alyssa_Milano). "If you've been sexually harassed or assaulted write 'me too' as a reply to this tweet." Twitter, October 15, 2017. https://twitter.com/alyssa_milano/status/919659438700670976.

Miller, Franklin G., and Alan Wertheimer. *The Ethics of Consent: Theory and Practice*. New York: Oxford University Press, 2010.

Miller, Jenni. "How *The Diary of a Teenage Girl* Creates Film's First *Real* Teenage Heroine." *Vanity Fair*, August 10, 2015. https://www.vanityfair.com/hollywood/2015/08/diary-of-a-teenage-girl-interview.

Miller, J. Hillis. "Narrative." In *Critical Terms for Literary Study*, edited by Thomas McLaughlin and Frank Lentricchia, 66–79. Chicago: University of Chicago Press, 1995.

Mitchell, Kirk. "Sexting Scandal Ensnares Hundreds of Kids at Cañon City High School." *Denver Post*, November 6, 2015.

Monaghan, Whitney. "Not Just a Phase: Queer Girlhood and Coming of Age on Screen." *Girlhood Studies* 12, no. 1 (2019): 98–113. https://doi.org/10.3167/ghs.2019.120109.

Morales, Wilson. "Exclusive: Singer Ryan Destiny Talks 'A Girl Like Grace.'" BlackFilm.com, December 18, 2018. http://www.blackfilm.com/read/2015/06/exclusive-singer-ryan-destiny-talks-a-girl-like-grace/.

Movement Advancement Project. "Equality Maps: Conversion Therapy Laws." Accessed July 27, 2022. https://www.lgbtmap.org/equality-maps/conversion_therapy.

Musto, Michael. "Michelle Hendley on Her Nude Scene, the Lesbian Stuff & Movie Stardom." OUT.com, February 2, 2015. https://www.out.com/michael-musto/2015/2/02/trans-actress-michelle-hendley-her-nude-scene-lesbian-stuff-movie-stardom.

Nabokov, Vladimir. *The Annotated Lolita*. New York: First Vintage Books, 1991. Original publication 1955.

Namaste, Viviane K. *Invisible Lives: The Erasure of Transsexual and Transgendered People*. Chicago: University of Chicago Press, 2007.

National Coalition for Women & Girls in Education. "Title IX Timeline." NCWGE Reports, January 2008. https://www.ncwge.org/reports.html.

NBC News. "Inside Dateline: To Catch a Predator III." August 4, 2010. https://www.nbcnews.com/id/wbna9878187.

Newstrom, Nicholas P., Steven M. Harris, and Michael H. Miner. "Sexual Consent: How Relationships, Gender, and Sexual Self-Disclosure Affect Signaling and Interpreting Cues for Sexual Consent in a Hypothetical Heterosexual Sexual Situation." *Sex Roles* 84, no. 7–8 (2020): 454–64. https://doi.org/10.1007/s11199-020-01178-2.

New York Times. "The A.P.A. Ruling on Homosexuality." December 23, 1973. https://www.nytimes.com/1973/12/23/archives/the-issue-is-subtle-the-debate-still-on-the-apa-ruling-on.html.

New York Times. "Censors Destroyed Evil Picture Films; National Board Weeded Out 2,000,000 Feet of Objectionable Motion Scenes." May 11, 1911. https://nyti.ms/3Bo8tnA.

New York Times. "Excerpts from Opinions in Ruling on the Child Pornography Prevention Act." April 17, 2002. https://www.nytimes.com/2002/04/17/us/excerpts-from-opinions-in-ruling-on-the-child-pornography-prevention-act.html.

New York Times. "Say Motion-Picture Censorship Is Lax; Board Which Passes on Films Paid by Manufacturers, Women Investigators Declare." November 8, 1911. https://nyti.ms/3zjDdUW.

New York Times. "What They're Saying about Sexting." March 26, 2011. https://www.nytimes.com/2011/03/27/us/27sextingqanda.html.

Ng, E. "Contesting the Queer Subfield of Cultural Production: Paratextual Framings of 'Carol' and 'Freeheld.'" *Journal of Film and Video* 70, no. 3–4 (2018): 8. https://doi.org/10.5406/jfilmvideo.70.3-4.0008.

Noreiga, Chon. "'Something's Missing Here!': Homosexuality and Film Reviews during the Production Code Era, 1934–1962." *JCMS: Journal of Cinema and Media Studies* 58 (2018): 20–41. https://doi.org/10.1353/cj.2018.0089.

NPR. "The History behind Sexual Consent Policies." *All Things Considered*, October 5, 2014. https://www.npr.org/2014/10/05/353922015/the-history-behind-sexual-consent-policies.

OK, Inc. *Sexting: A Documentary*. YouTube, September 8, 2019. https://www.youtube.com/watch?v=SS0UQRNWr3Y.

Orenstein, Peggy. "The Movies Discover the Teen-Age Girl." *New York Times*, August 11, 1996. https://timesmachine.nytimes.com/timesmachine/1996/08/11/711888.html?pageNumber=165.

Osenlund, R. Kurt. "Cancel Culture and the Dangers of Policing Art." *Playboy*, September 30, 2019. https://www.playboy.com/read/adam-cancel-culture-film.

Pahr, Kristi. "Is Teen Sexting Cause for Concern, or No Big Deal? How to Help Kids Stay Safe Online." *Washington Post*, July 12, 2019. https://www.washingtonpost.com/lifestyle/2019/07/19/is-teen-sexting-cause-concern-or-no-big-deal-how-help-kids-stay-safe-online/.

Palmer, R. Barton. "*Baby Doll*: The Success of Scandal." *Tennessee Williams Annual Review* 4 (2001). https://tennesseewilliamsstudies.org/journal/work.php?ID=37.

Patnoe, Elizabeth. "Lolita Misrepresented, Lolita Reclaimed: Disclosing the Doubles." *College Literature* 22, no. 2 (June 1995): 81–104. https://www.jstor.org/stable/25112188.

Paul, Jesse. "No Charges Will Be Filed in Scandal That Had No 'Aggravating' Factors." *Denver Post*, December 10, 2015.

PBS. "A Felony for a Selfie? Teen Sexts Pose a Paradox for Police." *NewsHour*, October 29, 2014. https://www.pbs.org/newshour/show/felony-selfie-teen-sexts-pose-paradox-police.

Petigny, Alan. "'Silent' Sexual Revolution Began in 1940s and '50s." University of Florida Research. Accessed July 28, 2021. https://research.ufl.edu/publications/explore/v10n1/pdfs/pg07extracts.indd.pdf.

Phillips, Lynn M. *Flirting with Danger: Young Women's Reflections on Sexuality and Domination*. New York: New York University Press, 2000.

Piluso, Robert. "An Education: Nick Hornby." *Script Magazine*, October 6, 2009. https://scriptmag.com/features/an-education-nick-hornby.

Planned Parenthood. "What Is Sexual Consent?: Facts About Rape & Sexual Assault." Accessed July 21, 2021. https://www.plannedparenthood.org/learn/relationships/sexual-consent.

PopBuzz. "Noah Centineo: 27 Facts You about the To All the Boys Actor You Need to Know." February 11, 2021. https://www.popbuzz.com/tv-film/features/noah-centineo/.

PopBuzz. "Where Is Jordan Fisher From?" December 3, 2020. https://www.popbuzz.com/tv-film/features/jordan-fisher/ethnicity-where-from/.

Popova, Milena. *Sexual Consent*. Cambridge, MA: MIT Press, 2019.

Projansky, Sarah. *Watching Rape: Film and Television in Postfeminist Culture*. New York: New York University Press, 2001.

Radi, Blas. "On Trans* Epistemology: Critiques, Contributions, and Challenges." *Transgender Studies Quarterly* 6, no. 1 (2019): 43–63. https://doi.org/https://doi.org/10.1215/23289252-7253482.

RAINN. "Child Sexual Abuse." Accessed July 28, 2021. https://www.rainn.org/articles/child-sexual-abuse.

RAINN. "How Does Your State Define Consent?" March 27, 2016. https://www.rainn.org/news/how-does-your-state-define-consent.

Ramos, Dino-Ray. "'The Half of It' Director Alice Wu Talks Returning to Filmmaking." Deadline, May 1, 2020. https://deadline.com/2020/05/the

-half-of-it-alice-wu-interview-netflix-saving-face-asian-american-lgbtq-inclusion-representation-diversity-1202922253/.

Reynolds, Daniel. "*Adam* Director Rhys Ernst Addresses Critics and the 'War on Nuance.'" Advocate, July 22, 2019. https://www.advocate.com/film/2019/7/22/adam-director-rhys-ernst-addresses-critics-and-war-nuance.

Rich, B. Ruby. *New Queer Cinema: The Director's Cut*. Durham, NC: Duke University Press, 2013.

Ringwald, Molly. "What about 'The Breakfast Club'?" *New Yorker*, April 6, 2018. https://www.newyorker.com/culture/personal-history/what-about-the-breakfast-club-molly-ringwald-metoo-john-hughes-pretty-in-pink.

Rooney, David. "'Adam': Film Review: Sundance 2019." *Hollywood Reporter*, January 28, 2019. https://www.hollywoodreporter.com/review/adam-review-sundance-2019-1178226.

Rose, Jacqueline. *The Case of Peter Pan or The Impossibility of Children's Fiction*. Philadelphia: University of Pennsylvania Press, 1984.

Rose, Sarah. "No. 1 Story of 2015: Cañon City School District Sexting Scandal." *Canon City Daily Record*, December 31, 2015. https://www.canoncitydailyrecord.com/2015/12/31/no-1-story-of-2015-caon-city-school-district-sexting-scandal/.

Rosin, Hanna. "Why Kids Sext." *The Atlantic*, November 7, 2014. https://www.theatlantic.com/magazine/archive/2014/11/why-kids-sext/380798/.

Rossetto, Kelly R., and Andrew C. Tollison. "Feminist Agency, Sexual Scripts, and Sexual Violence: Developing a Model for Postgendered Family Communication." *Family Relations* 66, no. 1 (2017): 61–74. https://doi.org/10.1111/fare.12232.

Rowe, Kathleen. *The Unruly Woman: Gender and Genres of Laughter*. Austin: University of Texas Press, 1995.

Rubin, Gayle. "Thinking Sex." In *Deviations: A Gayle Rubin Reader*, 137–81. Durham, NC: Duke University Press, 2012.

Rupcich, Claudia. "Deputies Bust Massive Teen Sexting Ring in Louisa County." ABC News, April 4, 2014. https://www.youtube.com/watch?v=7QDHqqDE-q4.

Russo, Vito. *The Celluloid Closet: Homosexuality in the Movies*. New York: Harper & Row, 1987.

Ryan, Patrick. "Why Did It Take So Long for Hollywood to Make a Gay Teen Story like 'Love, Simon'?" *USA Today*, March 15, 2018. https://www.usatoday.com/story/life/movies/2018/03/14/why-did-take-so-long-hollywood-make-gay-teen-story-like-love-simon/421300002/.

Saito, Stephen. "Interview: Craig Johnson on Triangulating the Triumph of 'Alex Strangelove.'" *Moveable Fest*, June 8, 2018. https://moveablefest.com/craig-johnson-alex-strangelove/.

Sandler, Kevin S. *The Naked Truth: Why Hollywood Doesn't Make X-Rated Movies.* New Brunswick, NJ: Rutgers University Press, 2007.

Sanjeevi, Jerusha, Daniel Houlihan, Kelly A. Bergstrom, Moses M. Langley, and Jaxson Judkins. "A Review of Child Sexual Abuse: Impact, Risk, and Resilience in the Context of Culture." *Journal of Child Sexual Abuse* 27, no. 6 (2018): 622–41. https://doi.org/10.1080/10538712.2018.1486934.

Sayers, Luke. "'A Brief History of the Nymphet's Tribulations': The Interpretation of Obscenity in the Early Reception of Vladimir Nabokov's *Lolita*." *Reception: Texts, Readers, Audiences, History* 12 (2020): 5–20. https://doi.org/10.5325/reception.12.1.0005.

Schaefer, Eric. "No False Modesty, No Old-Fashioned Taboos: The Sex Hygiene Film." In *Bold! Daring! Shocking! True!: A History of Exploitation Films, 1919–1959*, 166–216. Durham, NC: Duke University Press, 1999.

Scheiner, Georganne. *Signifying Female Adolescence: Film Representations and Fans, 1920–1950.* Westport, CT: Praeger, 2000.

Schoonover, Karl, and Rosalind Galt. *Queer Cinema in the World.* Durham, NC: Duke University Press, 2016.

Scott, Ellen C. *Cinema Civil Rights: Regulation, Repression, and Race in the Classical Hollywood Era.* New Brunswick, NJ: Rutgers University Press, 2015.

Seggel, Heather. "Ariel Schrag: On Her New Novel 'Adam,' Writing for the 'L Word,' and Trans Inclusiveness." LAMBDA Literary, July 30, 2014. https://lambdaliterary.org/2014/07/ariel-schrag-on-her-new-novel-adam-writing-for-the-l-word-and-trans-inclusiveness/.

Semonche, John E. *Censoring Sex: A Historical Journey through American Media.* Lanham, MD: Rowman & Littlefield, 2007.

Shary, Tim. "Course File for 'Film Genres and the Image of Youth.'" *Journal of Film and Video* 55, no. 1 (Spring 2003): 39–57.

Shary, Timothy. *Generation Multiplex: The Image of Youth in Contemporary American Cinema.* Austin: University of Texas Press, 2002.

Shary, Timothy. *Teen Movies: American Youth on Screen.* London: Wallflower, 2005.

Shelton, Jen. "'The Word Is Incest': Sexual and Linguistic Coercion in *Lolita*." *Textual Practice* 13, no. 2 (1999): 273–94. https://doi.org/10.1080/09502369908582341.

Siegel, Tatiana. "Weinstein Co. Finally Puts Transgender Teen Drama 'Three Generations' Back on Schedule (Exclusive)." *Hollywood Reporter*, March 3, 2017. https://www.hollywoodreporter.com/news/weinstein-finally-puts-transgender-teen-drama-three-generations-back-schedule-973463.

Simmon, Scott. "'The Female of the Species' D. W. Griffith: Father of the Woman's Film." *Film Quarterly* 46, no. 2 (1992): 8–20. https://doi.org/10.2307/1213004.

Simpson, Brian. "Challenging Childhood, Challenging Children: Children's Rights and Sexting." *Sexualities* 16, no. 5–6 (2013): 690–709. https://doi.org/10.1177/1363460713487467.

Smith, Frances. *Rethinking the Hollywood Teen Movie: Gender, Genre, and Identity*. Edinburgh: Edinburgh University Press, 2017.

Smith, J. Douglas. *Managing White Supremacy: Race, Politics, and Citizenship in Jim Crow Virginia*. Chapel Hill: University of North Carolina Press, 2002.

Smith, Sarah H. "Scripting Sexual Desire: Cultural Scenarios of Teen Girls' Sexual Desire in Popular Films, 2000–2009." *Sexuality & Culture* 16, no. 3 (2012): 321–41. https://doi.org/10.1007/s12119-012-9126-5.

Solzman, Danielle. "'Adam' Proves the Importance of Hiring Transgender Directors." *Out*, January 26, 2019. https://www.out.com/movies/2019/1/26/adam-proves-importance-hiring-transgender-directors.

Srinivasan, Amia. *The Right to Sex: Feminism in the Twenty-First Century*. New York: Farrar, Straus and Giroux, 2021.

Steinbock, Eliza. "Towards Trans Cinema." In *The Routledge Companion to Cinema & Gender*, edited by Kristin Lené Hole, Dijana Jelača, E. Ann Kaplan, and Patrice Petro, 395–406. New York: Routledge, 2018.

Stemm-Wade, Megan. "Careless Girls and Repentant Wives: Gender in Postwar Classroom Films." *Journal of Popular Culture* 45, no. 3 (2012): 611–27. https://doi.org/10.1111/j.1540-5931.2012.00947.x.

Sternin, Shulamit, Raymond M. McKie, Carter Winberg, Robb N. Travers, Terry P. Humphreys, and Elke D. Reissing. "Sexual Consent: Exploring the Perceptions of Heterosexual and Non-Heterosexual Men." *Psychology & Sexuality* (2021): 1–23. https://doi.org/10.1080/19419899.2021.1879911.

Stockton, Kathryn Bond. *The Queer Child, or Growing Sideways in the Twentieth Century*. Durham, NC: Duke University Press, 2009.

Strasburger, Victor C., Harry Zimmerman, Jeff R. Temple, and Sheri Madigan. "Teenagers, Sexting, and the Law." *Pediatrics* 143, no. 5 (2019). https://doi.org/10.1542/peds.2018-3183.

Stratford, Michael. "U.S. Names Colleges under Investigation for Sexual Assault Cases." Inside Higher Ed, May 2, 2014. https://www.insidehighered.com/news/2014/05/02/us-names-colleges-under-investigation-sexual-assault-cases.

Strub, W. "Black and White and Banned All Over: Race, Censorship and Obscenity in Postwar Memphis." *Journal of Social History* 40, no. 3 (2007): 685–715. https://doi.org/10.1353/jsh.2007.0072.

The Sun. "Students Accused of Sending Explicit Photos." November 28, 2013.

Tanner, Lindsey. "More U.S. Teens Identify as Transgender, Survey Finds." *USA Today*, February 5, 2018. https://www.usatoday.com/story/news/nation/2018/02/05/more-u-s-teens-identify-transgender-survey-finds/306357002/.

Thalberg, Irving, E. H. Allen, and Sol Wurtzel. "Don'ts and Be Carefuls." MPPDA Digital Archive, Record #341, May 24, 1927. https://mppda.flinders.edu.au/records/341.

Thomas, Sara E. "'What Should I Do?': Young Women's Reported Dilemmas with Nude Photographs." *Sexuality Research and Social Policy* 15, no. 2 (2017): 192–207. https://doi.org/10.1007/s13178-017-0310-0.

Timmermans, Elisabeth, and Jan Van den Bulck. "Casual Sexual Scripts on the Screen: A Quantitative Content Analysis." *Archives of Sexual Behavior* 47, no. 5 (2018): 1481–96. https://doi.org/10.1007/s10508-018-1147-1.

Today NBC. "'Teens Tell All' in Candid Talks about Drugs, Sexting, Hooking Up." YouTube, November 30, 2016. https://www.youtube.com/watch?v=YPoL_VGuTEA.

Tolman, Deborah L. "Female Adolescents, Sexual Empowerment and Desire: A Missing Discourse of Gender Inequity." *Sex Roles* 66, no. 11–12 (2012): 746–57. https://doi.org/10.1007/s11199-012-0122-x.

The Trevor Project. "Research Brief: Data on Transgender Youth." March 4, 2019. https://www.thetrevorproject.org/2019/02/22/research-brief-data-on-transgender-youth/.

Triplett, Hall. "The Misnomer of Freud's 'Seduction Theory.'" *Journal of the History of Ideas* 65, no. 4 (October 2004): 647–65. https://www.jstor.org/stable/3654273.

Turban Jack L., Stephanie S. Loo, Anthony N. Almazan, and Alex S. Keuroghlian. "Factors Leading to 'Detransition' Among Transgender and Gender Diverse People in the United States: A Mixed-Methods Analysis." *LGBT Health*, no. 8 (May–Jun 2021): 273–80. https://www.ncbi.nlm.nih.gov/pmc/articles/PMC8213007/.

Turner Classic Movies. "Ben Mankiewicz Intro: *The Moon Is Blue* (1953)." Accessed July 31, 2022. https://www.tcm.com/video/1338241/ben-mankiewicz-intro-the-moon-is-blue-1953.

Tzioumakis, Yannis. *American Independent Cinema: An Introduction.* Edinburgh: Edinburgh University Press, 2017.

UCLA School of Law. "Conversion Therapy and LGBT Youth." Williams Institute, June 2019. https://williamsinstitute.law.ucla.edu/publications/conversion-therapy-and-lgbt-youth/.

UCLA School of Law. "Prohibiting Gender-Affirming Medical Care for Youth." Williams Institute, March 2022. https://williamsinstitute.law.ucla.edu/publications/bans-trans-youth-health-care/.

United States Department of Education. "Dear Colleague." Office of Civil Rights, April 4, 2011. https://www2.ed.gov/about/offices/list/ocr/letters/colleague-201104.pdf.

United States Department of Justice. "Citizen's Guide to U.S. Federal Law on Child Pornography." Criminal Division, Child Exploitation and Obscenity

Section. Updated May 28, 2020. https://www.justice.gov/criminal-ceos/citizens-guide-us-federal-law-child-pornography.

United States Department of Justice. "Project Safe Childhood." Eastern District of Louisiana. Accessed July 2021. https://www.justice.gov/usao-edla/project-safe-childhood-0.

United States Sentencing Commission. "The History of the Child Pornography Guidelines." October 2009. https://www.ussc.gov/sites/default/files/pdf/research-and-publications/research-projects-and-surveys/sex-offenses/20091030_History_Child_Pornography_Guidelines.pdf.

Urban Dictionary, s.v., "consent culture." Accessed July 28, 2021. https://www.urbandictionary.com/define.php?term=consent+culture.

US House of Representatives. "Sexual Exploitation of Children over the Internet." Committee on Energy and Commerce, January 2007. https://www.govinfo.gov/content/pkg/CPRT-109HPRT31737/html/CPRT-109HPRT31737.htm.

US Supreme Court. Christine Franklin v. Gwinnett County Public Schools and William Prescott, 503 U.S. 60, 112 S.Ct. 1028, 117 L.Ed. 208 (1992). Available from Legal Information Institute, Cornell Law School. Accessed July 31, 2022. https://www.law.cornell.edu/supremecourt/text/503/60.

US Supreme Court. Davis v. Monroe County Board of Ed., 526 U.S. 629, 120 F.3d 1390 (1999). Available from Legal Information Institute, Cornell Law School. Accessed July 31, 2022. https://www.law.cornell.edu/supct/html/97-843.ZS.html.

US Supreme Court. Mutual Film Corporation, Appt., v. Industrial Commission of Ohio et al., 236 U.S. 230, 45 S.Ct. 387, 59 L.Ed. 552 (1915). Available from Legal Information Institute, Cornell Law School. Accessed July 31, 2022. https://www.law.cornell.edu/supremecourt/text/236/230.

US Supreme Court. New York v. Ferber, 458 U.S. 747 (1982). Available from Justia.com. Accessed July 31, 2022. https://supreme.justia.com/cases/federal/us/458/747/.

Valentine, Claire. "Lauren Tsai on 'Moxie' and Not Being a Side Character in Your Own Life." Nylon, March 12, 2021. https://www.nylon.com/entertainment/lauren-tsai-moxie-interview.

Varda, Agnès, dir.. *Ulysse*. 1983. https://www.criterionchannel.com/ulysse.

Vaughn, Stephen. "Morality and Entertainment: The Origins of the Motion Picture Production Code." *Journal of American History* 77, no. 1 (1990): 39. https://doi.org/10.2307/2078638.

Vogels, Emily A., Monica Anderson, Margaret Porteus, Chris Baronavski, Sara Atske, Colleen McClain, Brooke Auxier, Andrew Perrin, and Meera Ramshankar. "Americans and 'Cancel Culture': Where Some See Calls for Accountability, Others See Censorship, Punishment." Pew Research Center: Internet, Science & Tech, May 19, 2021. https://www.pewresearch.org

/internet/2021/05/19/americans-and-cancel-culture-where-some-see-calls-for-accountability-others-see-censorship-punishment/.
WCCO–CBS Minnesota. "Teen Shares Sexting Story, Tells Parents 'Don't Be Naïve.'" YouTube, November 12, 2014. https://www.youtube.com/watch?v=NSzeQUmMic4.
Weiler, A. H. "'69 a Bad Year for Good Films, Catholic Movie Office Finds." *New York Times*, January 2, 1970. https://www.nytimes.com/1970/01/02/archives/69-a-bad-year-for-good-films-catholic-movie-office-finds.html?searchResultPosition=2.
Weinman, Sarah. *The Real Lolita: The Kidnapping of Sally Horner and the Novel That Scandalized the World*. New York: HarperCollins, 2018.
Westen, Peter. *The Logic of Consent: The Diversity and Deceptiveness of Consent as a Defense to Criminal Conduct*. Abingdon, UK: Routledge, 2016.
Whitney, E. Oliver. "Susan Sarandon Says the Time to Tell Transgender Stories Is Now with 'About Ray.'" *HuffPost*, September 9, 2015. https://www.huffpost.com/entry/susan-sarandon-about-ray_n_55f83af4e4b09ecde1d9b50e.
Wickman, Kase. "How One Young Trans Woman Went from YouTube Confessional to Rom-Com Movie Star." MTV News, May 14, 2015. http://www.mtv.com/news/2159497/boy-meets-girl-michelle-hendley-interview/.
Wiederman, Michael W. "Sexual Script Theory: Past, Present, and Future." In *Handbook of the Sociology of Sexualities*, edited by John DeLamater and Rachel F. Plante, 7–22. New York: Springer, 2015.
Williams, Linda. *Screening Sex*. Durham, NC: Duke University Press, 2008.
Women and Hollywood. "Elle Fanning to Play Transgender Character in Multigenerational Drama." Accessed July 28, 2021. https://womenandhollywood.com/elle-fanning-to-play-transgender-character-in-multigenerational-drama-6e3c4aece83a/.
Wood, Michael. "*Lolita* Revisited." *New England Review* 17, no. 3 (1995): 15–43. http://www.jstor.org/stable/40243059.
Yakas, Ben. "This 'Teacher Trial' Rape Sketch on SNL Failed Miserably." Gothamist, April 12, 2015. https://gothamist.com/arts-entertainment/this-teacher-trial-rape-sketch-on-snl-failed-miserably.
Yardley, Jonathan. "Sugar and Spice and Not Nice." *Washington Post*, Nov. 16, 1981. https://www.washingtonpost.com/archive/lifestyle/1981/11/16/sugar-and-spice-and-not-nice/3b2572c8-0d87-4f22-b1a7-1af775c4460d/.
Young, Donald. *Motion Pictures: A Study in Social Legislation*. Buffalo, NY: William S. Hein, 1922.
Your Faux Mom (@JustBeNicer). "@Peoplemag Why isn't a real trans person cast? Things haven't changed since Boys Don't Cry w/H. Swank #3generations." Twitter, November 20, 2014. https://twitter.com/JustBeNicer/status/535250114550706176.

Zimmerman, Eilene. "Campus Sexual Assault: A Timeline of Major Events." *New York Times*, June 22, 2016. https://www.nytimes.com/2016/06/23/education/campus-sexual-assault-a-timeline-of-major-events.html.

Zuckerman, Esther. "Why *About Ray's* Director Cast Elle Fanning as a Trans Teen—Exclusive Poster." Refinery29, August 17, 2015. https://www.refinery29.com/en-us/2015/08/92441/about-ray-elle-fanning-poster.

Zurbriggen, Eileen, Rebecca L Collins, Sharon Lamb, Deborah L. Tolman, L. Monique Ward, and Jeanne Blake. "Report of the APA Task Force on the Sexualization of Girls." American Psychological Association Task Force on the Sexualization of Girls, 2007. https://www.apa.org/pi/women/programs/girls/report-full.pdf.

INDEX

abortion, 32, 34, 37, 50, 57, 60
abstinence, 41, 56, 72
acquaintance rape. *See* rape
Adam, 16–17, 150, 160, 162–65, 170–76
adolescent sexuality: omission in teen films, 9–10, 16–17, 22, 33–35, 55–56, 89, 112, 137–38; perceived dangers of, 8, 16, 18, 21–33, 185
adult sex with youth in films, 16, 45–47. *See also* child sexual abuse
affirmative consent, 1–9, 15–17, 62, 65–67, 72–73, 80, 89, 101–2, 106, 113–14, 180, 189
African American youth. *See* BIPOC
age of consent, 48–49, 55, 120, 124, 128, 146, 182
agency *See* sexual agency; subjectivity
AIDS, 22, 68, 74, 108. *See also* HIV
Alex Strangelove, 16, 18, 89, 93, 94, 95, 99–100, 101, 102, 113
All Over Me, 92
All Quiet on the Western Front, 34
Always in My Heart, 34
American Pie, 15, 55–56, 62, 68–70, 73, 77, 81, 128
American Pie: Girls' Rules, 15, 56, 73–74, 77, 81
Amy Fisher: My Story, 27
Amy Fisher Story, The, 127

Animal House, 44, 67
Antioch College Sexual Offense Prevention Policy, 5
Anything for Love. *See Just One of the Girls*
Anything's Possible, 160
Are These Our Children?, 34
Are You Popular?, 36
Arzner, Dorothy, 31
asexuality, 91, 100, 114–16, 138–39
Asian American youth, 81–87. *See also* BIPOC
As You Are, 94
audience, 7, 31, 33, 82, 90, 94, 149–150, 158–65, 170, 173–76; adults as audience of teen films, 10–12, 22–23, 45, 63, 98, 140, 142, 181; youth as audience of teen films, 15, 24–25, 46, 53–54, 67

Baby Doll, 40–41
Band of Angels, 42
Banging Lanie, 15, 18, 62, 74–76
Barrymore, Drew, 54
Basketball Diaries, The, 92
Bastard Out of Carolina, 137–38
Beach Rats, 94–95
Beatty, Warren, 42
Biden, Joseph, 17, 150, 151
Big Bet, The, 87

221

INDEX

BIPOC, 15, 29–32, 33–34, 42–43, 45, 52–53, 63, 81–87, 94–95, 112–13, 138
Birth, 128
birth control. *See* contraception
Birth of a Nation, The, 31
bisexuality, 9, 90–94, 100, 114–115, 175, 187, 191
Blame It on Rio, 16, 45–46, 127
Blockers, 10–11, 15–16, 61–62, 72–73, 76–77, 81, 89, 93–95, 98–100, 102, 112
Blue Denim, 34
Blue Lagoon, The, 34–35
Bob and Sally, 37
Bond Stockton, Kathryn, 145, 191
Booksmart, 57, 93, 113
Boy Erased, 12, 13, 16, 89, 94–95, 102–4, 107–9, 112–13
Boy Meets Girl, 16–17, 69, 150, 159, 165–70
Boys Don't Cry, 149, 157, 159, 161, 175–76
Boyz n the Hood, 53
Breakfast Club, The, 51, 61
Bringing Up Baby, 69–70
Broken Blossoms, 27
Brute, The, 30
Bully, 94
Burden of Race, The, 30
But I'm a Cheerleader, 53, 70, 98, 102
Butler, Judith, 121

cancel culture, 7, 17, 150, 160, 164–65, 171
Cape Fear, 127
Casualties of Love: The Long Island Lolita Story, 127
censorship, 15, 21–34, 37, 57. *See also* Production Code
Centineo, Noah, 79, 82–83
Child Abuse Prevention and Treatment Act, 123–124
childbirth, 25, 52
child pornography, 13, 14–15, 21, 43–44, 57, 68, 120, 186; accusations of, 47–48, 138–39, 184; definitions of, 48, 50, 184, 185; laws against, 55, 125, 181–82, 186
Child Protection Act of 1984, 48
child sexual abuse, 46–50, 118–46; definition of, 120; laws against, 123
cis sexism, 13, 17, 63, 150, 173–75
class. *See* socioeconomic class

Clueless, 52, 92
college, 5–8, 12, 29–30, 45, 53, 54, 64, 68, 74, 75, 80, 92, 95, 103, 108, 132, 149, 161, 176
coming out, 40, 82, 89, 94–97, 113, 116, 176
Coming Soon, 56, 70–71
Condor, Lana, 15, 79, 81
consent: definition of, 3, 8–9, 174 (*see also* affirmative consent); college and university policies, 5–7 (*see also* Title IX); consent laws, 3, 6, 13, 17, 47 (*see also* age of consent); as contractual notion, 57, 78, 79, 106–108; dilemmas of, 8–9, 14, 67, 98, 100–102, 114, 165, 174–175, 180, 184–86, 188, 189; invalidating consent, 5–6, 18, 47–48, 72, 127, 129, 137; jokes about, 1–2, 7, 18, 47, 70, 72, 80
consent culture, 7, 69, 180; definition of, 1, 3–5; flaws within, 7–9; origins of, 5–7. *See also* affirmative consent
Considine, David M., 34–35, 104, 180–81
Constant Nymph, The, 34
contraception, 53, 99, 171
conversion therapy, 13, 16, 89, 102, 104–5, 106–12, 152, 162, 163
Cooley High, 45
Cougars, Inc., 128
Crawford, Joan, 26, 28, 29
Cruel Intentions, 54
Crush, The, 16, 127
Curda, Piper, 15, 81
Curiosity of Chance, The, 93, 159

date rape. *See* rape
Davenport, Dorothy, 31
Dean, James, 38
Dellal, Gaby, 161–162, 166
Dern, Laura, 129, 135
Diary of a High School Bride, 38
Diary of a Teenage Girl, The, 13, 16, 57, 118–19, 129, 138–42, 145–46
Dirty Dancing, 51
disabilities, 6, 54, 156
discrimination in the film industry, 13–14, 22–23, 29–32, 93
dissent, 17, 149–50, 154, 156, 159, 160, 161–64, 173, 175–76
diversity in teen films. *See* BIPOC

INDEX

Doheny, Daniel, 101
Doherty, Thomas, 10
Dolorita Passion Dance, The, 23
double standard, sexual, 42, 63–64
Downing, Lisa, 9
Driscoll, Catherine, 11, 80, 146
drugs. *See* intoxication
Du er ikke alene / You Are Not Alone, 92

Easy A, 92, 94
Ebert, Roger, 35, 48, 60
Edge of Seventeen (1998), 53, 92, 100
Edge of Seventeen (2010), 83
Edison, Thomas, 23
education. *See* high school; college
Education, An, 119
Election, 16, 127
Ernst, Rhys, 162–64, 170–76

Fame, 45, 92
Fast Times at Ridgemont High, 45, 50–51, 70, 142
Fear, 127
Feder, Sam, 149, 154–155
feminism, 9, 13, 15, 71–72, 77, 80, 83, 84–85, 119, 122, 125–26, 142, 146, 160
First Amendment to the US Constitution, 24, 37, 48–49, 55, 185
First Girl I Loved, 117
First Time, The, 44
Foucault, Michel, 8, 50
Fox, Jennifer, 118–19
Foxfire, 53
Freak Show, 94, 159
Freud, Sigmund, 122–25

gender-affirming care, 2, 17, 151, 153, 161, 165–66, 169–70
Geography Club, 94–95
Ghost of Dragstrip Hollow, 38
Gidget, 33, 38
Girl Like Grace, A, 16, 18, 89, 94–95, 100–101
Girl Next Door, The, 56
Girls on Probation, 35
Girls Town, 53
Gish, Lillian, 27
GLAAD, 91, 93, 150, 154, 164

Gloeckner, Phoebe, 119, 139–40, 145
Goin' All the Way!, 44
Good Boys, 1–2, 11–12, 18, 55, 65
Goodluck, Forrest, 112
Graduate, The, 44–45, 128
Grease, 44
Griffith, D. W., 26–27, 31
Guess Who's Coming to Dinner, 43

Halberstam, Jack, 153, 175
Half of It, The, 15, 62, 77–78, 81–82, 93–94
Hall, G. Stanley, 24
Han, Jenny, 81
harassment. *See* sexual harassment
Hard Candy, 129
Harold and Maude, 44
Hays Code. *See* Production Code
Heller, Marielle, 118, 139, 141
Hendley, Michelle, 166–68
Henry Gamble's Birthday Party, 94
Hepburn, Katharine, 69, 158
Her Defiance, 25–26
heteronormativity, 38–39, 63, 90, 93, 166
heterosexual script, 15, 36, 61–67, 70–71, 81, 85
high school, 12, 45, 53–54, 64, 70, 77, 94, 99, 127–28, 160, 168, 170; teachers, sex with students, 7, 128. *See also* hygiene films
Hiraga, Nico, 83–84
HIV, 51, 52, 93. *See also* AIDS
Hollywood Reporter, The, 1, 162
homecoming, 73–74, 104, 159
Homesteader, The, 30
homophobia, 91–92, 94–97, 169
homosexuality, 16, 22, 35, 38–39, 89–111, 162–63
Horak, Laura, 157–58
Hot Moves, 44
H.O.T.S., 44
House behind the Cedars, The, 31
House Party, 53
House Party 2, 53
House Party 3, 53
House Party 4: Down to the Last Minute, 53
House Party: Tonight's the Night, 53
Hughes, John, 51, 61, 92, 158
Huston, Anjelica, 138
hygiene films, 32, 35–37, 46

Imitation of Life, 33
incest, 16, 35, 50, 122, 126–127. *See also* child sexual abuse
Incredibly True Adventures of Two Girls in Love, The, 53, 92, 112, 172
indigenous youth. *See* BIPOC
intergenerational sex. *See* adult sex with youth in films; child sexual abuse
intoxication, 5, 29, 31, 41–42, 61, 69, 72, 98–101, 115, 140, 144, 170–71
Irons, Jeremy, 55
It's a Boy Girl Thing, 159

James Boys in Missouri, The, 23
Jameson, Fredric, 11
Janis, Dorothy, 29, 30
Jenkins, Henry, 12
Jennings, Jazz, 154
Joy of Sex, The, 44, 70
Joy Ride, 38
Junction 88, 34
Juno, 58
Just Another Girl on the I.R.T., 52
Just One of the Girls, 159
Just One of the Guys, 159

Kazan, Elia, 40
Keegan, Cáel M., 155–56, 158
Kids Are All Right, The, 14
Kids, 52
Kincaid, James R., 50, 124–25
Kissing Booth, The, 11, 13, 56, 65–67
Kosciesza, James Aiden, 150
Kubrick, Stanley, 54, 126

Lady Bird, 18, 65
Lane, Sasha, 112
Last Picture Show, The, 44
Last Summer, 44, 91
Latinx youth, 15, 81, 83, 85, 94–95. *See also* BIPOC
Legion of Decency, 32–33, 37, 40, 44
lesbianism. *See* homosexuality
Lewis, Jon, 12
Little Darlings, 50–51, 70
Little Girl Who Lived Down the Lane, The, 47
Little Old New York, 158

Little Sister, 159
Littman, Lisa, 152–153
Lolita (1962), 54
Lolita (1997), 54–55, 138
Lolita (novel by Nabokov), 54–55, 119, 125–27, 136, 138, 145
Losin' It, 44
Love, Simon, 16, 89, 93–98, 100, 102, 112, 113
Love and Basketball, 56
Loverboy, 45–46
Lowe, Major Donald, 181, 182, 184
Lyne, Adrian, 54–55, 126, 138

MacKinnon, Catherine A., 9
Madison, Cleo, 25–26
Malle, Louis, 48–49
Manhattan, 16, 45, 46, 127
Manny & Lo, 53
marriage: heterosexual, 22, 25–26, 28–29, 30, 32–34, 36–37, 40–42, 56, 108, 115, 169; same-sex, 92
Marziale, Antonio, 101
masculinity, 29, 38–40, 63–64, 65–67, 83–86, 90, 158, 166
Masterson, Mary Stuart, 158
masturbation, 35, 48, 55, 68, 76, 97, 136, 138, 183, 187
Ma Vie en Rose (My Life in Pink), 157
Mean Girls, 92
memory, recovered, 122–23
#MeToo movement, 7, 160
Micheaux, Oscar, 29–31
Milano, Alyssa, 7
Miseducation of Cameron Post, 13, 16, 56, 89, 94–95, 102, 104–13
Mom and Dad, 36–37
Moon Is Blue, The, 40
Moonlight, 94–95
Moonrise Kingdom, 55
Moretz, Chloë Grace, 112
Motion Picture Association, 10, 43, 93; as Motion Picture Producers and Distributors of America, 25, 37. *See also* Production Code
Motion Picture Production Code. *See* Production Code
Motorcycle Gang, 38

Moxie, 56, 81–86, 159–60
Mystic Pizza, 45

Nabokov, Vladimir, 54, 119, 126, 136, 145. *See also* Lolita (novel by Nabokov)
Namaste, Viviane, 154–55
National Catholic Office for Motion Pictures, 44
National Film Registry, 13
National Velvet, 158
Nélisse, Isabelle, 130, 135
Never Been Kissed, 52
Never Rarely Sometimes Always, 57
"no means no." *See* nonconsent
nonconsent, 3, 15–17, 41, 45, 54, 65, 72, 75, 78–80, 100–102, 126, 137, 165, 180, 189. *See also* rape; sexual assault; sexual harassment; violence
Norman, Is That You?, 92
Not Wanted, 34
Novarro, Ramon, 29, 30
nudity, 10, 25, 38, 44–45, 50, 59, 168, 182–83. *See also* youth-produced sexual images

Obama, Barack, 6, 151
obscenity, 125–126, 181, 184–85; definition of, 49, 185
Once Bitten, 92
orgasm, 16, 50, 70–71, 75, 99, 106, 136–37, 142
Oscars, 13, 161
Our Dancing Daughters, 28–29
Our Modern Maidens, 28
Outsiders, The, 11

Pagan, The, 28–30
Painted Lady, The, 27
pansexuality, 91, 100, 114
parental consent, 17, 57, 151, 165, 170
Pariah, 93–95
Pascual-Pena, Alycia, 85
Patch of Blue, A, 42–43
Payne Studies, 27–28, 32
pedophilia, 48, 55, 100, 123–25, 139, 145, 168, 185. *See also* child sexual abuse
Peggy Sue Got Married, 51
Peirce, Kimberly, 149, 175
Perks of Being a Wallflower, The, 94

Pettis, Madison, 15, 81
Plan B, 10
Plaza, Aubrey, 15, 81
Poison Ivy, 16, 54, 127
Poison Ivy II, 127
Poison Ivy: Secret Society, 54
Poitier, Sidney, 42–43
Popova, Milena, 9, 64
pornography. *See* child pornography
Porter, Billy, 160
Powley, Bel, 141, 142
Precious, 13, 16, 137–138
pregnancy, 25–26, 28, 32, 35, 36, 37, 46, 50, 52, 56–57, 68
Premature, 56
Preppies, 44
Pretty Baby, 16, 44, 46–49
Princess Cyd, 16, 114–116
Private Lessons, 45
Production Code, 21, 22, 23–27, 32–37, 40, 41, 42, 46, 90–91
Projansky, Sarah, 4
prom, 68, 72–73, 78, 93, 94
Prom, 93–94
prostitution. *See* sex work
Protection of Children Against Sexual Exploitation Act of 1977, 48

queerness, definition of, 90–91
queer youth, 2, 13, 15–16, 39–40, 53, 56, 64, 82, 94–99, 100–102, 104, 108, 112–16, 159, 162, 169. *See also* homosexuality; trans youth

race films, 29–30, 33–34
race in teen films. *See* BIPOC
racism, 13, 24, 29–31, 32, 33–34, 43, 52, 81, 112. *See also* discrimination in the film industry
radical feminism, 9, 153, 155
rape, 28, 36, 43, 44, 45, 46, 47, 54, 63, 85–86, 101, 103, 108, 113, 118, 125, 149, 162–163; acquaintance rape, 1, 5, 42, 52; homosexual rape, 102–104; statutory, 16, 119–20, 125–27, 132, 137–38, 186
rape culture, 3–7, 9, 44, 54, 65–67, 69
rape revenge, 53, 76–77
Realization of a Negro's Ambition, The, 29

Rebel without a Cause, 38, 40, 91
Red Kimono, The, 31
Reign, Eva, 160
religion, 29, 32–33, 34, 72, 82, 102–10. See also Roman Catholic Church
Revenge of the Nerds, 44, 67–68
Rich, B. Ruby, 90, 92
Riding in Cars with Boys, 14
Right to Love, 28
Ringwald, Molly, 51, 61
Risky Business, 45, 70
Road to Ruin, The, 31–32
Roman Catholic Church, 32–33, 44, 124. See also Legion of Decency
Rosin, Hanna, 181, 183–84, 188
Rubin, Gayle, 21, 49

safe sex practices. See contraception
Sandlot, The, 22
Sarandon, Susan, 161, 170
Saturday Night Live (SNL), 5, 7
Save the Last Dance, 56
Saving Face, 82
Say Anything, 51
Schaeffer, Eric, 166, 167–68
Scheiner, Georganne, 10, 23, 28
School Daze, 53
seduction, 41, 50, 52, 54, 62, 66–67, 119, 123, 125, 128, 137, 140, 145
self-harm, 111. See also suicide
Sex Appeal, 15, 56–57, 62, 74–76
sex-critical approach, 7–9
Sex Drive, 56
sexism, 3, 13, 24, 63. See also discrimination in the film industry
sex-positive movement, 4, 9. See also affirmative consent; sexual agency
sexting, See youth-produced sexual images
sex toys, 1–2, 76, 162, 172, 174
sex trafficking, 54, 124. See also Victims of Trafficking and Violence Protection Act of 2000
sexual agency, 4, 17, 43, 63, 69, 71, 80, 139, 142–45, 146, 189; definition of, 120–22, 134
sexual assault, 3–4, 5–7, 28, 34, 35, 42, 44, 56, 66, 67, 76, 80, 101, 102, 114, 115–16, 123, 128, 187. See also rape

sexual harassment, 6, 8, 53, 56, 61, 76, 85–86, 154
sexualization, 16, 23, 120–21, 142–43, 185
sexual scripting theory, 9, 62–63. See also heterosexual script
sexually transmitted diseases, 25, 26, 38, 51. See also AIDS; HIV
sex work, 45–48, 120, 127, 143–44, 155
Shadows, 42
Shary, Timothy, 10–11, 12, 44, 52, 87
Sheedy, Ally, 51
Sheng, Leo, 170
She's All That, 52
She's the Man, 159
Shields, Brooke, 47–48, 49, 60, 184
Sierra Burgess Is a Loser, 15, 62, 77–80
silent films, 15, 25–27, 29–31
Sixteen Candles, 51
Skarsgard, Alexander, 141
Slums of Beverly Hills, 55
Smith, Frances, 21
Smooth Talk, 44
social media, 7, 17, 63, 149, 157, 160–64, 170, 176, 190
socioeconomic class, 13, 22–23, 33, 52, 85, 118, 149, 155–57
Some Kind of Wonderful, 158–59
Sorority Girl, 38
Speech & Debate, 94
Splendor in the Grass, 42
Spring Break, 44
Stand by Me, 22
statutory rape. See rape
Stolen Paradise, 34, 35
Strangeland 1999, 127
Stupnitsky, Gene, 1
subjectivity, 14, 121–22, 131, 138–39, 145–46. See also sexual agency
Suddenly, Last Summer, 91
suicide, 34, 37, 52, 91, 94, 110
summer camp, 50, 68, 137
Summer of '42, 1973, 45
Superbad, 56, 69
Supreme Court of the United States, 6, 19, 23–25, 37, 48, 55, 92, 151, 185
survivors, 7, 16, 118–23, 129, 135–36, 138–39, 146

Susan Slade, 34
Swain, Dominique, 55
Swap, The, 159
Sylvia Scarlett, 158
Szeto, Hayden, 83

Tale, The, 12–14, 16, 57, 118–19, 129, 132, 135–36, 138, 118–36, 145–46
Tambor, Jeffrey, 154
Tammy and the Bachelor, 33
Taxi Driver, 16, 46–47
Taylor, Elizabeth, 158
Tea and Sympathy, 39–40, 90–91
teachers, 6, 7, 41, 48, 86, 95, 106, 128
Teena, Brandon, 149, 159, 178
teen films: definition of, 10–14, 185; ratings of, 19, 33, 43, 44, 45, 57, 59, 77, 93, 138
teenpics, 10, 38
Teen Wolf, 92
Temple, Shirley, 33
These Three, 90
Thirteen, 11, 56
3 Generations, 13, 16–18, 57, 149–50, 159, 160–62, 164–66, 169–70, 176
Three Months, 93, 94–95
Title IX, 6–7, 151
To All the Boys: Always and Forever, 82
To All the Boys I've Loved Before, 13, 15, 57, 62, 77, 79, 81
To All the Boys I've Loved Before: PS I Still Love You, 82
To Do List, The, 11, 15, 56–57, 62, 71–72, 74–75, 77, 81
To Each His Own, 34
To Save Her Soul, 27
Totah, Josie, 85, 160
Totally F***ed Up, 53, 92
trans youth, 9–10, 13, 16–17, 57, 85, 149–76
Trapped: The Alex Cooper Story, 108–9
Trump, Donald, 151, 175
Truth about Jane, The, 94

Tsai, Lauren, 81–82, 85
Twilight, 67

Unpregnant, 56, 57, 113
Untamed, 26
Unwed Mother, 34, 38

Valley Girl, 59
Victims of Trafficking and Violence Protection Act of 2000, 16, 127
violence, 34, 46, 63, 66, 77, 94, 114, 169, 176; censorship of, 24–25. *See also* sexual assault
Virgin High, 87
virginity, 40, 44, 47, 50, 51, 52, 59, 65, 68–69, 70–74, 78, 98, 127–28
Virgin Suicides, The, 52
Viswanathan, Geraldine, 15, 73, 81
VOD (video on demand), 10, 13, 65, 82, 93, 154, 160, 170

Washington, Anjelika, 85
Weird Science, 51
Welcome to the Dollhouse, 53–54
Westen, Peter, 3, 8
We the Animals, 94
Where the Boys Are, 41–42
Wild Party, The, 31, 91
Williams, Linda, 57, 181
Williams, Tennessee, 40
Wood, Natalie, 42
Wrecked, 94
Wu, Alice, 82

Yes, God, Yes, 62, 72
"yes means yes," 1, 2, 4–5, 189. *See also* affirmative consent
youth: discourse about, 11–12, 17–18, 21, 22–23, 124–25, 151–52, 181, 187–90; studies about, 27–28, 64, 102–3, 114, 120–21, 152–53, 177, 186–87, 191
youth-produced sexual images, 17–18, 181–90
Youth Runs Wild, 34

MICHELE MEEK IS ASSISTANT PROFESSOR of Communication Studies at Bridgewater State University. She is editor of *Independent Female Filmmakers: A Chronicle through Interviews, Profiles, and Manifestos* and presented the TEDx talk "Why We're Confused about Consent—Rewriting our Stories of Seduction." For more info, visit michelemeek.com.

www.ingramcontent.com/pod-product-compliance
Lightning Source LLC
Chambersburg PA
CBHW030646230426
43665CB00011B/976